# Terminal Junction

## by

## *Steven Dushan Milakov*

aug 8, 2001
To Deenon:
next time your pop
gives you grief for something
you deel, just go to
pg 59 and reread him
to real it. He'll quiet
daem.

# Terminal Junction

By Steven Dushan Milakov

Copyright © 2001

Library of Congress Catalog Number: 566-369
Soft cover ISBN: 09636863-3-X
Pages: 226

Printed in the Republic of Singapore
First Edition: July, 2001

***

Published by:
Joe Vaughan Associates Publishing
PO Box 8524
Prairie Village, Kansas 66028-0524
Telephone Number: 1 913 384 6966
Facsimile: 1 913 384 6967
E-mail: flyingcrow@pobox.com
Web site: http//:www.terminaljunctions.com

Cover ilustration by Timothy Milakov

Sale Price:  US$18.95 soft cover edition

This book is dedicated to my "Uncle" Patrick Petrovich
and his devoted wife, Gertrude....

*They were always there for me...and I remain eternally grateful.*

# *Foreword*

Imagine a 24-year-old youth arriving in Kansas City, Kansas on January 20, 1951, after a decade of uncertainty and deprivations in war, and struggling in European refugee camps. And following a cataclysmic world war that left few stones unturned. Then being awakened in a bus along with about thirty others in the early morning hours by a loud greeting: "Good morning, brothers, and God's help!" This was the voice of one of the characters in Steve Milakov's book, **Petar Stepanovich**. We were quickly surrounded by other Serbs who had waited until the wee hours to greet their brethren – the first sizable group of newcomers after more than half-a-century of individual arrivals.

Father Dushan Milakov was there, and he was especially warm with his greetings. The church would afterward become the focal point of our lives for years. It was symbolic that the final destination on our long bus ride from New York would be the Serbian Orthodox Church, St. George. Without it and its parishioners, life in the United States – which we had been looking forward to as if we were survivors of a shipwreck, but now saved in this new land – would have been quite different, and certainly much, much harder. For this, all of us will remain grateful for the rest of our lives.

All of these recollections came back in full force while reading Steve's book. Although my stay in Kansas City was no longer than two years, the memories of it and the wonderful Serbs there are as vivid as ever. We were happy to find ourselves at home again several thousand miles away from our places of birth. These earlier immigrants were pleased and hopeful to see their relatively small colony rejuvenated, so to speak, with new blood. We were especially impressed by the large number of young people born here, but who were also Serbian in spirit. Even though we knew that eventually we too would become American citizens, the fact that those born here proudly called themselves Serb Americans made it easier for us to adjust to the monumental changes in our lives, saying goodbye to our fatherland (stari kraj), and hello to our new home. There was something reassuring in our knowledge that we did not have to forget our roots.

Steve's reminiscences about his experiences growing up as an American Serb are a valuable testimony to the process that has been repeated for centuries, and is being repeated by the millions today. The simple facts are *that he was born "here" and I was born "there"… yet we are able to share our experiences and arrive at more or less the same conclusions, and results.*

*What our children will be like remains to be seen. The syndrome of the "melting pot" will undoubtedly have its impact. Be that as it may, for us **Terminal Junction** will always be a unique, unforgettable experience of the miracle called Americanization.*

*Vasa Mihailovich Ph.D.*
*Professor Emeritus, Department of Slavic Languages & Literatures*
*University of North Carolina*
*Chapel Hill, North Carolina*

# Writer's Prologue

**Terminal Junction** *is a book that offers you, the reader, choices. It tells you about things at many levels. It's up to you to figure which one makes sense and what you like best.*

*That wasn't easy and the truth is even though I wrote the book, I'm still not sure I did what I set out to do. But then again I guess you can write that one off to a writer's insecurity. We never know…and that's why I keep writing, I guess.*

*The truth is, before you read the words on these pages, maybe I should tell you that there were at least three false starts over a twelve-year period. I'd get into the work, then abandon it – unhappy with the "feel" I was creating. It had something to do with syntax, structure, and, oh yes, genre – things we writers all like to wax heavy about in the classroom, and among ourselves. My original idea was to build a novel where everything was fiction. There was certainly enough there to get a book on the table using that approach. But each time I went down that road I hit the same dead-end. Something was missing…but what?*

*Finally, over a chance discussion one night, I gave what I had written to my Aussie friend and colleague, Dr. Tom Hogan. Tom is arguably one of the most well known hands-on practitioners in the radio field in Australia, and one who spent more than his fair share of years putting radio stations on line for islanders throughout the South Pacific. He's also had some luck stringing words on paper as a detective writer. Whether it's engines or pages of prose, Tom has that rare gift of knowing how to take apart and put together things carefully down at ground zero; yet when he puts his mind to it he can soar effortlessly in the stratosphere of academia.*

*Tom read the work, and in particular paid attention to where my journalistic background using the narrative descriptive style surfaced. He brought it back to me with a simple conclusion: "It's all there, mate," he said speaking in a measured way that reflected years of knowing how to work with fragile egos, and in other situations with men who sometimes had very different agendas. "But what I really think it needs is for you to tell this story – in* your *words."*

*"Go first person! Are you mad?" I blurted. Throughout my career as a practitioner and a teacher, I made it a point to lean hard on students who dared to bring their feature work to me using the first-person approach. Despite the fact that the new economy Dot.com world had put its blessing on it (these days they'll take just about anything) I dug in my heels when it came to that. It just wasn't on, I argued. Our craft isn't about finding ways to put ourselves in front of our stories. It's not us that make the news. Whenever you do – as one of my early mentors put it – "you end up with a bunch of* Tom Swifties *and* my gosh – my golly *syrupy work." It's the unmistakable sign of a rank amateur who hasn't a clue on how to*

*control words to really make them work for you. So instead, he or she relies on the first person to bury the obvious defects. Build a house with a lousy foundation – sooner or later it's bound to collapse…that's what I always say.*

*"You have the writing style of a story teller, and you're not a rookie…you do have something to say," he countered, deftly whittling at his point as if it were a fresh piece of balsa wood. "Write it that way – that's what's missing. You won't get in the way of your story…you know better."*

*I talked to others and their conclusions were the same. It was the missing link. Whether I liked it or not, I had to be there, and at times up close and personal. So I did…and then I did it some more… And today,* **Terminal Junction** *is a reality. (Thanks Tommy…)*

***

*Once I got over the barrier on how to write this work, the challenge was what literary devices I would need to use in recreating a world that existed more than five decades ago. For whatever reason those images of life between 1949 and 1953 are still burning in my mind's eye. It was as if they occurred only yesterday. I can't really explain that except to conclude that it was a pretty traumatic period for me. But it was also laced with joys and discoveries that have remained with me for a lifetime.*

*The question was how to bring them to life for others to recall who were there, and those who weren't to enjoy? That took a little doing, but in the end it eventually led me to my earlier work in fiction, namely short-story vignettes. They also have a place in this book. I used the approach to amplify what I had written in the narrative style. It was a technique I had learned over the years as a magazine writer. In some instances the characters are real; in others they are entirely fictional, a composition of many people I had known and more or less took literary license to make my point with one person who stood for all. Still again, with others their real identities are intentionally masked, but they are in my heart just the same.*

*It was a natural marriage of journalistic craft and literary techniques; at least that's how I would like to think it was, anyway. But I do want to add that whatever is there was also gleaned out of research – good old fact digging – library searches and interviews of those who were there, and remembered. As the axiom goes: accuracy…brevity…clarity…it's the journalist's sacred* Powers of Three.

*Still, I don't think* **Terminal Junction** *is a history book in the purest sense. I write about historical events – the Great Flood of '51 – the life and time of working folks and, of course, the Serbian people who toiled in the West Bottoms and built futures for themselves. But as a thesis where every word hangs on absolute historical accuracy where the penalty is that the entire book will blow up in your hands? No, that wouldn't be right to assume, nor would it be fair to the scholars in the region who know far more about historical fact digging and assembling than I do.*

*But if you're the type that insists on classifying everything that you read, then could I suggest that at its core it is an* **autobiography**, *but one that also incorporates fiction along the way to make it more comfortable for you to see – and* *maybe even feel, what I saw.... I do my best to keep me out of it along the way. On my end, I suppose I can live with that compromise. Deeply held beliefs are always hard to give up.*

*More to the core of the work, I would like to think that in many ways* **Terminal Junction** *is really a book about American values as they might have existed during those times. It was a period of the American adventure where a new generation was coming into view. They were asking the early questions that in the decades that followed reshaped the nation's social mosaic – sometimes in disturbing and disruptive ways.*

*Happily, though, we are all pretty much still in one piece, despite our compulsion to smack ourselves in the face. We are all collectively using our feet and hands to climb the bottom rungs up and into an exciting New Millennium. That should count for something, shouldn't it? I happen to think what went on back then had a lot to do with how we got to this momentous point in time. That's one of the reasons why I wrote this book.*

***

*There are a few other structural factoids you need to know about this work before you plow on.* **Terminal Junction** *is built in three sections: Home...Friends...and The Immigrants. Each can stand more or less independently as an editorial offering, yet each is also intertwined with the other. Collectively, you might try and imagine the structure as being a diminishing circle, beginning with Home...moving to Friends, and ending with the Immigrants. Depending on what I wanted to achieve, I emphasized either the narrative or short story fictional approaches to bring forward the era.*

*Finally, a note about my frequent reference to trains in the book: I see them as more than that...on one level they are one of man's most creative tools that binds communities, even today in our jet-age world. They underscore and reveal the power of our commerce and lifestyles, and to a lesser degree they put people in touch with one another. For me, though, they were a way to allow my imagination to soar and see beyond the horizon. They continue to do so, even today. They are the essence of life. They are Kansas City....*

*I hope you enjoy reading* **Terminal Junction** *as much I did writing it.*

Steve Milakov

# Part One

# HOME

## The Missouri River Eagle


*Eagle.*
*Blue and gray it is — a creature of the rails. Its*
*colors understated, historical — elegant.*
*Perfect for the master it was meant to serve —*
*Man.*


*Eagle.*
*Part of America's rich, abundant Heartland.*
*Farmer's Heartland, Salesman's Heartland.*
*Quantrill — Vigilantes!*
*Slavery.*


*Eagle.*
*Pride of the Missouri Pacific Railroad.*
*St. Louis, west along the Missouri River —*
*into Jefferson City.*
*Then Independence. A handshake for Harry?*
*Kansas City.*


*Eagle.*
*Mid-afternoon — gliding on the Highline.*
*Soaring, above the West Bottoms.*
*Spiraling downward, skimming the Kaw — Then*
*Speed.*


*Eagle.*
*Traveling North.*
*Again, the Missouri beckons.*
*Passing through Atchison, Nebraska City —*
*Omaha's night lights — journey's end.*
*Rest.*

*Eagle.*
*On Board — Classy décor. Food.*
*Waiters dressed in white*
*jackets — coal black faces.*
*Silver trays perched on broad shoulders.*
*Huge hands — workman's hands;*
*Freedom.*


*Eagle.*
*Glory Years — 1949 – 1954.  Inside the*
*"Planetarium Dome" America unfolds.*
*Block signals loom.*
*Crimson Red!*
*Then Emerald Green again —*
*Onward!*


*Eagle.*
*Glides gracefully —*
*Steel rails bending with nature.*
*Harmony.*


*Eagle.*
*Kids — walking along gravel farm roads.*
*Friendly waves from the crew.*
*Reliable, trustworthy — a friend.*
*America.*

# Chapter One

**B**ethany Street, Kansas City, Kansas was the center of my universe. At least that's how it seemed to me and the kids I grew up with in the summer of 1949. As streets go, it wasn't nothing much to look at. The neighborhood had to be at least sixty years old judging by the fact that the widening holes in the road's tar-covered surface generously revealed dull looking red-orange bricks that were put there at the turn of the century, maybe even earlier.

Pops came to Bethany in 1942, the year I was born. Our simple looking and freshly painted white, two-story wood-frame house at *50 S. Bethany* sat next to the small, red brick *Serbian Orthodox Church*. The tree-lined street was full of neatly manicured homes that cost all of $4,000 brand new and that included attics, front porches, and basements.

To tell the truth, the church really didn't look like it belonged there. Not that its steeple and the wooden cross sitting on top of it were so ugly, or violated the rights of others.... To the contrary, you could make a case that it was as about an American scene as you'd care to get – a genuine *Rockwell* inspiration. No...it had more to do with where the church was built – dead center in a typically Midwestern workingman's neighborhood, and in the heart of rows of simple, unimaginative-looking homes with uniform-looking yards. *St. George's Church* and its spacious grounds violated the simple, yet effective man-made geometry that had been imposed on the landscape.

Our house was no different from the others except for the silver colored cyclone fence that stood no more than three feet – defining our property line. The neighbors, though, mostly relied on neatly manicured hedgerow bushes to do the same.

Aside from the neighborhood's physical appearance, there were other man-made intrusions as a result of *God's* neighborhood presence. Every Sunday – and often going well into the late afternoon – the surrounding streets were clogged with cars. The neighbors didn't seem to mind. If there was one thing most Bethany Street folks were pretty good at, it was minding their own business and leaving things be.

Anyone who strolled down Bethany's brick sidewalk could tell this wasn't a place where the rich and famous lived – although since then a few of these types could rightfully claim their roots were right there. Bethany Street was really a working man's neighborhood, a world where unions felt right at home.

The sidewalks that lined both sides of the street told their own stories. I used to spend hours playing a kind of hopscotch on them, jumping from one of the six-inch bricks to another. It wasn't easy to do. Nature had taken its toll on those dull orange bricks. They heaved and dipped unevenly from years of tough weather – bone-chilling winters and oppressive summer heat. The price they paid for their resistance to nature had been high. Many were cracked in two; others were frayed and chipped on their edges. And yet, the foundry stamps were still visible, etched in the stone, a declaration of quality that came from within. In a way, the bricks were a lot like the people who lived on Bethany Street. They had also endured many hardships over time. Yes, there were casualties along the way and the scars were there for all to see. Yet, they survived. When the *Yoke Vit Company of Coffeyville, Kansas,* forged bricks from its kiln, they were expected to last an eternity. Few argued they couldn't....

Bethany Street was full of railroad families and there was a good reason for that. Railroads put Kansas City on the map. They conquered the mighty *Missouri River* with their steel bridges and shimmering rails; they opened the Great Plains; they hauled the cattle to slaughter from Texas and they moved war machinery to New York and San Francisco. Working on a railroad meant security. It was the community's bedrock work. If you went to work for a railroad it meant you had a job for life. Fathers saw their sons follow them to the yards. There were switchmen, car knockers (car repairmen), engineers, firemen, and telegraphers. The odds were that in Kansas City everyone had at least one relative who worked on the railroad.

As the crow flies, Bethany Street ran almost directly north and south and couldn't have been much more than a half-a-mile long. It began within line of sight of *Bethany Hospital,* and I guess that's where the street got its name. But on the other end, it terminated in a meandering rutty dirt road that ran parallel to the *Union Pacific* and *Rock Island Railroad* yards. There was a telegrapher's shack just a stone's throw away and adjacent to two shiny main line tracks that stretched east and west.

The railroad companies called it *Terminal Junction,* named for a local switching railroad that controlled the movements of a lot of trains in and out of the majestic *Union Station* over in Missouri. They had put a telegrapher's shack at the beginning of their right-of-way to notify people down the line of all the train movements, and especially those that were about to go over the passenger *Highline* leading into the terminal. The bridge was long and in its own way graceful, spanning high above the *Kaw River* and then punching into the Missouri bluffs to the station beyond.

Actually, there was nothing *terminal* about Terminal Junction. The truth was that few travelers stayed long in Kansas City. It was a little like landing on the *Just Visiting* block in a *Monopoly* game – go in and get out as soon as you can. Maybe Kansas City wasn't exactly the garden spot of the world, but the folks who lived there didn't see it that way. They took pride in their community. They knew their neighborhood had more going for it than the track-side blur of little homes and factories travelers saw through the train windows as they scooted out of town.  After all, *Harry Truman* was their President, well, at least sort of....

Even though he hailed from nearby *Independence* over in Missouri, Bethany Street folks were quick to point out that his no nonsense style and common sense solutions was Kansas City thinking at its best.  No matter that Harry was a Democrat.  He could be forgiven for his political miscalculation. Kansans have pretty much gone Republican ever since damn near the dawn of time.  But not in Kansas City.... This was a place where the Democrats had a lot to say about things in local government, especially after the War.  Truman was a working man's President, and they believed him when he spoke.  He was one of them, and nothing would ever change that.

Several miles east of the telegrapher's shack was the mammoth Union Station.  The station's 90-foot tall marble ceilings and stone arches stood as a monument to an era that still existed.  For years it was the showpiece that stood apart from the Kansas City, Missouri skyline.  During the war years, Union Station was at its zenith when millions of *GIs* and travelers passed through its gates en-route to points on every direction of the compass.

But by the early forties there were signs that significant changes werse on the horizon.  The station's days as a focal point for travelers were numbered.  Yet long before then, Union Station had accumulated more than its fair share of colorful, regional history.

Carved into the terminal walls just a few feet from the station parking lot and main entrance, bullet holes allegedly told the story where on June 17, 1933, hoodlums from the *Pretty Boy Floyd* gang, the *Kansas City police*, a small town *Oklahoma Police Chief*, and federal *G-men* shot it out during a botched attempt to free a captured criminal.

Armed with machine guns, Floyd and two other accomplices were trying to free *Frank Nash* who had been captured earlier in Southern Missouri after breaking out of federal prison in *Ft. Leavenworth,* Kansas.  He had been transported to Kansas City on a *Missouri Pacific* train arriving at 7:45 a.m.  As they left the main station entrance and put Nash into a waiting car, the gangsters converged on the officers and opened fire.  When it was over, four law enforcement officials and Nash lay dead.  The prohibition years, gangsters, booze, women and gambling were big time stuff in Kansas City and the Union Terminal massacre was part of the local folklore.

In truth, what might have occurred on that day was a testimony to the local folks – and also the media's ability – to grow stories taller than Kansas corn.  By the time it was over, the only facts that held up were the names and number people who were killed.  But after that it was a case of *Liar's dollar*...everyone was coming up with their own version of what happened that fateful day.

The players came from everywhere.  There were eyewitnesses a-plenty who swore that *Pretty Boy Floyd* and a host of other well-known thugs had come together to form the shooting team.  But latter accounts suggested he wasn't there at all. Instead, two St. Paul, Minnesota gangsters, *Verne Miller* and *Harvey Bailey* seemed to be behind the ambush. They, along with Nash, had earlier been part of the same gang up north. One other alleged gunman, *Adam Richetti*, a partner of Floyd's, was also reportedly in the group. In the end Richetti was the only one who was later captured, tried, convicted, and then sent to his death in the Missouri gas chamber for his part in the massacre. Floyd himself died in a gun battle in Southern Ohio. Yet, despite the FBI's detailed report to the contrary, no one was ever able to confirm without a doubt who the three shooters actually were on that fateful Saturday morning.

The Union Station Massacre was an event that fueled a nationwide media frenzy, inspired manhunts, and a series of *kangaroo court* convictions engineered by *FBI Director J. Edgar Hoover* and politicians out to make themselves well known in the name of law and order. *Crime Does Not Pay*...was the slogan repeated over and over in the weekly editions of the *Gangbusters* radio program, real-life stories that chronicled the wild and wooly era where law and order prevailed, or at least was trying to…. The hoodlums were gone but the stories that carried on for decades about the Great Massacre swirled around Union Station with the force of a Midwest tornado.

***

All the inbound trains had to cross the Kaw or Missouri River basins to get to Union Station. Just beyond the telegrapher's shack, the trains rolled onto a long steel bridge, the *Highline* the locals appropriately called it. Terminal Junction was the last place the trains rolled on solid ground until they finally stopped under the tarnished steel train shed inside Union Terminal, high in the Missouri bluffs.

For the trains traveling west, the mystery to me was what lay beyond. The red oscillating rear car light of outbound trains sprinting to California conjured thoughts of places I thought I'd never see. As the engineers opened the throttle of their trains, passengers got their final, *terminal glimpse* of a Kansas City they probably didn't notice, anyway. But I saw them.... And I dreamed.

Railroaders left home at all hours of the day and night. The one thing they all seemed to have in common outside of their jobs were their scratched, heavy, metal lunch pails they carried to work with them. You got used to hearing the sounds of their flat-head Ford engines as they sputtered to life on chilly winter mornings and then drifted down the narrow street toward the yards.

Bethany Street's inhabitants were a generation of work-oriented Americans who believed that sticking to the basics and doing the same thing every day was fine with them. And it was these bedrock principles that gave my friends and I who grew up there a feeling of security that life had a certain predictability about it. We felt we were invulnerable to the changes that we sensed were out there somewhere in the distance. We were protected by the replays of life going on as usual. You could put your watch to the precise routines of the railroaders who went off to work.

When I went to bed on those winter nights and heard the cracking sound of a steam locomotive cutting through the chilly air, I felt warm and secure. I dove even deeper into my blankets. Through my bedroom window, the pale, blue glow of a full moon on a cloudless night bathed my tiny bedroom. It was all I needed as I imagined what the engineer and firemen must have looked like in that locomotive cab. Every time the fireman opened the boiler gate to shovel another batch of coal, their hard, weathered faces were etched in a fiery red-orange glow. His workman-like hands had magically turned the darkness into light. I saw the engineer with his hand on the throttle as he looked out of the cab window at the emerald green block signal in the distance, confident and determined that he could handle whatever lay ahead. He was in total control. He could see into the future.

Railroad families took pride in living lives that were just as predictable. On Sunday nights, when the air hung heavy after a late afternoon summer storm, they would pile their broods into their *Fords, Chevys* and *Plymouths,* and head to *North Kansas City* to buy a tank full of ten-cent-a-gallon gas. Later it was off to the *Dairy Queen* for a chocolate-covered soft ice-cream cone. Then, back home again to get ready for another workday.

It wasn't always those predictable periods that I most remembered about Bethany Street. Once in a great while things got a little sparky, and one of the more notable flash points had to do with religion. In terms of pure numbers, the neighborhood was composed of two types of Christians – Roman Catholics and Protestants. My own Serbian Orthodox Church was seen as an anomaly which I later learned worked for and against me. The Catholic congregation was composed of the most recent wave of Polish immigrants who arrived during the early twenties and thirties. There was also a sprinkling of Italians and Croatians. For those two ethnic groups who chose to settle in another area of Kansas City, it's still known today as *Strawberry Hill.* It was the Polish more than any of the other Slavic groups that dominated Bethany's ethnic composition. But no matter what your background was, if you were a Slav you were called a *Bohunk.*

Bohunks, or *Hunkeys* as we were sometimes called, were monikers we learned to live with, and I learned about those terms in my own way. The N...*word,* for example, and all its derivations thrived. Italians were *Dagos,* and the sprinkling of Mexicans that found their way to the area were called *Spics.* The Chinese, in fact almost all of the Orientals were *Gooks,* but the opportunity to use that term was rare since I can't remember seeing a single family in the neighborhood. Jews, of course, were always called *Kikes,* but here again, they weren't really a part of the neighborhood either, except maybe when Pops went to buy something from an appliance store at *18th and Central.* He'd come home complaining about the haggling he had to do to buy his new *Zenith* TV. But whatever the irritation was, it was soon forgotten. In fact, to tell the truth, I think he enjoyed the mental jousting. He just hated to lose, at anything.

And, of course, there were the Japanese, but they were different from the other Gooks. They had a special status. With them, things got personal because of Pearl Harbor. The word that we used to describe them wasn't as denigrating as how we said it. We did it with a hiss...those *Nipssssss*...kind of like the sound a bayou *Water Moccasin* makes when it's about to strike. Learning that one began early and it was reinforced everywhere...at home...with my buddies...on the radio...and in the movies. And it was all for the right reasons, folks argued. The sneak attack made all of the neighbors pretty mad and a lot of people went off to war to fight them because of it. Those *Nipsssssss* were the one group that everybody agreed needed to be taught a lesson. Nobody fooled with the USA. And if anybody had any doubts about that, all they needed to do was go to church and hear about it right from the pulpit. *Let Freedom ring....*

We Bohunks lived alongside neighbors who were typically German, Scottish and Scandinavians, plus a large contingent of Irish families whose forefathers came to the US generations earlier. These groups came to the region to work as common laborers who built the city and worked in the burgeoning slaughterhouses, mostly down in the *West Bottoms* district near the confluence of the Missouri and Kaw Rivers. Some had come even earlier when they built the railroads that tamed the West. The more recent arrivals, though, were the whites who migrated out of the deep South, an influx caused mainly as a result of the Great Depression and the Dust Bowl era that turned Oklahoma, Texas and Arkansas into a succession of poverty pockets that dealt endless pain and suffering. Today, I refer to these times the *Woodie Guthrie* era of American history. His ballads of life on the road as a migrant worker best described the hard times all around and before Pearl Harbor jolted the nation into its furious era of unprecedented productivity which was still rumbling along nicely in 1950. All these white majority families didn't get by without being tagged with racial labels, too. We simply called them *Heinz 57s.* Just like the juice brand with the same name that advertised itself as being made out of fifty-seven ingredients, these families were concoctions of ethnic backgrounds that, in the end, told us Serbs they were really nobodies. What made matters worse was that whenever they began to recite their litany of ethnic origins, they would always throw in the name of a recognizable American Indian tribe to spice it up.

*"I'm also one-sixth Indian.... My great-great-great-grand-daddy on my mother's side was married to a Shawnee...or a Kickapoo, or a Sioux...."* Whatever tribe sounds snazzy, that's who they were related to. It always struck me how mechanical and silly these people sounded as they spouted on about their phony Indian relatives. Ironically, they were talking about an assemblage of so-called distant relatives who a hundred years earlier had been systematically hunted, murdered, raped, and then banished to reservations throughout the United States in a territorial war that the Indians had no realistic chance of ever winning. Yet here they were today, reborn, rejuvenated and now cozy family additions in the white man's family trees,

even enjoying damn near celebrity status. Being there performed a vital service; they validated their white relative's Heinz 57 identities with a touch of Wild West Americana. That ensured their family names were indeed a part of history. I often wonder how these Indians might have reacted when they heard these people talk about them in modern America.

The dominant Polish ethnic group built their churches and sent their kids to Catholic schools. The biggest of them all was *St. Benedict's*. After completing the eighth grade, they would go on to the all Catholic *Ward High School*.

The Protestant churches were more diverse and ran the gamut in terms of their Christian philosophies. There were the *Methodists*, probably the most liberal and sensible of the lot; so were the *Presbyterians*. The mostly German immigrant *Lutherans* weren't in the majority and tended to go their own ways with little fanfare.

But the majority *Baptists* were something else again. Many of these congregations were direct offspring of churches born out of the Deep South, *Hard-Shell* Baptists folks called them. Churches that perfected hellfire and damnation as the cornerstone of their teachings. Unless you followed the Bible's teachings to the letter, your road to heaven will detour right into *Satan's* clutches!

There were also churches that fell into the category of *Evangelical.* These were by far the most radical of the Christian groups – those who believed in speaking in tongues and the power of touch healing. I think these groups were the direct descendants of the television evangelists that swept America in the seventies and eighties, and are still going strong at the turn of the century. Somebody figured out how to stick a camera into the building and polish up their Godly act. But essentially, it was all right there and working fine in 1949.

Children of all these groups typically attended the public schools, *Central Junior High School,* then later *Wyandotte High,* located a few miles from our Bethany Street neighborhood. With such divergent views about religious beliefs, it was inevitable that there would be times when things got sparky. Some of the more radical Baptists were convinced that the Catholic priests had a secret mission to convince the other faiths that their way of educating was better than the public school system. By forcing youngsters to memorize their Catechism and using the rod liberally when they didn't, the results yielded better student performances all around. And if that logic prevailed at the lower levels, it would surely be effective in high school.

I listened on the sidelines as I heard my folks talking about all this. Historically, the Roman Catholic and Serbian Orthodox faiths in Yugoslavia were always at odds over who was on first...and who was on the chosen path to preach the faith with no arguments...and who really had a divine right to spearhead God's work. It was always there, this rivalry wrapped in the holy cloth, latent, festering and potentially ugly. When World War II erupted, the percolating turned into an eruption – a bloody Civil War that, in fact, at war's end led to a Communist takeover. Communism was ushered in as if it were some kind of societal referee to keep all sides from bludgeoning each other. It was an economic system and a totalitarian noose that society willingly slipped around its neck without complaint. And why not? Anything was better than the carnage that had preceded it. The adoption in turn numbed everyone equally into a homogeneous, bland, and uneventful lifestyle that put a lid on the ever-bubbling nationalistic cauldrons. Yugoslavia was a social fault zone where frequent and violent movements were the only guarantee. It also signaled the beginning of a tightrope walk between the East and West that was to last for decades. *Yosip Broz Tito* knew how to cut a deal with the best of them.

All of that I could sort of appreciate – the religion and the communism part. Pops made sure of that during his countless and never-ending lectures on the life and times of Serbs, their religion, the Croatians, and their religion, and what he was absolutely convinced God was talking about in the pursuit of spiritual totality for all mankind. It was heavy stuff but the pieces were still visible enough for my nine-year-old intellect to assemble in child-like ways. At that age you don't see the entire movie, but the key parts are out there in living color. But for the life of me, what I couldn't understand was why people got so upset when it came to school things. I hated school, no matter who dished it out.

Yet among many of the Bethany Street neighbors, religion was a hot issue. Once, two of the families who liked to mind their own affairs – the very Baptist *Mr. Schnyder* and the pious and very Catholic *Mr. Danowski* – almost got into a fistfight over God. Every evening they would meet and exchange small talk over trash burning the in back of their facing yards. Then one night the schools issue crept into their light talk.

From the beginning there seemed to be no thread of reason to their argument, but we all heard both sides clearly enough. They were nose-to-nose, yelling so loudly that the neighbors went out to their back porches to see what the fuss was all about. The Polish carpenter and Heinz 57 railroad switchman finally stormed off in a huff to their respective back porches. It was a hell of a scene that had everybody talking about it for weeks and over many suppers that followed. Mom recounted the event as if she had memorized every word, saying what a shame it was, and that they had been on such good terms before all this had happened. Mom was the type who liked to play peacemaker whenever she could. But she knew her limitations. This one was out of her hands. The men hadn't so much as uttered a word to each other since that fateful August night two years earlier. In fact, they even passed on the nightly burning chores to their wives. It didn't matter there, either. Every night at six o' clock, Mrs. Schnyder lugged her trash out and dumped it into the empty can. Seconds later Mrs. Danowski would show up with hers. The two oil barrels were barely five feet from the other. They came out and lit their trash, then folded their arms like Genies, glaring at each other through the growing flames. They never said a word, holding their ground until the fires died. Then they turned for home, slamming their back porch doors behind them.

These *trash can wars* were an important learning lesson. It showed just how far people would go to protect their false pride. I'm quite sure that if you asked them, neither would have been able to explain why things got so out of hand in the first place. Yet they still were willing to stand and face each other in stony silence, night after night, month after month, and year after year. Far as I know, I don't think those families ever spoke to each other again. And that was even after Mr. Schnyder lost both of his legs up to his knees five years later, when he fell under the wheels of a boxcar on yard-track sixteen…on the *Rock Island Line.*

***

The north side where Bethany Street began told a different story – it was all about dying. I never knew much about *Bethany Hospital* except that I didn't like it very much. Pops would go there to see sick people. The parishioners settled in homes around the neighborhood near their church. Some came back from their hospital stays. Others didn't. By that time Mom had taken a job down at the *Simmons Mattress* factory in the *Fairfax District,* and that meant Pops had to keep an eye on me over my summer school vacation. Whenever I was unlucky enough to get trapped into going with Pops to see sick people, I knew I was in for a boring day. He would always leave me to wait by myself in the hospital lobby area. I guess that's why I learned to talk to myself when I was a kid. It didn't take me long to figure out that I would have to be creative in finding ways to entertain myself during those long absences in public places. When you're an only child and a priest's son, there's lots of things you have to do that you would just as soon avoid. Going to Bethany Hospital was almost at the top of the list.

Once, I remember standing in the hospital lobby with nothing to do. Then I spotted something called an *iron lung* the hospital had put on display. The tubular machine looked like a torpedo with windows and it scared the hell out of me. I wondered what the poster next to it meant when it said that this machine was a lot of help to people who had polio. I walked from one end to another and peered inside the thick glass, imagining what it would be like to have to stay inside it all my life. I didn't know much about polio but I hoped I'd never get it.

But it was really the smell that I disliked most about Bethany Hospital. That super clean antiseptic odor that settles in for a lifetime in your olfactory senses and never, ever leaves.

Maybe the folks who built the hospital and planned the city knew about it, too. At any rate, they put a nice big park in front of it. *Central Avenue* ran on the park's south side, and that's where the streetcars ran to the Missouri side of town. That was another world completely and getting there was an adventure in itself.

Bethany Street terminated into Central Avenue at a "T" intersection. It was all neatly laid out and typical of the kind of sensible, ninety-degree neighborhood planning that the founding European settlers liked to employ throughout the Midwest.

The park was spacious but generally not very crowded, especially in the fall and winter. There was a run-down, pebble surface tennis court on the far end, but nobody used it much. During summer my buddies and I would occasionally take our busted wooden rackets and try to hit, but the call for baseball, football, and the biggest of them all – basketball – always lured us to other places, inspiring dreams of fame.

It was really the gentle rolling terrain and aging big Oak trees that gave Bethany Park its appeal. Kansas City was full of Oaks. They were like giants. How many times had we taken refuge among them and used their massive roots and broad trunks as resting places, the ideal spot for a *Hostess Cup Cake* and *Nehi Cola* on a sweltering Kansas summer day.

It was also on the park's dying grass in mid-Fall that I figured out something else: I wasn't a football player. We used to occasionally go there to play touch football, but that invariably led to some smart-ass upping the ante into a full-blown tackle.

It got worse. Bethany Park was neutral ground for kids living in the area. They were all from similar neighborhoods that flanked the east and west sides of the park. Whenever somebody showed up with a football, kids would show up from out of nowhere, and the inevitable followed.

At first the tackles were tolerable and *gentlemanly,* but as the game wore on, so did the pain merchants' tactics. The combination of the crisp fall wind and cool temperatures took its toll on my skinny body. I can still feel the biting sting on my ears and those rough hands scraping across my face as I was unceremoniously gang tackled to the hard ground. I wore glasses and it was a miracle they were never broken. Football is a great sport to watch, but it all stopped there as far as I was concerned.

To all of us kids who lived there, territoriality was an important rule to respect. I didn't like the other neighborhood kids much and was intimidated whenever I chanced an encounter with them. They were rough and tumble and always looking for a fight, and ever willing to see somebody get whacked for their troubles. All of them were white – and most were children of parents who came out of the rural South. Sons of dirt farmers and laborers who had migrated north looking for work. Even at ten and eleven they were well on their way to understanding the realities of a hard life, with little chance of it being much else. I suppose that was one of my most important discoveries as a kid growing up there. *Poverty and ignorance are really colorblind.*

I also learned another lesson that lasted a lifetime. Down near the railroad yards, Bethany Street's rows of tiny houses gave way to muddy hills, the perfect playground for young boys determined to see how dirty they could get. The twenty-foot high ridges were ideal for playing war games. I was on the hill with the *Fry* boys, *Jimmy* and his younger brother, *Phillip.*

Both of them lived on *Lowell Avenue* behind our parish house, and just on the other side of the cinder alley that separated our properties.

We were having a time of it, lofting the plentiful dirt clods like grenades over the rim of the hill to the ground below. It was an old playtime scenario. I imagined I was John Wayne in the **Sands of Iwo Jima** pulverizing the enemy when suddenly, the clods started coming back faster than we were throwing them. We peered over the top and saw several boys looking at us. One was *Ray Sadecki.*

Sadecki was Polish, Roman Catholic and naturally ornery. He was also known for something else: He could throw a heck of a fast ball. Ray Sadecki was neighborhood news.

Nobody messed with Sadecki. He was a natural left-hander and scared the hell out of anybody who challenged him at the plate. I did that – just once. Like my football fantasy, the sizzling fast ball that whizzed by an inch from my nose was all I needed to abandon my baseball dreams. I was down to basketball or nothing at all.

***

*Years later I saw why I had been so intimidated as a kid when Sadecki's name popped up on the World Series winning 1964 St. Louis Cardinals pitching rotation. He and baseball legend, Bob Gibson, showed the Cards the way over the Yankees, and it was Sadecki's 20 – 11 won-lost record that went a long way to get them there. Gibson was right behind him with a 19 – 12 result.*

*Sadecki went on to play for 17 years in the majors with the Giants, the Mets, Kansas City A's and Milwaukee. No surprise to me. He had the gift.*

***

But none of that mattered back then. Sadecki was just a hometown Little League star, not a World Series champion. He was a tough neighborhood kid with a *Howitzer* for an arm. And now, there he was looking up at us. He was holding a dirt clod about the size of a baseball in his left hand and sporting his best: "I got your ass now " smile.

We thought we had the high ground and the advantage, but that fantasy didn't take long to evaporate. I hovered below the lip of the ridge and peered at Phillip who had just thrown a fresh barrage of clods over the top of the ridge. He cautiously stuck his head up to check out the results. That's when Sadecki's clod smashed him flush in the left eye. He grabbed his face and opened his mouth, but there was no sound, nothing. The howl that eventually followed sent chills down my spine. I had just been introduced to the ugly face of terror.

***

Every neighborhood has at least one grocery store and Bethany was no different. In fact, we had even better service. There was also a sort of door-to-door fruit and vegetable service.

A couple of times a week you could hear *Chica'* (Uncle) *Milovan Yovetich* at the top of the street beckoning Bethany's housewives to come outside and peruse his panel truck full of fruits and vegetables.

*"Cheereee-up...Cheereee-up,"* he would call. His voice was never irritating. It blended into the neighborhood, kind of like a robin does chirping on a tree branch on a Kansas morning in early spring. Those kinds of sparkling days that make you glad to see what's coming next. Where the dew from the night before kisses the leaves as if it were being anointed by God. To this day I'm not even sure what his words meant. But they worked. Chica' Milovan was a gentle soul who made his way through life without fanfare, letting his humility show him the way.

The fruits and vegetables peddler was tall and rangy, standing maybe six-four, and who lived with his family in a well kept two-story, wood-frame white house over on *Twelfth Street*. A Serbian immigrant who settled near his church in the twenties, he was rarely absent from Sunday services. His beliefs were as simple as his lifestyle, and he liked it that way.

When I saw him the first time, he was already well into his sixties. He always wore a pair of starched blue bib overalls with a print shirt underneath. His sparkling blue eyes, full white mustache and full head of silver hair gave him the look of a Senator when he stepped out of his olive green Dodge panel truck and quietly stood by as the neighborhood housewives rummaged through his fruits and vegetables.

Bethany Street folks knew his produce was the best that money could buy and Mom was continually amazed at how he managed to do it over and over again. His tomatoes were bigger and redder, his long stem onions were greener – even his apples were juicier. And come late spring when the cherries were in season? Well, that's when Chica' Milovan really showed his stuff.

My Mom's declaration about his superior products was a bombshell. If there was any place on earth where you could find top grade fruits and veggies, it had to be in eastern Kansas. Yet somehow, this quiet, soft-spoken man had managed to outdo everybody else. It's a secret that he no doubt took to his final resting place.

Whenever Mom sent me off to buy a quart of milk or loaf of bread, there was only one place I would go. It was to *Mrs. Evango's* little store on the corner of *Lowell* and *11th Street*. There was another store a little closer on the corner of Bethany and *Pacific Avenue*, but somehow it didn't have the feel that Mrs. Evango's did. It was operated by the *Hall* family, and although they were nice enough to me, they were still Heinz 57s. Anyway, Mom never encouraged me to trade there much and I suspect she may have felt the same way, even though we never talked about it.

Mrs. Evango was different. She lived behind the store in an attached red-brick apartment. I never saw her husband in all the years I went there.

Nobody ever talked about him, but I assumed she was married because she had a daughter in her twenties who also lived nearby.

The walk to the shop took only a couple of minutes and it was the perfect time for me to play trains – pretending I was the *Twin Star Rocket* or *City of St. Louis* rolling down the mainline to everywhere and nowhere. Sometimes I rode my bike and I'm sure that people thought I was a little nuts – especially when I included the sound effects of a whistle, bell and a rumbling diesel locomotive as it sped away from Terminal Junction.

There was only one distraction along the way. About half way down the *"mainline,"* I'd pass *Jenine Jensen's* house, a single-story faded green-frame home that always looked perpetually abandoned. From the outside the simple, traditional wooden front porch and its uneven row of cement steps looked dirty and uninviting. The narrow sidewalk leading to it was cracked and appeared to have been permanently fractured as a result of hard times. The lawn was scruffy looking with weeds growing everywhere. The thin stand of hedgerow bushes along the leading edge of the public sidewalk was brittle and dying from a lack of care.

Two sisters lived there, but I only knew one of them. Once a month, *Jenine,* the younger of the two, would knock on my folk's front door holding an armful of comic books. She wanted to trade and her supply was the best in the neighborhood, no doubt about it. There were always several editions of *Plastic Man, Superman* and a complete collection of *Terry Lee and The Pirates.*

We would sit on my front porch for hours during those hot summer months thumbing through our collections. At eleven, Jenine was a little older than me but already becoming a woman. I remember how I felt hot all over when she bent over to pick up another comic and I saw her boobies. We always did our trading on my front porch spreading the supply of comics in front of us. Together, we would slowly look them over. When she spotted one out of arm's reach, she would stretch herself and more or less crawl toward it. Her flimsy blouse sagged, and that's when I got a peek. I couldn't seem to get a handle on my feelings, but I still liked the way I felt every time they popped into view.

If I was lucky, I'd get two or three shots in a single sitting. When it was over I got all that plus some good comic trades for my effort. So it was only natural that I kept the comic trading going, and I always worked it out for her to come to my place. I can't say for sure, but I think she knew what I was up to and she really didn't mind too much, either.

No matter how deep I got into my streamliner fantasy on the way to the store, I always came out of it the moment I passed Jenine's house. I hoped she might see me and come out. But she never did. And then one day she wasn't there at all. The house was abandoned. Just as mysteriously as she had come into my life, Jenine disappeared. We never touched or explored anything beyond our comic book collection. Yet she would have to qualify as my first genuine sexual fantasy. Although I didn't realize it then, thanks to her, my life had taken a turn that would lead to many more fantasies and realities, too. But Jenine was the first and, as they say, you never, ever, forget your *first*.

Inside the corner shop, Mrs. Evango was almost always there. The Russian-born immigrant stood about five feet and, on a good day, weighed no more than eighty pounds. She always wore a simple, plain dress that did absolutely nothing for her rail-like figure. Her graying hair was much too long for a woman in her late forties to be put into a ponytail.

The store's narrow aisles and shelves revealed the typical dry goods of the times – boxes of cereal, canned goods and bakery products. None of them looked very fresh, and the store had a peculiar smell, a sort of *mildewy* one that was mixed with stale food odors.

Near the far side and away from the entrance, there was a small chiller where the milk and cheeses were kept. Ironically, it was inside there that I discovered progress creeping into our neighborhood. For as long as I could remember, I would bring home a quart of milk in thick, glass bottles. The bottles were heavy but there was something different about how the milk tasted, fresh and wholesome, as if it came right off the farm.

Then, one day, all the bottles were gone. In their place were milk cartons made of a wax paper with the company's logo stamped on both sides. Mrs. Evango put on her best PR smile and assured me it was the latest thing and that the milk would taste the same. But I didn't believe her. Later I tried it and I was right; it tasted funny. To tell you the truth, I'd make the same argument today. Milk that comes out of a bottle still tastes better.

In the back of the store there was another larger chiller where Mrs. Evango did her butcher work. When I ordered a pound of ground meat, she opened the door and pulled out a hunk of rump roast. Then she turned to a nearby wooden chopping block, cut off a piece with a big knife, and stuffed it all into a meat grinder that looked a little like a *Pilgrim's Blunderbuss*. The machine whirred away, churning out long strands of hamburger meat on the counter. They looked to me like a never-ending parade of little red worms. While the grinder was still working, she tore off a piece of thick white butcher paper from a roll that was mounted on the back wall and laid it next to the growing pile of stringy meat.

When the grinding was finished, she scooped it all up with cupped hands and dumped the meat dead center on the wrapping paper. Then she lifted the package to a silver colored weight scale pan that was on top of the meat counter. She intentionally left it there several seconds, making sure I had enough time to check its weight. Mrs. Evango worried that her customers might think she might cheat them, but far as I know, she never did. No one ever asked.

"One pound ground meat, *honey please look*," she said.... "One *feefty*...honey please look...One dollar *feefty* cents you owe me. Okay?"

That was really the only time she looked directly at me, searching my face for some kind of acknowledgment that what she was saying was the truth, the whole truth and nothing but the truth, so help her *God*. Sure that I got it, she folded the loose edges of the paper and scribbled down the amount on its front. She smiled and held up the package next to her tiny face. It was more of a mechanical looking gesture rather than something genuine on her part. Then she turned toward to the table to complete her most dramatic act of store business. Back then, scotch tape wasn't plentiful, so I waited a few more seconds while she cut a piece of string from a piece of sharp metal on the end of the butcher table. She deftly flipped the package around, ending up with a perfect little knot at the top. The amount she wrote down earlier on the paper were also there in perfect position. Without speaking, she turned for the cash register counter near the front of the store. Her steady stride was full of purposeful energy, a sure sign that she was now totally engrossed with the work at hand.

If anybody else happened to come in to her shop while she was working in back, they just waited. Nobody worried much about stealing. There were no hidden cameras, or alarms. You lived by a code of honor. If you stole, people figured you really needed it. It was a kind of donation. So you just hung around and waited, and waited, and waited – until it was finally your turn.

The counter was near the doorway entrance, positioned at an angle in front of a plate glass window the local sign painter used to advertise her weekly special. Actually, her specials were nothing *special* at all. I think Mrs. Evango did it as a sort of sales promotion gesture. It was her way of keeping up with the changing times. No matter…. We didn't go there because of that, anyway. We went there because it *was* Mrs. Evango, but I don't think she ever figured that out.

In front of the cashier's table and off to one side, there was an assortment of candy bars and other five-cent sweets. Once in a while Mrs. Evango would get in a supply of candy beads. They were actually strips of thin, white paper about two inches wide and a couple of feet long. Evenly spaced down the length of the strips, there were little red, blue, green and yellow beads of semi-hard candy made almost entirely out of sugar and color coating. There was something special about those candy beads. Maybe it was how they tasted after I bit them off one at a time. You couldn't help but get a little paper mixed in with the candy. I think that was the real secret of their taste.

Generally, it was Mrs. Evango who did the cashier work, but once in a while her daughter helped out. She showed up during the rush hours between five and eight o'clock at night, and just before she closed.

What I vividly recall most about this small store owner was her precise and methodical way of doing business, and that was really the case when it came to exchanging money. I suspect that this interaction between two people was probably as intimate as she cared to get with folks in the neighborhood. To Mrs. Evango, money was a very personal thing. Giving it up for any reason was something that demanded careful preparation and focused execution.

Her money exchange ritual was as precise and methodical as a surgical procedure. First, she quickly moved in behind her big NCR cash register – a shiny black one made of heavy cast iron with ornate designs burned into its framework. Her small stature was nearly overwhelmed by the bulky register, but she had long ago showed the NCR who was boss.

When she took my money she put her tiny fingers on the register buttons and pushed a couple down. It sprang to life with a penetrating *cheeng-cheeng* that was far too loud and definitely out of place in her little store. The register drawer flew open with a thud as if rudely awakened. Then two metal banners inside a small glass case at the top popped up… *$2.50….*

Mrs. Evango peered into the open register till. It was as if she was only now discovering a hidden treasure buried inside. Then she carefully took out the change due me, only to put it all back and do it over again. To this day, I don't know why she did that. She may not have been all that confident with her arithmetic; but then again it could have had something to do with not wanting to part with her dollars at all, even though she had no choice. Anyhow, she finally nodded her head and took out the money, telling me to open both hands.

"You give me five dollars, *honey please look,*" she began. "I give you back your change…*honey please look.* You hold your hand and I count…*honey please look….*"

Then, dollar by dollar, quarter by quarter, dime by time, nickel by nickel, and penny by penny, she put the change dead center into my cupped hands, all the while finding a way to squeeze in another *honey please look* as she did her counting.

Mrs. Evango's little store held on, despite the relentless march to embrace mass marketing that was starting to nibble at the fringes of our little neighborhood by 1950. When they opened the new *A & P Supermarket* on Central Avenue, she looked like she was a goner for sure. But after a while the people got tired of gawking at the wide aisles full of food and the neatly displayed rows of frozen meats that were pre-weighed, cut and ready to go. Pushing metal baskets around to gather our groceries was lots of fun to us kids, but the novelty didn't last with my folks. They still preferred the simple, personal touch. These new stores, well, they were just too…*sterile.* Too easy…too efficient. Eventually, most of her customers drifted back to her corner shop. Mrs. Evango was still a part of the neighborhood, and that counted for something. Mom would simply send me on my way, telling me it was worth a few cents more for a quart of milk. Back then, we took care of our own.

# Chapter Two

**K**ansas City in the late forties was also a treasure trove when it came to public transportation. Since the turn of the century the city's founders decided that the best way to get around both sides of the river was on an efficient network of streetcars. The lines took shape, crisscrossing the entire twin cities area in a web of steel rails, bridges, and a tunnel. The system even included a cable car – an interesting fact because cable cars were typically associated to be something people used in places such as San Francisco, not the Midwest. Truth is, Kansas City is built on hills – bluffs really, that ran along both sides the Kaw and Missouri Rivers.

I'll leave it to the historians of the region to detail in more precise terms where all these lines went and when they were built. Or when the *Hallmark Card Company* went into business. But I will offer this one small factoid: During the zenith of Kansas City's streetcar era, the passion had become so intense that you could take an interurban ride as far away as *St. Joseph, Missouri,* or *Atchison, Kansas.* By the late forties and into the early fifties, the network had been reduced to serving the greater metropolitan area. That was still a respectable operation. In fact, it had to rank as one of the nation's best.

Pops loved streetcars, and since neither of my parents drove a car, it didn't take me long to get hooked, too. Every once in a while he would go to the Missouri side to see a parishioner. Sometimes he would look my way out of the corner of his eye as he opened the front yard gate. No need for talk! I was like a horse out of the gate. It was our own private little game, and he loved it.

We went to lots of places but I never really knew where we would end up. Was it to be *Swope Park* and the zoo? The line there was a direct one, dropping us off no more than a hundred yards or so from the entrance. When I asked Pops if that was in store for today, he simply shrugged and smiled, and in his thick Serbian accent answered:

*Zoo today? Maybe yes, maybe no – maybe rain, maybe snow....*

No matter where we went, the rides typically took an hour or more each way from our house. Sometimes we'd take the *Country Club* line to the end, a ride that was as close as you could get to riding on a real railroad.

I liked the Country Club run a lot, but we didn't go there very often. First, we went through a rich section of town. Modern, spacious and with plenty of specialty shops, *The Plaza* smelled of money. I would hang my head out the trolley window and spot the *Kansas City Public Service's* steeple cab electric engines as they pulled freight cars into building sidings. I didn't know it then but it was the last streetcar line that would run in Kansas City.

Sometimes, though, we would take another line to *Dodson, Missouri,* and I thought that was the end of the earth. The line was ancient and the wooden trolley car swayed precariously as it rumbled over the aging roadbed, struggling mightily to get to its maximum twenty-five per as it negotiated eastern Missouri's thickly wooded terrain, finally terminating on the edge of town near the main street. Once I got to that nowhere town, well now, that's when the fun really began.

The moment we stepped off the trolley steps, Pops would beeline into a beer joint up the street to see a parishioner and have a cool one. But even before he did, I was on my way, too. I knew exactly where to go. I was on my way to a battered, splintered and unwanted puke green park bench that as far as I could tell served absolutely no useful purpose any more except one: *to serve me.* It had been unceremoniously dumped at the edge of a grassy patch just a few steps from where the streetcar track looped for the trolley's return run. There, where the grass always seemed to smell as if it were freshly cut, and the summer dew wrapped itself around my shoes, on this very spot – where the sounds of life came alive – I would settle in for the afternoon, protected by the graceful limbs of a big Oak tree. I was no more than thirty feet from the two-track mainline of the *Missouri Pacific Railroad*. This was where the *Eagle* streamliners roamed! A world where the addictive aroma of creosote oozing off wooden railroad ties drifted into the humid summer air. The main running tracks of the blue and white speedsters; the glass domed beauties that carried its passengers to points south and west of Kansas City.

It was a busy track and I didn't have to wait long. The growling locomotive was on me in a flash, heading due south. Its unmistakable silver *Eagle* emblem on the face of the elegant blue and white diesel shimmering in the afternoon sunlight. For an instant, the train seemed to pause in its assault on the track. It was as if it had momentarily noticed me standing trackside, then discounted it as nothing important as it roared onward through an equally unimportant town on its way to its long distance destination. Blue, gray and yellow pinstriped colored passenger cars followed, and then they too quickly disappeared into the tree-lined countryside. I relished it all as one who savored the haunting aftertaste of a vintage wine. *Eagle....*

***

The *West Bottoms Line* car line revealed another interesting mosaic of a very different sort. It would cut across the Kaw River on the *James Street* Bridge, and then sort of meander toward Missouri, crossing the border through the lively packinghouse district. *Armour, Fowler, Wilson and Swift & Company,* and a myriad of other different kinds of businesses had set up shop there during the early 1900s, and even earlier. You could make money in the Bottoms, but you had to work for it. Not even the relentless pursuit of the accountant's pencil could negate its potential. The ever-important economic formula of available transportation, cheap labor, yielding respectable bottom line results held fast.

Actually, the term – *packing house,* was a colorless way of explaining what really went on there. It was, in fact, where animals were brought for slaughtering, their carcasses prepared and packed, and then shipped, mostly by rail, throughout the nation. It was a place nobody bragged about, and yet provided thousands of jobs to immigrants who were eager to find their ways in a new land.

The city fathers knew where their roots were and they also understood there was no getting away from them entirely. But they tried, anyway. They built a long bridge over the Bottoms. And they called it the *Inter-City Viaduct.*

The Viaduct ran from downtown Kansas City, Kansas, to the Missouri side. The four-lane bridge was the perfect engineering solution. People who lived in Kansas always talked about their cross-state neighbors and, I suppose they talked about us, too. There was this natural rivalry, especially when the *Kansas Jayhawks* played the *Missouri Tigers* in basketball. Outside of sports, however, it was more a comparative thing about their own state's prosperity versus ours. That, in turn was reduced to a common denominator such as who had the best roads.

Whenever we traveled on the Viaduct from the Kansas side, about a mile or so passed and a big neon lighted sign appeared on a telephone pole. Its simple message read, *"Welcome to Missouri...."*

No sooner the sign flashed by and you noticed something else: the ride was *smoother.* The car tires whirred effortlessly over the fresh tar surface, where moments before they bumped and banged over the potholes and tar patches that were typical of the Kansas side.

There were other reminders that our side of town was coming up short in the comparison game. The Kansas light poles were unevenly spaced across its section of the two-mile long viaduct. Not only that, on our side the light bulbs they used were a sort of flat-white color. They worked, but weren't very efficient, especially when rain, sleet, and snow hit during the heavy winter months.

But on the Missouri side, well now, that was another story. Their lights were a yellow-orange color. Perfect for cutting through anything, even the spring fog that always seemed to hang around.

Still, there was one viaduct feature that neither side could avoid, or wanted to claim: It was that unique *West Bottoms smell.* I could describe it as a sort of sweet smell and be partially right. Almost, but not quite. It was sweet, but it was also pungent, so much so that it could turn your stomach if whiffed in too large a dose. I knew those Bottoms *smellies* had a lot to do with the meat packing plants that were directly under the bridge. And I loved it!

Depending on how the wind blew, sometimes it would just hang around the whole of the viaduct and make everybody sick. Kind of like somebody who has BO and nobody wants to tell him. You just live with it.  Fine by me...I'd roll down the neighbor's car window and load up.  Mom would pull me away, holding her fingers to her nose.  Then she'd ask how in God's name I could stand it, even enjoy it!  To me, the Bottoms smell was anything but nasty.  It was Kansas City, warts and all.

***

When it came to potholes in the road, though, nothing could beat the West Bottoms.  It was a war zone created by nature and the endless march of capitalism.  The roads were often flooded because of too many torrential summer rains that had nowhere to go; concrete that was chipped into submission thanks to the relentless snowy, icy, and rainy winters.  It all resulted in too many cars that lost their shock absorbers trying to survive the holes in the ground.  Too many heavy trucks and trailers that battered the land, and too many trains running down the center of its brick laid streets.  Too many spur tracks long since abandoned and leading to no place in particular, except into the shells of neglected buildings, or disappearing into a patch of overgrown weeds where nature had taken back what it once had owned.

The square-shaped, red brick buildings with their faded whitewash company signs painted on their exteriors were all the advertising companies needed to demonstrate their presence.  This was big hands and strong backs country; long sleeves and the land of corduroy and denims, where heavy boots and even heavier coveralls were the office dress.

For all of these reasons and a thousand more, I loved to explore the West Bottoms.  There were plenty of *beaneries* where you could get a great hamburger steak, mashed potatoes, and homemade apple pie, for a song.  The coffee was steamy and always smelled fresh and the men who sat on the simple counter stools did it with one eye on the kitchen window, and the other on the clock on the wall.  It was there where I learned about the balancing act between economic survival and racial equality.   The men and women who worked as packers, stevedores, truckers, and railroaders, knew all about skin color.  But it was the green of a dollar bill that really caught their attention.  They generally treated each other with civil respect, no matter who they were.  Yet it wasn't a love feast, either.  It was what it was, and nothing more: a respect for the job and for those who did it every day.  There was no need to talk about their whiteness and blackness, no time to delve into *"tell me how you really feel about it"* types of conversations.

Back then, that type of touchy-feely social intercourse was looked at as being pretty useless stuff.  If it went on at all, it was behind closed doors.  It had nothing really to do with getting that truck trailer loaded on time with tons of beef destined for Chicago; or off-loading another train car full of cattle into the stockyard pens; or slitting the throat of a terrified pig as it dangled helplessly on an assembly line of death; or using a sledge-hammer to smash the skull of a confused steer trapped in a wooden chute where there was only one way out, and only one outcome. These slaughterhouses were where nature and man collided. Ugly in the raw and unsightly, yes, but still necessary. It was *Darwin's Survival of the Fittest* and an African game hunt played out in unison. And all of it occurring dead center in America's Heartland. Day in and day out, year-in and year-out, the orderly slaughter went on with brutal assembly-line precision. And the people who sat inside their glass-enclosed world in the cars above knew it. And they just kept on rolling...*Illusions*...*Progress*.

Getting out of the West Bottoms to the Missouri side by streetcar took some doing. The limestone hills that straddled the east side of the river basin were fairly high and steep. And it was on the tops of these ridges where much of downtown Kansas City, Missouri, was built.

The streetcar would meander through the Bottoms down its main street. Then it would enter its own right-of-way, a slowly rising steel trestle that climbed straight toward the hills.

I remember watching through the open window as the trolley climbed higher and higher, swaying precariously from side to side as it always did, slowly making its way toward the summit. Ahead was the mouth of the tunnel leading into *Quality Hill* that was constructed at the turn of the century.

By the time we entered it my heart was pounding. No matter how brave I tried to be, I always ended up putting my hands over my face. The clacking sound of the wheels on the tracks inside was deafening.

But it was those damn tunnel walls that really got to me. They seemed to be no more than six inches from the open trolley window. They whizzed by revealing their dank watery sides in unpredictable patterns, some dark and brick exposed, others patches of pale, white cement. When I finally worked up the courage to look out, it was as if I was hypnotized, watching the mosaic of earth flash by in front of me. Then, just as I thought I was getting my fear under control, we'd pass a spot that always did me in. It was a gaping hole. The abrupt change in the wall pattern sent a new surge of terror through me. The gap lasted only a couple of seconds, but I couldn't move. Then those whizzing walls would return to haunt me again!

During all of this Pops would watch, laughing and encouraging me to be brave. I really don't think he understood the depth of the trauma I was experiencing. Had he, I'm sure he would have acted much differently. He did explain that the gap was, in fact, a place where workmen could safely wait until the car passed. I thought it was more like looking into the entrance of hell!

***

Just east of Kansas City, Kansas, *Highway 32* meandered through the rich farmland, and never far from the banks of the lazy *Kaw River*. The two-lane highway began at the outskirts of town, passing by *City Park*, then over the north bluffs that eventually gave way to the fertile river basin below. Once in the valley, little towns popped up along the way – *Muncie, Edwardsville,* and *Bonner Springs.* Farming towns yes, but railroad towns, all the more.

Running parallel to the highway the steel rails also stretched west. These were the running tracks of the *Union Pacific* and *Rock Island Railroads.* And a two-track, high stepping mainline it was for sure, with sturdy ties and ballast to support the never-ending march of trains that kept America on the move. Once these trains cleared the yard tracks, it was out there running parallel to Highway 32 that the engineers opened their throttles, hurtling their long trains on appointed schedules. The long gently curving mainline was a sure place to pick up a minute here or there as the engineers fudged their speed limits to meet their advertised arrival times at Union Station and out west. Hours away were the sprawling prairie lands that eventually led to the Rocky Mountains and the Continental Divide.

To the unaware, Highway 32 and the railroad lines signaled nothing out of the ordinary. They both revealed *Rockwellian-like* scenes of mid-America in the late forties. But there were secrets hidden here as well. This was where the great journey west began. It was formerly the right-of-way of the *Kansas Pacific Railroad,* the 1800s trunk line that took the adventurous to the gold and silver mines of Colorado, and eventually connected to the fertile farm lands in California.

There was a local history buried in the valley soil, a region that had been explored centuries earlier by *Coronado* in the mid-1500s. He and his explorers had chosen this peaceful valley as their winter camp near *Bonner Springs.* Coronado never found the gold and treasures he was looking for, but he felt the beauty of the *land of the Kaw.* He also left behind the many tools and artifacts of his time that gave archeologists a road map to yesterday.

Recent times also revealed a historical mosaic of a different kind. This was what was left of the dilapidated *Kansas City Kaw Valley* electric interurban railroad. It was an ancient trolley line that began somewhere in Kansas City, Kansas, and ended up in Bonner Springs. The genesis of the *Kansas City Kaw Valley Railroad* began in 1904 when it was originally called the *Kansas City & Bonner Springs Electric Line.* Throughout the early twenties in the Midwest, the expansion of interurban lines formed a unique part of the nation's transportation mosaic. In this case the road's founders had their eye on tapping the lucrative Bonner Springs, Lawrence, and Topeka passenger traffic.

Getting underway took years of legal, financial, political wrangling, and more than one name change. A year after the company was formed and work began, in a move to financially and politically strengthen the corporation to accommodate its aggressive plans to expand beyond Bonner Springs, the road was legally chartered as the *Kansas City Western Railroad.*

By 1908, the line began its interurban operations to Bonner Springs. In keeping with the achievement, another name change was required, this time as the *Kansas City Kaw Valley Railroad.*

Back in the robust heyday of the electric line, the times were good and the ambitions of the interurban moguls were seemingly unlimited. The *Model T* had not yet forever altered the nation's perceptions about its transportation needs and the *Boeing 747* belonged in a science fiction book. Distances weren't measured on a global scale. *Topeka*, approximately sixty-eight miles away from Kansas City was still considered a long ride.

For the Kaw Valley executives, the infusion of investor dollars allowed the road to pursue its goal west. By 1917, the electric line had made it to *Lawrence*, forty miles away and, in keeping with that, it went through yet again another name change: the *Kansas City Kaw Valley & Western Railroad.*

But the expansion dreams all ended in Lawrence. In the years that followed, *Henry Ford's* invention came to town, and the interurban line felt his presence. The line never made it to Topeka. In fact, by 1949 the line had even abandoned its Lawrence leg, leaving only the Bonner Springs segment to generate the now all freight line's revenues. That being the case, the lawyers reverted to the earlier *Kansas City Kaw Valley* moniker, the road name it kept until its demise on December 28, 1961.

By the early fifties, the electric line that ran a total of 14.9 miles was in a bad state, a victim of deferred maintenance that had gone too far and was now on the edge of being safe, maybe even sensible. The unevenly spaced wooden ties had decayed to the point where one wondered how in the world anything could roll on it without derailing. There were only thin patches of rock ballast to support the ties and rails; none of the traditional signs of structural uniformity and engineering integrity so typical of a financially sound, well-run railroad. To the contrary, it was an existence kept together by *maintenance Band-Aids* and a fifteen-mile-per-hour (or often less) speed limits. Despite its decrepit condition, it was still hanging tough, a unique reminder of Midwest tenacity. In its own way it had a story to tell during those final years of operation, and I suppose that is what intrigued me about it so much. It was a fascinating little line that violated all the rules. Kind of like discovering a *T-Rex* rumbling along in the middle of civilization – it should have become an extinct species long ago, but it was there just the same.

The Kaw Valley's spindly rails twisted and bent all the way to Bonner and its remaining customers, the *Lone Star Cement* plant just east of town, the *Lauhoff Grain Company*, and the *Safeway Cereal* plant on the western fringe of the small community. That is where the car barn was too, and the three locomotives that were serviced, and left each morning to do their daily chores.

Once every day a faded yellow steeple cab Kaw Valley electric locomotive and string of cement cars would slowly crawl through downtown Kansas City, Kansas, and work its way to Bonner Springs, or the other way around. I never knew exactly where the yards were in town or where they connected to the major lines. I suspected it might have been a *Missouri Pacific* spur that ran into the busy *Fairfax* industrial district on the northeast end of town.

The big problem was that it was a long way from Bethany, and it was where a lot of the *colored* people lived. Although I had thought about going there to satisfy my burning curiosity, I also knew that it was a neighborhood I would never, ever enter by myself.

I didn't know much about the coloreds except they liked to go to *Swope Park* a lot. They would come in by the hundreds, and then take over the swimming pool. Folks on Bethany always acted nervous whenever they talked about them. They knew what happened at Swope Park and they didn't like it one bit, no sir…. They saw it as a bad sign. They talked about it a lot – pointing out that someday they would *take over the whole of Kansas City unless we white folk didn't do something to put them in their place good and proper.*

It was a dramatic declaration – a convincing, universal act of white power that underscored their commitment to putting things back where they thought it all belonged. Something *they* would do together that would make them remember it for a long time. So they took clear and decisive action: *They quit going there.* They starting going to *Wyandotte County Lake.*

I guess all of that talk did a lot to make me afraid to go around *them,* too. When all you hear is something bad, it's hard to be brave and see for yourself what was true, and what wasn't. It sets up a mindset that can last a lifetime.

\*\*\*

If I were really lucky, sometimes I would spot the locomotive when it popped out from behind a row of buildings, tooting its tinny horn at the double crossings at *Minnesota Avenue* and *18th Street.* Then it disappeared just as quickly along its narrow right-of-way into a gully below *Wyandotte High School.* Beyond was Highway 32 and the rest of the rocking, creaking journey through the Kaw River Valley to Bonner Springs.

The little engine would tote its five or six precariously swaying cement cars with great care, and before the sunset it would generally return. All along its journey, during those sweltering summer months the train's snail-like movement blended perfectly with the Kaw Valley lifestyles. The searing heat kept most everybody who could manage it indoors. Folks would buy a block of ice from the town ice locker and tote it home in the backs of their pickups. Then they would haul it into the living room and drop it into a battered porcelain pan. Back then an ice pick was an indispensable tool. It was the man of the house's main chore to punch and poke the big block of ice into several large pieces. The final step was taking the electric table fan and pointing it right at the pan. The bouncing breeze took the edge off the summer heat.

When the locomotive crawled through the bluffs and slithered into the wide fertile river plain through *Muncie* and *Edwardsville,* nobody paid it much mind. On a good day they might take a moment to glance through their front room windows. The real task was to keep one's head well inside the path of the cooling fan breeze.

***

Kansas towns in the late forties and early fifties were testaments of orderliness and common sense. They always seemed to mushroom alongside the tracks, but over time the social needs and business contracts that brought them together initially were redefined to suit the era. The results were a gradual series of changes and a peaceful coexistence of sorts, borne out of mutual expectations. Only the clanging bells of the railroad signal crossing on *Edwardsville's* main street served notice that one was about to impose itself on the other.

The intrusion was only temporary, but nevertheless dramatic enough. Union Pacific and Rock Island trains zipped dead center through town. Just a few yards north of the line was the local post office. On the same side, the town diner did a brisk early morning business.

There was an assortment of other stores that typically dotted both sides of the tracks in these kinds of towns; a feed and farm supplies store, a gas station, and a beer joint.

Even today beer joints are different from bars. Bars are clean. The walls are whiter and the floors swept clean. The chrome on the barstools is shiny, and the wooden bar counter has a polished, commercial luster. The bartender wears a nice white shirt and a bow tie. He always uses a clean towel to wipe down the glasses and stacks them neatly on the shelf behind him. Off in another area, there is entertainment – a jukebox, or maybe a sawdust-covered shuffleboard table. Civilized stuff…the kind of place you would go to comfortably whittle away a few hours.

Beer joints are ugly, dark; they have a heavy, earthy smell to them. It's a world where windows are never opened and the sun never gets in. Over time, the odor leaches into the walls and fades into the cracked and warped floor tiles. It's a dark and solitary place. You know that when you walk through the door. You go there to be alone, not to be social. You go there to wrestle with the reality of a failed crop or a busted marriage. You go there to cope with your darkest fears and your bitterest disappointments.

The bartender knows that. He puts a long-necked Falstaff beer bottle in front of you, takes your money, gives you your change, and disappears into the woodwork. If there is a jukebox inside, it's only cosmetic. The records it spins makes it official: you are in a time warp. Nothing's current. Nothing to do with the real world out there. It plays only an endless hit parade of painful memories. And that's okay with you. It's why you went there to begin with. The customer is always right.

None of that had much to do with the Kansas City Kaw Valley. Its passing through town was more of a non-event. Like the impact when an ear of corn falls off its stalk, or a swirling quarrel of sparrows settle in a tree for the night, or the gurgling sound of a creek as it meanders toward the *Mother Kaw*. It was just there, a notation on the pages of Kaw Valley life.

***

Sometimes, though, there are other events that impact everyone. Tornadoes and floods are like that. Kansans learned to take the weather in stride. Every summer when we saw the huge thunderheads building in the west and rolling our way, folks on Bethany Street naturally talked about the tornadoes. The black funnel clouds that appeared out of nowhere were a common occurrence in the western part of the state, but few, if any actually struck Kansas City directly. Old-timers believed we were safe because tornadoes rarely formed where there were large bodies of water.

Tornadoes were one thing, but a flood was something altogether different. Whereas tornadoes are powerful, natural events that can cause untold destruction, as bad as they can be, the damage is generally limited. But the sheer scope of a flood destroys the lives of many, many more. It's never ending. It's a slow kind of death-dealing natural event that erodes and undermines our sense of security and well being. In its relentless onslaught of waterpower, it washes away the arrogant assumption that we can control the natural world around us. Only an earthquake or hurricane can equal its potential path of destruction.

You can also *see* a flood doing its work in slow motion. Its unyielding process allows enough time to really show you what it can do. Its power and destruction are portrayed in front of you like a B-grade movie. Except it isn't a movie. It's the real thing.

At nine, this was a difficult connection to make. Water was a natural friend to me. I saw it as a calming, gentle element, linked to peaceful activities. I saw my father use it almost every week baptizing a newborn baby. Sometimes I'd ride for miles just to go swimming down at *Lake Quivera*, or boating at *Wyandotte County Lake*. Water was a friend that brought all of us kids relief during the hot, sweltering summer months.

But water is also deceptive, and that's where its terror really resides. Its rhythmic, flowing movement disguises how much real pain and destruction it can deal. It was only when I eventually saw it in places where it didn't belong that I began to really comprehend its vast destructive potential. When it was indiscriminately tearing down monuments that I thought were supposed to be there forever – the freewheeling destruction of homes, buildings, bridges, roads, even entire communities, and along with it a way of life. That's how it was in the *Great Flood of '51*, a time when nature took total control, and brought Kansas City to its knees.

My first real appreciation that a flood was coming began in the early spring. I made the discovery in a lot of ways, but mostly it was the neighbors and their actions that told me something was going terribly wrong. Nature was the reason why. Day after day the rains came, first arriving in the mid-afternoon, and then lasting longer and well into the night. There were few breaks. One storm followed another. As the days progressed into weeks, and as we passed from spring into early summer, the neighbors began to pay more attention to the changes that were being imposed on their daily routines. These weren't just the seasonal rains that everyone expected. They were occurring everywhere, west of us, and to our north and south, in fact throughout the great Midwest.

The rains kept coming, and they got worse. Now they started in the morning and hung around all day. I sat on my front porch by myself for hours at a time, with nothing better to do but thumb through Jenine's stale stack of comic books. I was past reading at this stage. It was more like scanning over the pictures, with nothing in particular catching my eye. Nobody to play with except with my brown and white mongrel, *Brownie*. I had already picked every flea off him I could find. Brownie was clean, happy, and snoozing by my side. I was bored. And the rains kept coming.

The *Kansas City Star* newspaper talked about it, and Mom and Pops talked about it. And when the neighbors took their walks at night during the brief lulls between storms, they talked about it, too. When I got up in the morning I ran to my bedroom window hoping to see the sun. No luck...just more rain....

People were getting edgy, partly because they were spending too much time inside, and maybe because they also knew a little about Kansas geography. West of Kansas City, the lands opened up into millions of acres of farm country. To the naked eye, these vast prairies that were seasonally full of golden fields of flowing wheat fields appeared to be flatlands with no extreme changes in the topography. But they weren't.

In truth, if you traveled west, the elevation rose a few feet every mile. At the far western end of the state, and into Colorado more than 600 miles away, stood the mammoth *Rocky Mountains* and the *Continental Divide*, the birth place of streams which eventually turned into rivers. Melting snow off the eastern slopes was normally all it took to keep these prairie streams and rivers full by late spring. But this year nature upped the $H_2O$ ante.

Rain clouds that were parked over the Midwest from the Dakotas into Oklahoma were hammering the region. The gentle terrain and levies that normally corralled and herded the water eastward in reasonable, predictable patterns were in an expanding struggle to keep it in check. The Kaw River was, in effect, a catchment basin formed out of tributaries that merged from all directions in the center of the state. It was showing signs of having a serious temper tantrum. Its bulging waters churned and challenged the dikes and levies as the water flowed eastward, ushered still more by the non-stop rains along its path.

North of Kansas it was the same scenario, only this time it was the even more formidable *Missouri River* that was starting to flex its watery muscles. Together, the Kaw and Missouri Rivers formed a natural pincer as precise as a military maneuver in the heart of Kansas City.

Now, as spring turned into early summer, I sat in our compact dinette and listened to the small radio. I looked up and watched Mom making dinner in silence. She was cutting small pieces of dough into noodles on her wooden chopping board. It was a precursor for her homemade chicken soup and dumplings. The steady *tick, tick, tick* of the cutting knife and the radio announcer's solemn voice merged into a doomsday cadence. Still, Mom's soup was no pushover. The aroma filtering throughout the kitchen created a temporary distraction. Even if only for a few seconds, I felt secure.

But the announcer's voice was pursuing an aggressive counter-attack. He slashed through my fragile sanctuary getting his razor results. Mom sensed my uneasiness. Her smile and dark eyes always did the job.

"Don't worry, honey.... It'll be okay.... We'll be safe.... We live on a hill," she said, sealing her declaration with yet another tick of her knife on the board. Her expression abruptly changed into a worried look.

"But those poor people down in *Argentine* and *Armourdale*.... I don't know...." she said, crossing herself and then looking toward the heavens.

Her calming smile was back again.

"God will help them, too...I know he will."

I hoped she was right. Even as my mother proclaimed her confidence that things would turn out okay, the radio announcer was busy telling me that things weren't looking good at all. God, I concluded, was obviously busy tending to something else. Kansas City was about to be overwhelmed by tons of uncontrollable, churning, muddy, silt-riddled, angry water.

As I sat in the dinette and fiddled with our old *Philco* table radio, every time I turned the dial the tuner would *twang* in a little more bad news. The announcer's robot-like reading listed the latest casualties, except these weren't people...they were entire towns, communities where people lived and worked: *Dodge City, Great Bend, Salina, Topeka,* and now *Lawrence*...only 25 miles away. Mom's chicken soup, the last line of defense, was in a lot of trouble.

During those rare interludes between storms, I rode my bike in the neighborhood for a first-hand look. What I saw worried me even more. There was a crackling urgency in the air. The neighbors seemed to be moving about in more deliberate ways; the housewives compulsively swept their front porches in an act of defiance that would somehow magically push their fears aside. The worried looks on their faces matched nature's ugly mood. There was none of the relaxed, easy going mannerisms I had grown accustomed to – no friendly waves, no hellos when we met on the sidewalk.

On Central Avenue, people were walking in nervous, purposeful ways, eyes darting to and fro, hands buried deep in their pockets and shoulders hunched. Open umbrellas partially hid their concerned expressions. It had all become a private matter. Nobody looked at anybody. They were too busy coping with their widening net of fears. It was coming....

Even the neighborhood birds were on to it. All day long you could count on them chirping away high atop the big Oaks. Family quarrels of sorts.  Especially the aggressive little *sparrows* that seemed to be on every rooftop gutter.  But now there were none of the usual territorial squabbles. Just silence.  And it was deafening.

***

It began with the sound of a siren.... I shot up in my bed, trying to comprehend something I had never heard before.  The siren's wail drifted over Bethany Street, riding the morning wind, trailing off, and then coming back even louder with its mournful sound.

I jumped out of bed and ran into the living room.  Mom and Pops were already up, and through the screen door I saw them standing on the front porch.  I ran outside.  Streams of people were walking down on both sides of Bethany.  They were strangers, all of them, and yet they all reflected the same worried looks as they solemnly made their way toward the railroad yards.

Pops looked at me.

"Come, we go...we go now...*Stevica'*.  We go to see the flood."  He looked at Mom who was fixed on the crowd passing in front of her.

"We come back, soon.  You call *Tooky* and see if anyone needs help."

She cupped her hands on the sides of her face and looked at him, nodding to Pops through her grim expression.

Pops opened our front gate and we joined the human stream.  I wasn't sure what we were going to see, but I could tell by his expression that whatever it was, it was serious.  The flood had come.  It was time for us to pay our respects to nature.

"See Stevo...water everywhere," Pops said, pointing to the widening torrent of a new river that had just been born where man once claimed was his alone.

"The crest won't hit until tonight," a voice muttered from out of the crowd who watched on in respect at the unfolding spectacle.  "It's gonna get a lot higher before this one's over."

Now, as I stood next to Pops and looked out over what was once the Union Pacific and Rock Island rail yards, I was horrified at the sight of the ugly brown river that had consumed it.  Already the tops of railroad boxcars and familiar buildings were nearly totally submerged.  The water was rolling on an uninterrupted path of its own choosing.  The entire *Armourdale* and *Argentine* districts and working man's neighborhoods had fallen victim to the flood.  From my vantage point I could see the *10th Street Bridge* spanning both yards.  It was only a few feet above it all, and the water was closing the delta fast.

Pops grimly surveyed the spectacle unfolding in front of both of us. He pointed to a floating two-story wood framed house just like ours that was being carried by the swift current.  There was a cow on its roof.  The sight of the animal lying on its side as if it were resting in a pasture was pitiful. The critter was on a journey which meant that certain death was only a few minutes downstream. Once the Kaw converged with the rampaging Missouri, the current would surely tear the wooden-framed farmhouse into shambles. I'll never forget its sad expression as it floated by us no more than twenty yards from the bottom of Bethany Street.

I felt an overwhelming sense of helplessness as I watched the power of nature in full fury, the cars, trees, church steeples, pieces of torn out bridges, and the piercing shrieks of terrified hogs stranded atop small islands of floating debris. Their almost human sounding cries for help made my hair stand on end.

To be totally helpless and unable to do anything is a humiliating experience. It violates the spirit of man, and chews at the core of one's self worth. I had only once before felt something similar, the time a kid a lot bigger and meaner threw me onto the hard winter ground, pinning my arms and shoulders with his knees. There was nothing I could do but look into his angry face as he raised his fist. The pain of the blow bothered me far less than that feeling of helplessness.

As I stood on Bethany and looked at the horrifying site in front of me, I understood where the power of our destiny really resided. It wasn't with us, that bully, or the spectators standing with me. It was out *there*, in the tons of muddy, angry water that was swallowing all that stood in its way. There was nothing we could do except to watch in awe and submissive silence. Change was being imposed on all our lives, and it was non-negotiable.

Later that afternoon at home, as the images of the torrent of water were still racing through my mind's eye, I heard the unmistakable voice of *Ljubica' (Libby) Zuzich,* one of the church's most successful and influential parishioners. She and her quiet, soft-spoken husband, *George,* owned *Zuzich Truck Line,* a frozen meat carrier that specialized in delivering loads mostly from Kansas City to Chicago. I came out of the house and saw them in the middle of the front yard talking to Pops and Mom. Mom was trying to comfort Libby as she cried.

At first I almost laughed. Mom stood just a tick over five feet, but Libby was a big-boned woman, slightly plump, and standing near 5'8". Mom was awkwardly reaching up, trying to wrap her arms around her big shoulders.

The big, black four-door *Buick Century* sedan that she used to haul Mom and me to her house in Missouri was parked along the street curb, and I could see the thick mud covering its silver hub skirts. The rains had temporarily halted, but the cloudy skies above signaled more was on the way as they talked.

"The river took everything in the Bottoms," Libby said, sobbing, then struggled to pull out her handkerchief buried deeply inside her big black purse.

"It covered our building terminal…Nicky, Sammy and Gene managed to get most of the trucks up to *Seventh Street,* but not everything. We didn't have enough time. Nobody thought it would come in so fast." Another torrent of tears followed. Libby blew her nose, then bent forward and buried her face into Mom's tiny shoulder.

In the days and weeks that followed similar stories unfolded; personal accounts revealed through the media as the full scope of destruction unfolded. Once, when I went on my own down to the Bethany *riverbank*, I saw a *Kansas National Guard* soldier on duty. He stood by himself on the grassy knoll in his green fatigues, wearing his helmet liner, and looking no-nonsense with a big rifle slung on his shoulder. He was ready to go to war. But there was no war he could fight this time. This was an enemy that had brought him and his kind to their knees in short order. To me, he was a daily reminder that his kind of power had its limitations.

"What's that?" a spectator asked, as he pointed to a huge ball of fire erupting along the bluffs near the Missouri side. Dark, thick ugly clouds of black smoke laced with orange flames shot high into the afternoon sky. Another explosion followed...and another...and yet another.

"Looks like a refinery fire to me," another voice said. "It's over in the *Southwest Boulevard* area."

Later, I learned the fire erupted inside a chemical plant that was situated in partially flooded waters. For days, stories on the radio talked about how the firemen fought bravely – and around-the-clock, to control the flames. But the battle was being severely hampered because of the dangerously low and unpredictable fire hose pressure. Ironically, they were fighting a blaze standing knee deep in water! Nothing was predictable.

When the waters finally passed and Kansas City struggled to regain its balance, the true destructive force of the *Flood of '51* became all too evident. The sun was back and I had the time to do some exploring. Riding my bike down to the bottom of Bethany, I saw the results first hand. Gone was the water. In its place were tons of silt and mud. As I walked into the yards, I felt the thick, red mud pulling at my battered tennis shoes. Everywhere I went, there was a heavy, earthy smell, noxious and overpowering. I tied my cowboy handkerchief over my nose as I slogged on deeper into the heart of the destruction. The mud sucked at my shoes and stuck to my jeans as I tried to reorient myself to familiar landmarks. But there were few. It was as if the yards had been hit by a nuclear blast. Boxcars were turned on their sides like toys and tossed about every which way. Tracks were ripped from their ballast and ties, then twisted into unimaginable shapes. Rails were pointing toward the heavens – their contorted shapes pleading for mercy from the watery onslaught. Switch posts lay on their sides, their green signal bulbs shattered, unable to communicate that all was well – to proceed with predictable confidence; buildings were barely standing now with entire walls gone, revealing only gaping holes where men once worked inside.

Yet some of man's monuments of self-importance somehow did manage to survive. The Rock Island's twenty-six-stall roundhouse had taken its hits, giving up a portion of the roundhouse wall to the water's wrath. But its ninety-foot engine turntable was still intact. Already, track gangs were busy trying to get their crippled railroad back on its feet. They worked at a fever pitch. It was as if every tie they put in line, every track they put back in place, and every building they re-commissioned was a piece of *themselves* being restored.

As the streets opened and more of the stricken areas came into view, I sat in the back seat with Libby and Mom in front, and we saw for ourselves what happened in the West Bottoms. We were touring a battleground. I guess I understand now how *General MacArthur* must have felt when he surveyed the aftermath of a war. But this wasn't *Iwo Jima* or *Saipan,* or the *Philippines.* It was the working class communities of Armourdale, Argentine and *Turner, Kansas* that had been under attack. The *Buick* meandered along as we lurched over the potholes and ruts and stared at the foundations of homes that weren't there any more. A few of the remaining buildings revealed where the high water left its mark just below their roofs. Gas stations where pump islands still existed, but the pumps were long gone, committed to the current. Cars plowed nose first into corner sewers, and that's where they stayed. Bridges that began but never ended. Telephone poles that were sheared off at the base and dead power lines lying on the ground that connected nobody to nowhere. But most of all it was that smell...that penetrating, putrefying, stifling, nauseating smell that told me this was where nature had left its calling card. *The Great Flood of '51* was history, but it would live in our minds forever.

***

*Looking back, I can see it all as if it happened yesterday. Once you have been consumed by a catastrophe, then things start to happen. It sort of becomes a video recording. You go into a frame-by-frame mode. Things slow down to the point where every image becomes an eight-by-ten portrait, precise in its composition, full of rich, vibrant color, and razor-sharp focus. Each one leaves a unique imprint in your memory that lasts a lifetime. When it happens like that, that's when you understand what it means to have been an eyewitness to history. And I was....*

**Home...**


*Sketches from the past...*

# Dance of Death

**N**othing made sense today as Belinda Hawkins looked up and down *Minnesota Avenue,* in downtown Kansas City, Kansas, trying to understand where all the people had gone. The stores were nearly empty – in fact many had shut down. It was close to high noon, Friday the 13th – normally a bustling time that saw folks walking up and down the street shopping and having lunch at one of the stores. To some folks Friday the 13th was bad luck for sure, but at barely 11, Belinda really didn't know about such things. To her it was the usual time to find her Mom and spend the afternoon reading in the back of the clothing store until she had finished her work for the day.

She had come to town from her home near *Kensington Park* on the streetcar. Ever since her Pop had died a couple years earlier, her mother, Norma, took on a job to make ends meet. With school out for the summer Norma felt more secure if her daughter was nearby rather than letting her whittle away the hours until she got home.

Belinda picked up the streetcar on *18th Street* after riding the old rickety line that stopped a block or so from her house. The car route angled toward the main part of town and eventually made its way through the West Bottoms, over the *James Street Bridge,* then climbed again into the bluffs beyond into Missouri.

But not today. When they arrived near *Minnesota Avenue* the car came to a halt. The conductor told all the riders that this was as far as he was going this day. There was a flood on the way and the *Bottoms* would be hit for sure.

Belinda got off the car and walked the few extra blocks to where her Mom worked down at the bottom of Minnesota Avenue and a stone's throw from the *City Viaduct.* When she stepped inside, she saw Norma hurriedly putting the balance of the cash from the register drawer into a brown bag, then into the small safe on the floor. She slammed the door shut, turning the combination lock several times and pulled the safe handle for good measure. Then she reached for her small black purse under the counter and stood up, stuffing the pocketbook under her arm and tidying up the counter area as she looked around one more time. She smiled at her only daughter as she approached her, holding out her hand.

"C'mon sweetheart."

"Why are we leavin' now, Mama?"

Norma flashed a nervous smile as they exited the front door together. She pulled the ring of keys out of her bag and pushed several aside until she found the bright gold one she was looking for. She stuck it into lock and turned it, then twisted the doorknob for good measure. She stuffed the keys back into her bag and looked down at her daughter

"It's the flood sweetheart...customers aren't coming in today. Mr. Davies called and told me to close early. Folks bein' so worried about it and all, no sense in staying open. It's all people are thinking about."

Belinda thought about her mother's statement. But in truth it was her expression that worried her more. She hadn't seen anything quite like it since her Pop had died in a car crash. It was a combination of sadness laced with fear that something bad was happening, and there wasn't much she or anybody else could do about it.

"The conductor said he can't go into Missouri any more, Momma," Belinda added matter of factly. "He said the water is coming up really fast."

Norma took her daughter's hand, but instead of heading up Minnesota like they always did, she turned right.

"Where we goin', Mama?"

Norma pointed to the viaduct.

"Over there...not far. Where all those people are standing."

Ever since her husband had died, Norma had taken it upon herself to raise her only child with the kind of loving care that would normally have come from two parents. She was always looking for ways to help her understand life and the unfolding world around her. At night she read to her from a stack of children's books – during the summer school break when she wasn't working to make ends meet, she made sure that their time together was meaningful. She talked to her quietly about lots of things – in particular about the power of *God* and nature. And most about life and its unpredictabilities. Norma was a religious woman and it was her way of preparing her daughter for events she knew she might not understand too well right now, but later they would become the building blocks of her own survival, and inner strength.

"Those folks are standin' right over the flowing water, honey," Norma said, as she picked up the pace. Belinda was finding it hard to keep up with her mother's gait as she made her way onto the bridge. She held her hand tightly as they trotted along the bridge sidewalk. When they stopped next to the knot of spectators, Belinda edged closer to the railing, holding her Mom's hand now as if it were a lifeline. Through the bridge rail bars she could see the ugly, muddy water churning at will. By now it had spilled well over the dikes and was inundating the rail yards that hugged the bluff just to the west below *Strawberry Hill*. The entire area had become a river more than 2½ times the size of the Kaw that normally ran through town, where under normal conditions few even noted its presence. But not now. The tops of the railroad boxcars were inundated by the watery mass. An old girder span bridge that led to nowhere into the Bottoms was gathering debris along its southern flank.  The water now easily topped the bridge's rail bed where only a few months before there were at least twenty feet separating it.

Belinda looked up at her mother who was also fixed on the unfolding spectacle of nature.  When she noticed her daughter, she forced a weak smile.  Belinda saw her mother's lower lip tremble as she fought to bring out the words.

"It's the Power of *God*...sweetheart...nothing can stand in *His* way."

Belinda looked down again at the deluge, gripping her Mom's hand even tighter.

"Look! Out there!  That house floatin' down near the *Central Avenue Station*. There's people on the roof!" someone in the crowd shouted.

The house was still some distance away but already Belinda could see it helplessly bobbing along with the current, literally floating over the same space where rail yards once existed.  It was a small country farmhouse, something she remembered seeing once when she and her parents took the Union Pacific to Denver to see her cousins.  The kind that sat by itself in western Kansas, accompanied by a clump of old Oaks in the front yard, a battered white picket fence in front, and built alongside a nameless dirt road that led into the vastness of a prairie land that stretched into infinity.

"Look, he's right," Norma said.  "See...it's a man and a woman...and a little girl! "

Belinda edged closer to the bridge rail.  The house was coming into clearer view now. The little farm girl was about her age.  She saw the ugly brown blotches of mud all over her plain cotton dress.  Her mom and dad were between her, wildly waving their arms and pleading for help.

"We gotta help 'em!" one of the men shouted.  "If that house gets to the Missouri, they're gonna die for sure."

Two men bolted for the bridge entrance, flagging down a passing police car.  Belinda looked back at the approaching house, which by now was no more than thirty yards away. From their vantage point, they were almost directly above them.  It was a bird's eye view of an unfolding tragedy.

The little girl held on to both of her parents' hands the same way Belinda held her mother's.  When the house floated closer, the farm girl picked out Belinda from the crowd.  They riveted onto each other just as the house began to slowly spin counter-clockwise in the churning, unruly current.

Belinda pulled herself free from her mother's grip and grabbed the bridge rails, leaning forward as far as she dared between the railings.  The little girl was almost directly below her now.

For an instant Belinda was transfixed by the red ribbon still in the stranded girl's long strawberry blond hair.  She focused on it with a jeweler's stare as she watched her begin to perform a pirouette below her.  It was a slow dance of death – a spinning symphony orchestrated by the flood's current.

In desperation, Belinda stuck her hands and arms through the bridge railings, hoping that somehow, some way, she could pluck her out of harm's way.  The little girl understood the gesture.  She pulled away from her mother's grip and lifted her hand arm toward her. The last thing Belinda saw was her pleading eye as she disappeared under the bridge.

"Oh, Mommy…what will happen to her?" Belinda said as she looked up and then buried her face into her side, sobbing. "Please Mommy, don't let her die. She won't die, will she?"

Norma pulled her daughter closer and wrapped her arms around her tiny shoulders, fighting to hold back her own torrent of tears.

"God will watch over them, sweetheart…don't worry…they'll be fine."

Belinda held onto her mother, too terrified to look back out into the watery torrent below. She knew that if she did, she'd only see the eyes of a frightened little girl and her  outstretched hand – reaching for salvation.

# # #

# Part Two

# FRIENDS

# The Southern Bell

*The Bell.*
*Strutting smartly into the South.*
*Cutting through the piney woods.*
*Jasmine…mint juleps…*
*Mardi Gras calling…*

*The Bell.*
*Kansas City's own… Queen of the Ball*
*Parasol twirling…debutante*
*Sashaying…leisure living…*
*Into Confederate Gray.*

*The Bell.*
*Southern Comfort on the way…*
*Leaving the Union…*
*Gliding into Missouri…Kansas …Arkansas*
*Climbing…*

*The Bell.*
*Rolling hills and farmland…Then…*
*Heavener…Mena…Dequeen…*
*A Crow's flight…into Southern breezes…*
*Kissing the land – golden brown…*

*The Bell.*
*Night views… alone…no fears…*
*Shadows …private thoughts*
*Rolling through the memories…*
*Sleep…safe…*

*The Bell.*
*Good Morning Red Stick!*
*Skimming over the bayous…*
*Wooden trestles…sturdy, strong*
*Pirogues gather…Cajun calls…crawfish…*

*The Bell.*
*Big Easy welcome...*
*Benois in the Quarter*
*Dixieland...parades...life...*
*Rest...Then Home again... Union calling.*

# Chapter Three

Sunday afternoons on Bethany Street were always special times for the Nichols family and, in a way, for all of us. That was when all the family who were still living in the area gathered to enjoy *Grams Nichols'* special Southern Fried chicken and all the trimmings. It was an affair that lasted pretty much most of the day. The gathering was a natural extension of neighborhood life, and as predictable as the seasons. No one paid much attention when the cars began to arrive.

*Grams and Gramps Nichols* lived next door to us. Over the years they minded their own affairs, but there were also tight bonds between us. The kinds that were forged out of years of predictable friendship and reliability. If you needed something and it didn't violate the rules of the Bible or give Satan any assistance, you could count on them being right there. Mom and Pops felt the same way about them.

There were other connectors that brought us together and the times we were living were as responsible for that as much as the people. For one, their daughter *Aunti-Mac (Maxine Bowers)* and Mom were roughly the same age. Her first-born son, *Denny,* and I were born barely a month apart. With the war on, people had to work together. *Bob,* her salesman husband, went off to the Army. Like so many others who were caught up in the war, it meant the women folks had to make do more than usual. Mom did her share watching Denny and me while Maxine worked, not to mention the two of them pooling their resources at finding other creative ways to keep things going. Practical stuff such as sharing their ration cards whenever one or the other ran out of something essential.

*Uncle Fuzzy,* Aunti-Mac's oldest brother, had been exempted from military duty because of his job as a fireman on the Rock Island. After his divorce – a matter that caused considerable family pain and embarrassment but was rarely discussed – he brought his identical twin sons, *Ronald and Donald* to live with his mother at the Bethany Street house. The boys slept in an attached bedroom in the back of the house and that was where they stayed until both of them joined the Navy after completing a couple of years at *Kansas University.*

Once in a while Denny and I would spend the night there, too, and I always felt that the room was special. Everything was virtually identical and always spic-'n'-span. Above the twin beds were tiny airplane models hanging from strings. They were perhaps early indicators that they were destined to carve out careers as aviators.

The family patriarch, *Clint Nichols,* ran his home in a traditional way. But folks who knew better would tell you that it was Grams who had quite a fair bit to say about what went on in that house. Quiet-natured, resolute and a Hard Shell Southern Baptist to her very core, Grace kept the faith, and ran her home and life with the precision of an orchestra leader who knew how to get the best out of every instrument in her ensemble. She offered no apologies in claiming that it was the *holy score* of the *New Testament* that she blindly followed and never, ever questioned. And she always encouraged anyone to join her who had a mind to. But she never pushed and she never, ever put her husband in a bad light, no matter what transgressions he occasionally slipped into over the years. Her rules of living were black and white and always anchored in the teachings gleaned out of the *scriptures.*

When Sundays rolled around it was natural for me to be included in most of these family gatherings. The idea of getting a plate full of Grams' chicken, mashed potatoes, an ear of corn, and a tall glass of lemonade made me more than happy to be considered an extension of their family tree.

But it was Grams' homemade applesauce that got to me every time. She used to pick up the apples that had fallen out of the old tree in the back yard. She had a special talent for finding just the right ones, not too sweet, and not too sour. Far as I know, she did it without ever taking a bite.

When the dinner officially began Denny and I connived to get our food quickly and went outside to our favorite spot on the front porch. He sat on the porch swing and I picked one of the chairs, using the porch railing to balance my plate as I ate. The soft breeze that suddenly came up thanks to a patch of clouds bathed my face as I used both hands to dig in. I didn't mind it a bit when some of the corn kernels found their way to the sides of my mouth, and then to the porch floor. It was all part of the process.

Behind us and through the front window, we could see the family gathered around the rectangular table with Gramps in his customary head-end position. Grams was in and out of the room bringing on an endless stream of food. It was a perfect afternoon until I saw the screen door fly open and a little girl pop through it. She was back! Denny's three-year-old sister, *Dee-Dee* barged into our world again.

Dee-Dee strutted toward us using her already familiar mix of authority and dramatic star qualities. It was that same kind of confident presence that Denny also reflected, but hers was even more pronounced. As if she were entering – *down stage, center.*

Aunti-Mac saw it too, and was tickled pink. From day one, she had a plan to make sure whatever this quality was that her daughter had, she would give her every opportunity to bloom. Truth was Aunti-Mac was a firm believer in the arts and ever ready to fully encourage the depths of her kids' creative talents. And it wasn't restricted to them alone. More than once, she happily included me in the exercise.

Aunti-Mac had also adopted many of Gram's simple philosophies on Christian living, but also stepped around the brimstone and fire talk that accompanied Southern Baptist teachings.  It was evident that her spiritual cup was overflowing.  She was a stalwart in the Methodist Church, and long before it became fashionable and commercial to help the poor and oppressed, she was on the firing line doing volunteer work for the less fortunate.  She was that rare type of human being who genuinely liked anyone and everyone she met, no matter what their color or persuasion.

Dee-Dee walked up to us, but her attention was riveted only on her older brother who she adored. She stood there, relying on her *Bette Davis blues* to register a plea for Denny to play with her.  It was quite possibly her most patented performance.  The kid had range.  And she was quick on the turn, too. Depending on what kind of response she got, she would decide what to do next.  Sometimes it meant going into her *super pleads mode,* and here again it was her eyes that led the way.  If he decided to go stupid and look the other way, then she kicked in her *I'm getting angrier mode*, a combined tactic that still relied on her eyes as the main weapon, but now introduced a low-level whimper.  No need for talk. Dee-Dee already figured out that her non-verbal signals could work wonders.  She simply revved up the decibels and let her vocal cords do the rest.  When that happened, we both knew it was time to clear the deck.  Dee-Dee Bowers could be very convincing.

***

*Apparently there are millions of others who in the years that followed also agreed, although I had no idea back then what was coming.  After graduating in Speech Communications from the University of Kansas, she packed her bags and went to New York to study acting.  Years later I spotted her four-color poster photo and name plastered on a theater marquee in downtown Geneva, Switzerland. As a stage and screen star,* **Dee Wallace Stone***, captivated millions as the mom in the Steven Spielberg's box office smash,* **ET***.  She has since been a feature actress in countless movie and television appearances. Just like fire-baller Ray Sadecki, Dee-Dee had the* **gift***.*

***

Back then Dee-Dee was still years away from stardom, although with us she was doing an Academy Award job at being a pain in the butt.  We saw that she was ramping up for the full treatment and started looking for a way out. Then suddenly, for no apparent reason, she abruptly turned and left, slamming the screen door behind her as she went inside.  Maybe it had something to do with getting to know more about her two cousins, Ronnie and Donnie who were seated side-by-side at the dining room table.  The conversation among the family members was brisk and full of catch-up news. Having the twins on hand was the big event of the summer, and everybody wanted to be in on it.

Later that afternoon, Gramps adjourned into the living room and settled into his favorite high-back chair with arms that were worn down to the padding from all the years he propped his elbows on them. The battered, gray cloth-covered chair was his and his alone. It bore the personal imprint where his behind had shaped and contoured the seat pad like a river cuts through a gorge. The chair was positioned just so, almost touching – but not quite – the family's stately *Philco* console radio. On the other side of the room there was the new *Zenith* ten-inch TV. A gift from Aunti-Mac, its circular eye looked stupid and uninviting. Judging by its backwater location, it was obvious the new invention, good as Aunti-Mac swore it was, had not been given much of a welcome in the Nichols household.

By 1950, television was making its mark on Bethany Street, but Gramps was a hold out. In those days, radios and televisions weren't just communication tools. They were, in fact, expected to be pieces of elegant furniture, hand crafted and designed to accentuate quality in the living room. The *Zenith* was no different.

Yet the Philco had a fascinating quality all of its own. It was a bona-fide stand-alone machine right out of the vacuum tube era. Its shiny mahogany cabinet reflected a classy luster like the waxed hood of a big, Cadillac sedan. The black plastic dials on the front looked like movie props Dr. Frankenstein might have used to pump electricity into his handcrafted monster. The radio design in itself made a statement about where the notion of quality fit in the manufacture of American products.

But it was its oval shaped tuning dial that was the real grabber. The yellow light mounted behind the glass cover turned everything amber and mysterious looking. The numbers, short wave, FM and AM frequencies – the names of faraway places on the dial monitor tugged at my imagination. Tokyo, Hong Kong, London and Paris – wherever my mind dared to wander, it was there on the dial, waiting only to be discovered. The old Philco could make it a reality, pulling far beyond the rolling hills of Eastern Kansas. All that was required was a patient fiddling with the dials and a keen ear zeros in. The voices from beyond filtered into the room, riding on the backs of airwaves that moved at will.

Gramps knew how to get the best out of the old radio, and everybody knew it. But it wasn't places on the other side of the globe that caught his fancy. It was the tiny hamlet of *Blue Eye, Arkansas,* on the state's border with Missouri. How he did it, nobody ever quite figured out, but every Sunday he locked into the *Arkansas Jamboree.* He never missed. Once he got it, he upped the volume and the house echoed with the staccato rhythm of *Blue Grass* music and a banjo lead playing at breakneck speed. Between each tune the MC's voice was so heavy with a thick Southern drawl that few of us in the room could understand what he said. But Gramps could.

As the afternoon wore on he tapped his foot to the steady pulse of the music that faded in and out of the room. Next to his chair were his pipe stand and a stand-up ashtray. As the music blared he picked up his small silver penknife on the lip of the tray, selected his favorite pipe and methodically began to carve out the inside of the wooden bowl.  Then he took his felt covered metal pipe cleaner out of its box on the stand and worked it through the stem, all the while bending forward to pick up the music.

Secure that all was in order, he opened the metal tin and stuffed a wad full of *Sir Walter Raleigh* tobacco into his pipe bowl.  Gramps liked to light up using the long-stem wooden matches he kept alongside the tray.  The kind that fizzled and half exploded into a cloud of blue sulfur, then into a bright orange flame.  He puffed away, holding the match flame over the bowl and letting the smoke meander throughout the house.  Then he settled back into his chair and shut his eyes.  The look of tranquility on Gramp's face told us all life was in order.

# Chapter Four

S chool…it takes no prisoners, no matter where you are or what you think you may be. Once you enter the bricked, academic, sterile hallways of education, you're on a level playing field. No fantasies…no deals. If you've got it, you're in. If not, then think about a job in a good trade. That's what school does. It's the great leveler. Slowly, like an iceberg inching its way to an unknown destination, the reality of where you will fit in the big picture begins to unfold. There's no escape.

As places of learning go, *Prescott Grade School* was not among the most notable of educational *prisons* that existed in Kansas City in the late forties and early fifties. Yet in some ways it did resemble the classic *Little Red Schoolhouse* that so often depicted life in the Midwest and the underlying educational processes that went on inside these types of buildings.

To that end, one could call Prescott a qualified distant relative. To be sure, the rural schools were still out there and operating. Country folks who lived in the small farming communities such as *Savenberg, Abilene, Council Grove* and *Genesco* owed their futures to these protectorates of fundamental education that seemed to percolate out of these simple yet highly effective teaching houses. They were a natural and consistent part of the Midwestern landscape with their bell steeples and wood framed one-story construction. To most they were a reflection of America in its most basic form. When the school bell clanged the children knew that the fun and games were over. The time had come for grinding out the infamous Three Rs: *readin', writin' and 'rithmatic….*

Prescott was erected in the twenties. Despite the *Great Depression* and the hard times all around, the money was set aside to keep the local system operating and to train the young to face a still uncertain tomorrow. A staff of homegrown elementary teachers – most who came from small teachers' colleges in the region, dug in for the long hard pull to rear yet another generation of Kansans.

These dedicated people heard the call and held the line, re-introducing the fundamental teaching principles that seemed to survive, despite new ideas and approaches suggesting that it was time to put aside the old ways and try something new. But the fundamentals held fast. It really stemmed from a core belief that *if it ain't broke, don't fix it.* Those views kept the learning machine well oiled and working smoothly. Simple designs like a Ford with a *flat-head V-8* engine. An economical approach in car engine propulsion, yet stunningly effective at getting results.

In Kansas City the learning progression was systematic. Actually, it was automatic. It meant that anyone going to Prescott would be part of its hallowed halls for six years, and from there move on to *Central Junior High School* to cover the seventh, eight and ninth grades. After that it was the top end for most – the final three-year stint at *Wyandotte High School,* the showcase example of what a good high school education was all about in Kansas.

But it was at Prescott where the foundation was laid. It was also at Prescott where those first glimmers of reality began to seep into the wild-eyed imaginations and unpredictable antics of impulsive kids with emotional rudders that didn't work very good. Just tons and tons of energy coupled with a pinhole sized understanding that boys are boys and girls *are* girls. Still, the game being learned was deadly serious. Parents reminded their children of the importance of school as consistently as the nine-o'clock *Proctor and Gamble* whistle that blew every night. Inside the small rooms, teachers stood at the head of their stark wooden classrooms and behind their simple desks. On the tabletops the hand written comments they made about us charted our futures. It was an academic roadmap – our own *DNAs* that revealed our individual potentials. Clinical…a place where no prisoners were taken – unforgiving, and most of all terrifying every time a pencil was picked up and notations were made.

The dark mahogany pupil desks already had the scars of imprints from other *prisoners* who had passed through and left messages to the newcomers. This was the road into the unknown – to knowledge, books, and mastering those thick, rounded, soft lead black pencils to record what we had learned. Nothing came easy. Nothing was a hand-out. War is hell!

\*\*\*

Her name was *Clementine Petsick.* She was a broad-shouldered, heavyset woman with laughing eyes and a stern mouth. If there was anyone who was born to be a teacher, it had to be her. I came to know Mrs. Petsick after going through three years of grade school. The kids I was grouped together with were from all over the neighborhood. We learned how to be civilized – well sort of, in kindergarten. I soon figured out that they were pretty much like me, all except the fact that they didn't like trains. That is except for *Frankie Gibbons.* He liked trains, a lot. His dad was an engineer for the Union Pacific and that meant a free ride to the roundhouse on more than one occasion.

The climb up the academic ladder through our first and second grades was fairly uneventful until I got into the middle of my third year. The problem that popped up then stuck around forever.

It was my eyes. One night during supper I told Mom that I was having trouble seeing the blackboard, and that was all it took. Next thing I knew I was in an optometrist's office and his eye exam confirmed it. I was nearsighted as hell and the prognosis wasn't good.

"You must have got it after you caught the measles and mumps one behind the other last year," Mom told me, as she tried to find the words to console me. "That happens to people sometimes."

She reached down and hugged me, doing her best to eliminate the pain of my having to wear coke bottle glasses for the rest of my life. When I walked into the classroom and heard the snickers from the kids, it told me that things were going to be very different from now on.

All except Frankie. He was a nice person...gentle by nature and generally the quiet sort in school. A stocky lad, Frankie had deep set blue eyes and a shock of dark, almost black hair. We got to know each other pretty well by the time we both went into the Fourth Grade. He sat right next to me in class and once in a while we would get off into our own world. Frankie would pull out a comic from under his desk and while Mrs. Petsick wasn't looking we would scan the pages. They were action comics...*Plastic Man...Superman...Batman*.... What generally got us into hot water, though, wasn't the story line. We would lock into one of the character drawings and begin to critically analyze it. More often than they looked idiotic and out of that we began to build story lines of our own. Inevitably, it led to both us working into laughing jags that were so intense I peed my pants more than once. It also got us into trouble, but stern as she could be, Mrs. Petsick never took her anger all the way to her full potential. She seemed to understand the sometime idiotic direction kids with fluid imaginations could go.

In a strange kind of way there was something *spiritual* about going to school back then. Almost...but not quite.... Every day we stood up and made our *pledge of allegiance* to the US flag. With our right hands placed across our chests, we were more than ready to belt out the lyrics to *America...the Beautiful,* or *The Star Spangled Banner...*or *My Country 'tis Of Thee.* We learned it in school and nobody seemed to mind. But it didn't stop there....

Every Wednesday our class would take a two-block walk into the neighborhood. Two-by-two we made our way down the tree-lined neighborhood street until we came to a tiny Baptist Church. The teacher trooped us down into a small room where we were all given hymnbooks. For the next hour we sang as a group...familiar, traditional Bible Belt songs that had simple messages and melodies. Easy to work into harmony. And it really didn't matter what we were...Methodists, Serbian Orthodox, Lutherans.... Wednesday afternoons meant it was time to get in touch with our spiritual selves.

Bible Belt songs seemed to permeate in every religion. They were the glue that kept Kansas City culture together. You could hear them every day on the radio, and on Sunday there was little else to hear. Using school time to sing them was only natural and I soon discovered that I had an ear for music. When it was over and we started our walk back down the tree-lined street to school, I felt...well...kind of liberated.

\*\*\*

Despite the fact that learning was more often than not a painful process for me, there were moments where wonderful things occurred inside the classroom.  Sometimes it had something to do with Mrs. Petsick, but it also had a lot to do with what went on in the world in general.  I was essentially a nosey kid and found out pretty early that if you asked the right questions to the right people, you could save yourself a lot of time.  You could learn the easy way, and I was always on the lookout to do things as easily as possible.

Education was an important goal.  All us Kansans were acutely aware of where we were in the big picture, at least geographically speaking.  This *dead center* reality worked for, and also against us. On one side we were quick to point out how the state and its people represented the true *Heartland* where common sense invariably prevailed and that these decisions were in keeping with *God's* teachings.

On the other hand, there was also an underlying insecurity that seemed to be part of the social fabric.  Country bumpkins…a place where nobody spent much time…yet among us all an insatiable need to be the best in the US…especially in sports.  As the song goes, *Everything Is Up To Date in Kansas City*.  It was, in fact, more than just a cute jingle.

All of that percolated in the classroom and it was probably a major underlying factor why I was so curious about so many things during those early years.  To be sure, there were lots to learn, and plenty of places that only the imagination could bring to life back then.

For whatever reasons all of this lateral growth – learning how to make connections from a lot of different directions, suited me just fine.  I liked to wander around the world in my mind's eye.  Once, during class I stood in front of the entire group of kids and made a spot presentation on why I thought Palestine would become the world's next hotspot. It was all quite impressive and I really didn't know what I was taking about. But it was fun just the same.

It pretty much stayed that way until the fourth grade.  That's when Mrs. Petsick, doing her duty as a dedicated teacher, introduced us to something that changed my life forever: *arithmetic.* When she did, the comfortable, predictable, and reasonably successful life as I knew as a student took a lifetime nosedive.

It was to be a struggle that crept into my very soul – the mastering of linear numbers and then putting them in order – correctly.  No mistakes allowed, ever; no mind drifting.  Just the quest to make sure that *two times two* always equaled *four.*

The rigidity of the discipline ran against the grain of my flying imagination and growing compulsiveness.  It wasn't long that Mom and Pops discovered there was a glaring hole in my academic portfolio.  Try as I might, I simply couldn't put things right and the grades reflected my dismal performance.  As I struggled to get the best out of a series of addition and subtractions – and labored over multiplication and fractions, I found myself nervously pressing on the tip of my thick pencil.  The *tickity-tick* sound the lead made on the wooden table sounded a little like a telegrapher's *Morse Code*. The rhythm paced the images I conjured of an outbound passenger train. The relief – as it was, invariably led to more pain. With each passing hour thinking about what was happening *out there*, I was falling behind *in here*.

It all came to a head one fateful day when Mrs. Petsick handed me my report card. There it was…a big, ugly **"4"** posted next to the arithmetic grade. A **"1"** was tops – **"5"** and you've totally bombed out. It was devastating and the tears came on too suddenly to do anything about it. (*I've hated the number* **"4"** *ever since.*)

Later that week Mrs. Petsick came over to the house and talked with my folks, carefully explaining to them what had to be done to make things all better. Pops listened but it was obvious by his expression that what I had done was a sign of out-and-out failure. Mom was more forgiving, but the truth was, I was in trouble.

###

*I only discovered more than fifty years later why I had so many problems. Quite by accident a neurologist friend observed the way I typed and did other things; it was a sure sign that I had dyslexia. It was a mild form, he said, but enough to wreak havoc for a kid who was trying to keep his numbers straight and accurate. At least now I know what was behind it, and I'm grateful for that!*

***

**Friends...**


*Sketches from the past...*

# The 'Over The Can' Wars...

The fireflies that blinked in the cloudless nighttime sky were everywhere. They always showed up by the thousands in late spring, when the earth was coming alive and the temperatures were just right. They danced on the tops of hills and in the small yards throughout the neighborhood. I spotted one just above my head and snatched it out of the air, stuffing it into the *Libby's* fruit preserve glass jar. In a flash I screwed on the copper lid tight and held up the jar for everybody to see. The orange lights inside were blinking a Morse Code of their own.

"I did it!...I got my twenty...I won. C'mon you guys...you know the rules..."

Out of the darkness I saw that Denny had done pretty well, too. He had at least fifteen."

"Okay, what now?" His voice was even, controlled, but there was also a tinge of growing impatience to it. Denny was never the type to stick with something too long. His bright, restless mind was coupled to a bundle of endless energy. Life was a never-ending exploration of discoveries, and sometimes he got right on the edge of right and wrong. Nothing was off limits.

"Yeah...so you won...so what?... You wanna have a circle jerk?" chirped another boy's voice out of the darkness.

I didn't bother answering. I knew that it was just *Emory-Emory* trying to crack another one of his silly, unimaginative jokes.

I walked across *Lowell Avenue* and stood under the lone street lamp leading to the entrance of the cinder alley that ran behind my house and next to the Fry boys' home. I saw another kid coming my way. *Mikey Dodig* didn't live in the neighborhood but he might as well have been one of us. He actually lived in Strawberry Hill, but he and I were pretty good buddies. For one thing, both of us were altar boys. For another, he was a Serb. Some of the parishioners said we even looked alike. I never told him but I always thought he was a lot better looking than I was. He was bigger and more rugged and didn't wear coke bottle glasses like me. I couldn't see the comparison.

Mikey was a survivor and nobody to fool with either. His home turf over on *Splitlog Avenue* offered more than enough survival challenges. Kids from Strawberry Hill were known to be mean, especially the *Croatians* and *Italians* who went to the Catholic schools.

"How about *Kick the Can?* We ain't played that in a long time," he suggested. The idea caught on. Several of the neighborhood kids appeared out of the darkness.  Most were dressed in plain cotton shirts and an assortment of baggy, flannel pants.  The one thing we all had in common were our battered, black *Converse* high top tennis shoes.  They gave us a kind of togetherness, not to mention making a statement about our economic status.

Emory-Emory was at it again.

"Okay Mr. Big Shot, you wanna play kick the can?  Then you're the can. And I'm gonna kick it!" he said, as he guffawed at his own joke, slapping his knee in self-congratulations at being such a wit.

Mikey glanced at Denny, who glanced at me and rolled his eyes.

"You stink...." Denny muttered.

Emory-Emory stomped toward him.

"Wha'd you say? You talkin' to me, boy?"

Denny held his ground.  Although he was a good four inches shorter, he was lightning fast and probably the best athlete of the bunch.  What really made him lethal was that he didn't have enough sense to know when things were getting out of hand.

"Hey, you guys gonna play, or what?  Or are you just going to stand around playing with yourselves?"

The boys wheeled around to see *Annie Jean Polanski* pop in under the street lamp's dull glow.  *AJ*, as she was known to us kids in the neighborhood, had both of her hands characteristically stuffed in her back jeans pockets. Willowy and with fiery blue eyes and shoulder length auburn hair, at eleven she was caught somewhere between being a first-class *"Tom Boy"* and on her way to becoming a sensual women.  Her already developing bust stretched her flimsy white T-shirt.  But it was her natural command presence that kept us riveted to her every move.

"Well, what you gonna do?" she demanded, standing legs spread in a command posture.

When no one spoke she pointed an accusing finger at Emory-Emory.

"You got a big mouth, Emory-Emory.  You got the guts to back it up?"

Emory-Emory looked around trying his best to hide the blush that was obvious, even under the street lamp's dull glow.

"Who me?  Shit, I ain't afraid of nuthin'...or nobody.  My Dad was a *Marine...* He taught me lots of things."

AJ paused before she spoke, glancing at the rest of us.  Her piercing glare was a sure sign she was looking for trouble.

"Yeah, what kinds of things?"

"Just...things, okay?" he said, glancing at us with retreating eyes.

"Like what...?"

"What's it to you, anyway? Emory-Emory sneered.  It's war stuff...things girls don't know nuthin' about."

"Can you shoot a machine gun?" she persisted, imitating the recoil action with her hands.

"Sure," he snapped.

"How about a knife? Did he teach you how to kill all those *Japssss?"*

Emory-Emory was getting cornered fast and knew it. He bit his lip in a futile attempt to bury his boiling rage. But all he saw in return was AJ's devilish smile. She was moving into her full-blown kill mode.

"C'mon, Emory-Emory, you can tell us. We wanna learn, too," she chided.

"Look, I ain't talkin'...it's war stuff. What my daddy taught me ain't none your business. He learnt it fightin' those dirty Nips."

"Like the *Sands of Iwo Jima,* right Emory-Emory?" We all laughed. Emory-Emory winced.

I knew from my own encounters with her that AJ was more than capable of engineering untold damage with her never ending barbs. She loved to set traps and then bury me in them. Once I got a snoot full when I went to stay at her Grandma *Schneider's* farm in *Baker,* in southern Kansas. She led me into a barn where she and her three cousins ambushed me, unmercifully teasing me, bringing out my temper to its limit, then making me look like a fool. Worse still, all three were girls, but AJ was definitely the leader of the pack. I moped around the farm by myself for days, depressed as hell, but AJ didn't care. The more she saw me suffer, the happier she was.

Then one morning in an unexpected and welcomed lull in her torture tactics, she changed directions. Like a fool, I let her talk me into climbing on the backside of a pony with her. Once on top, she told me to kick it, and I did. How was I supposed to know you're not supposed to kick a horse in its flanks? After we both flew sky high, she got up mad as a hornet, kicking me in the shins and chasing me around the farmhouse yard. I yelled for help, but nobody was around. Grandma Schneider and the girls had gone into town to pick up supplies.

That farm stay was the worst trip of my life. My only salvation was that on the northeast perimeter of the property, there was an isolated Rock Island spur track. In a weak moment, Wanda, the oldest of the Schneider girls, and the one with the best chance of having a little heart for a tortured kid, told me that once in a while a freight came along and picked up grain cars. She said that sometimes there was an old passenger car on the end of it.

That was all I needed to hear. I merrily trotted the quarter-mile or so along the gravel country road until I reached the track. The faded, white wooden railroad crossing sign that protected the road was battered and listing on its side. But like an old war-horse, it was still on the job. I carefully inspected the track, noting that the ties had seen better days. The rust on the rails indicated this wasn't *Terminal Junction* country, for sure.

But still, it *was* a track, and that meant sanctuary. If I was lucky, sooner or later something would show up. I found a large rock and quickly turned it into a little seat. Then I sat...and waited...and waited some more, sometimes for half a day or more. Whenever I got bored I stood up and looked around. The open spaces and rich farmland made me feel small and unimportant, but I didn't mind that so much.  I felt I was part of something much more interesting, even though I had no idea what it was.  Above, the blistering Kansas summer sun battered the farmland through a cloudless, azure sky.  Shimmering heat waves coiled and rose into infinity.  As I sat on that rock peering down the mile or so of track that parted the tall stands of corn on both sides of the roadbed, I was being serenaded by thousands of locusts and birds that had made this remote part of Kansas their homes.  No train ever came.

***

Now, as I watched Emory-Emory's eyes as AJ closed in, I wanted to help, but held fast. This wasn't my fight.  Still, none of us relished seeing someone getting systematically cut to ribbons, especially by a girl.  But then again everybody knew all about Emory-Emory and what he was up to.  And especially by AJ…. She figured out a long time ago how he had injected his father into his own private *"Iwo Jima"* hero tale.  In truth, the closest his dad ever came to World War II was watching troop trains whiz by his small farm west of *Salina.*  That was before the family of four packed up and came to Kansas City, busted.  Emory-Emory was the eldest of four, and in a weak moment, the old man decided to give his son the same first name as his last.  According to Emory-Emory, he said his dad did it because he thought it would make him unique.  He was certainly right about that.  Emory-Emory *was* one of a kind.

But there was one thing you could say about Emory-Emory.  He was resilient.  He was like a fishin' bobbin'.  He'd go under for a second or two, but you could always count on him to pop right back up.  The movie fantasy he had contrived was his way of getting respect and finding a little internal equilibrium.  All us kids saw the film together at the *Jayhawk Theater,* and it left deep impressions on the group.  But none so deep as it did on old Emory-Emory.  The film star, *John Wayne,* was a Marine who had fought, and died, for his country on *Iwo Jima* island.  The film revolved around the famous photo of four Marines hoisting the American flag on a hill.  It was perhaps the most moving symbol of the war in the Pacific.  And *"Big John"* was there.

It was first-class drama, but a far cry from reality, and Emory-Emory's real-world father.  These days, old man Henry Emory was living on an island of his own making.  A couple years earlier, he caught a mysterious stomach illness that no doctor could cure.  Emory-Emory touted it as a recurring case of malaria his Pop contracted during his jungle wars.  Now the old man stayed at home on permanent disability from his laborer's job at the silo storage tanks, content to fan himself on the front porch and acting like the neighborhood watch dog.  That is, when he wasn't on a drunken binge beating the shit out of his wife, and poor Emory-Emory.

AJ moved in for the kill.  Her angelic face turned hard, almost evil looking.  "Well, what you gonna do?"

"Okay, okay!  You want me to go first?  We'll play!  Sure.... And you know what?  You're gonna be the first one I catch!"

Out of nowhere, one of the boys tossed an empty *Heinz 57* quart-sized can at his feet. The label and top had been removed completely, revealing only its dull silver colored metal skin.  Emory picked it up and put it directly under the street light, hands on hips and straddling the can.  Sporting his patented sneer, he looked us over as if he was a field general considering his battle tactics.  Then he suddenly covered his eyes with both hands and began counting to a hundred by tens.  We all knew what to do, exploding in all directions into the darkness.  The game was on!

I ran full speed up the alley, looking for a place to hide.

"...A hundred!" Emory-Emory shouted.  I dove for the low standing row of hedge bushes next to the Fry boys' house.  When I did, I landed directly on AJ's well formed behind.

"Get outta here!  This is my spot!" she hissed.

My right hand was stuck between her thighs.  It felt good, but I fought off the fantasy that was coming on fast.  I focused all my attention on Emory-Emory who was peering our way straining to see the shadows in the darkness.  Suddenly, he whirled and darted for the can, straddling both sides with his legs.

"Over the can for Phillip...over there, behind the tool shed."

Emory-Emory pointed an accusing finger at the captured player.

"C'mon.... I got you fair and square.  Come out."

*Phillip Fry* came slowly into view, hanging his head like a POW.

"He won't get me," AJ mumbled as she saw the little guy walk up to Emory-Emory.  As his prisoner, he was duty bound to help him capture others who were still at large.

"Me neither," I replied, trying to sound just as confident.

She turned and looked up at me.  In the soft light she looked like an angel, but I knew better.

"Look, I got an idea.  Maybe we can draw him out."

"You wanna make a *detour?*"

She scowled at the comment.

"You mean...a *diversion.*  Detours are what cars use, not people, you big dummy.  What do they teach you at Prescott, anyway?"

"You know what I mean."

AJ looked up the alley and saw Emory-Emory standing under the street lamp.  His back was to us.

"Look, you go in one way and I'll take another.  While he's looking at you, I come in from behind and kick the can.  He can't get us both, and Phillip won't do anything too dumb.  He wants to get away, too."

I thought about it, then nodded.

We both crept toward the street lamp, keeping as low to the ground as we could, using the row of hedge bushes for cover.  Suddenly, my shoe caught the tip of an empty *Falstaff* beer bottle. The glass spun like a top on the alley cinders, then rolled down the natural slope, falling into a small ditch with a *clang.* The sound sent Emory-Emory whirling, peering into the darkness for the source. We dove for cover again under the bushes.

"I know somebody's out there. You might as well give up. You ain't gonna get away."

AJ punched me in the arm.

"Dummy!" she hissed.

She jumped to her feet.

"Where you going?" I asked.

"Just stay here. Count to a hundred. When you finish, go for the can. I'll do the rest."

"Start countin'...now!" she whispered as she disappeared into the inky darkness.

I began to count, looking for some sign of her, but she was gone. Her direction told me that she was sprinting around the Fry house and making her play from the opposite direction. With Emory-Emory concentrating on me, she had a good chance to kick the can right out from under him.

"Eighty-five...ninety...ninety-five...a hundred!"

I sprang to my feet and bolted for the can that was several yards in front of me. My tennies churned on the loose cinders as I sprinted full speed toward him, hell bent and determined to kick that damn can. But despite all the noise I was making in my dash, Emory-Emory wasn't interested. He was fixed on something else somewhere in the opposite direction. Then, he casually stepped over the *Heinz 57* can.

"Over the can for AJ! Over there...comin' right at me."

I was still more than five yards away when he whirled around, straddling the can and at the same time blocking my path. I ran full tilt, hitting him square on, then bouncing off him like a cue ball on a railing and landing on my butt.

"Over the can for Stevie!" he said as he looked down at me revealing his buck ugly grin.

"You dumb shit!" AJ screamed. "You got us both caught! Where you been?"

I helped myself up, dusting off my pants, trying my best to avoid her killer-bee glare, then back pedaled fast as she closed in.

"I counted to a hundred." The meek excuse sounded tinny and unreal. It incensed her even more.

"Yeah, sure...preacher boy. Then why were you late?"

I looked at the ground, shifting my feet as if I were standing in the front of class and getting a dressing down from the teacher.

"I dunno what happened, AJ. I did what you said. I counted...by *fives* and...."

"You did what?" she shrieked. "No wonder! You always count to a hundred by tens!"

Emory-Emory watched on with glee.  He slapped his knee and bellowed his most prized guffaw, pointing his finger at the two of us as the rest of the kids gathered to watch.

"I told you!  I knew I'd get you, big mouth AJ!"

AJ whirled and focused her laser glare on Emory-Emory.  Even in his finest hour, he instinctively stepped back when he felt her heat.

In the distance I heard the sound of the ten o'clock whistle coming from the *Proctor & Gamble* plant.  Right behind it was Mom's melodic voice calling me home.

"I gotta go," I said, turning for the alley leading to my backyard.

"Yeah, you better.  It's time for mommy's little boy to go," Emory-Emory chirped as he strutted around the can.

AJ's glare felt like a flame-thrower on my back.  I was relieved to get away and bury myself in the alley's darkness.  I opened the back yard gate and ran for the house porch, thinking about the piece of apple pie that I figured was in the fridge.  It hadn't all been a disaster, I thought.  But it was still Saturday night.  No school tomorrow…and time for another episode of *"This Is Your FBI"*.

###

# The Campaign...

The big apple tree behind Grams Nichols' house had been growing at a severe right angle for years, but its roots were deeply buried in the eastern Kansas soil. Just like the working man's neighborhood surrounding it, the tree had survived. Its deformed limbs stretched out well beyond its bowed, arthritic trunk. Its saving grace was that it was out of harm's way in the far corner of the back yard. The thick tree limbs and long, narrowed trunk made it the perfect tree for Denny, Mikey and me to shimmy up to our choice spots in its branches. Once inside its thick foliage, we felt safe and secure. During the height of summer, the scent of tree sap drifted through the neighborhood. To us, the pungent odor was more like an aphrodisiac.

There was really no need to build a clubhouse in Grams' tree. It was already built in. The old apple tree had grown into a natural two-story mansion. We simply moved in.

Denny bent under one of the branches when he heard the sound of the creaking garage door. I watched him dispassionately as he tried to master the sour taste of the green apple he had plucked off a nearby branch.

He was on his favorite limb, a thick, leafy branch that grew outward, then abruptly shot into the air, terminating at treetop level.

"It's just Uncle Fuzzy," he declared with an air of official finality. It was a kind of supreme understanding that none of us challenged.

"He's going to work."

His analysis was validated by the sound of the old Ford's flat-head engine coming to life inside the house garage. The sedan's loose tappets knocked in protest when Fuzzy pressed on the accelerator and slowly rolled out of the garage. The engine growled and the tires crunched on the soft driveway gravel, then faded into the sounds of the afternoon.

Denny casually continued his treetop surveillance. He gracefully used his leg to swing himself up and over the limb. Acting as if the branch were his personal cot, he crossed his legs, then stuck one arm under his neck like an armrest. It was all sort of matter-of-fact, uncomplicated, what you would expect from any high achiever who saw life as nothing more than a series of positive challenges. All of that had been inculcated into him by his Mom, Maxine, herself a disciple of positive thinking.

He finished his readjusting, shutting his eyes to the world, keeping his left hand locked tightly around the branch...just in case. I was also trying to snooze. I liked the wall of leaves protecting me on all sides. The thick branches ambled upward near to the top.  In the late afternoon, shafts of soft light and a gentle breeze filtered into our hide-away world, perfect for keeping the heat of the day at bay.

The late June day had turned into a predictably muggy one, a sign that before sunset, the towering thunderheads building in the West would shower Bethany Street with rain and bring at least partial relief from the sticky humidity.

I turned my head and looked down at Mikey who was lying mummy-like on his branch. He must have sensed it and opened one eye.

"What?"

"Nuthin'… But I bet you're in la-la land again…thinking about … *Adriana Scalfaro.*"

"Shut up!"

"See, I told you, I was right.  You were thinkin' about her *big* boobies. Go on, admit it…."

"I think you're right," Denny added, picking up on Mikey's irritation.

Denny shot up on his perch from on high, looking down at us.

"I bet you've never even seen her boobies, or anything else."

True enough…. Mikey's heartthrob wasn't from his neighborhood. She lived near *10th Street,* not far from the bridge. Her pop was a car repairman for the Union Pacific. Mikey's story was all too familiar to us by now. It all started a year earlier when he happened to sit next to her during a Saturday matinee at the *Granada Theater* on Minnesota Avenue. The way he told it, things got hot and heavy in the back row. Lots of smooching and stray hands moving around. After that red-hot encounter, Mikey kept going back to the Granada every Saturday, but she never showed up again. It didn't matter. He kept the story alive and every time he told it, he tried to add a little more spice. She had become his mystery sex fantasy. He held up that one fun-filled afternoon as being his finest hour. It was enough to earn him bragging rights among the guys who were busy building their own sex portfolios whenever they got the chance.

The search went far and wide.  Stories were floating around about another willing lass, *Marla Hunt,* who lived near *Bethany Park.* She went to *St. Benedicts* parochial school, the Catholic's version of Prescott and Central Junior High combined. Her reputation at being a hot ticket was more than conjecture. Not only was she pretty, she was *willing.*

Among us kids, Denny was by far the most aggressive and experienced. He was a bit short, but his stocky build, dark hair and eyes and infectious personality made him a winner with the girls. It was really that overwhelming, almost cocky confidence that won him the favors. He could turn a lady's eye.

He also had a scheming mind and the guts of a cat burglar. I could tell by his expression that the gem of an idea was already percolating.

"Maybe we should scout around tonight."

"Where?" I asked, not sure I wanted to hear his reply.

"Over by the park."

Mikey sat up, still trying to unravel what Denny was getting at.

"You mean over there – at *Marla Hunt's* place?"

Denny nodded.

"I hear her old man is always out drinking.  When her mom died, she was left all alone and he likes to go up to Central Avenue to booze it up."

"Shit, that stinks," Mikey said.  The tone in his voice revealed another story.  These days he was living with his grandmother over on Strawberry Hill.  When his mother and father split up, he and his dad moved in with her.  The Splitlog house had been there ever since the family had finally managed to make enough money to get out of their small and overcrowded West Bottoms house.  *George Dodig* was known to be a decent but stern man.  Pretty much a copy of his father who raised all of his sons with the staunch belief that if you spared the rod, you will definitely spoil the child.

For Mikey, it was more of the same.  He had to share a room with one of his uncles, and nobody in the house except for the kindly *Mom Simica'* really paid too much attention to his comings and goings.  Her gentle hand, no doubt, kept him on the straight and narrow, and probably did more good than the strap when things got out of hand.  Still, through it all Mikey was a good-natured guy, and a loyal one to boot.  I always knew my backside was covered when he was around.  There was a gentleness about him, and a genuine zest for life and curiosity about things that led to continual discoveries.

"I heard she likes to do it with lots of guys at the same time," Denny continued.

"Who told you that?" I asked.

"*Ronnie Marsh.*"

"That big bully from Armourdale…the one who jumps kids after school?"

One gray, cold winter day, Marsh was lying in wait for me.  He was a tough guy and not one to fool with.  He put me through hell.  Ever since then I did everything I could to avoid him.  Marsh was a loner, a rogue, and the kind of guy who didn't respect territories.  Wherever he went, nobody challenged him.

"Yeah…I get along with him okay," Denny said matter of factly.  "I saw him down at *Hassig's Drug Store.*  He said he was there last week.  She let him and a couple other guys in he didn't even know."

"What happened?" I asked.

Denny looked down at me from his power perch and laughed.

"They played, *'Old Maid,' "* he said, his voice dripping with sarcasm.

"Very funny."

He edged closer to the two of us, letting his legs dangle freely.

"So, how about it?  You wanna see for yourself?"  It was more a challenge than a question.

"I dunno, Denny.  What if her pop shows up?" I asked.

"He won't…he'll be up on Central getting tanked.  My dad knows him.  He says he's a real drunk.  He always comes home after midnight and we'll be long gone by then."

I looked at Mikey.

"What do you think?"

He thought about it, then nodded.

"Okay. We meet here at nine," Denny said, acting fast before we changed our minds.

The idea of sneaking around an unfamiliar street made me uneasy, but the prospects of the *reward* was an even stronger pull. If we did it, maybe then I'd have something to brag about, too. My track record wasn't that good in this area. As we looked at each other for support, I felt a surge of excitement. It was worth the risk – but what if it all got fouled up? I brushed away my fears and slithered down the tree trunk. As usual, Denny was already on the ground, leading the way.

***

The narrow street that led to a "T" intersection was dark, and that was a good sign. Nobody could see us as we worked our way on the opposite side of the street toward the house. Only a single lamppost cast a dim glow on the corner. In the distance, we could tell that somebody was inside. The living room light was on and there was a crack in the front door. A row of cars was lined up along the curbing.

Denny appeared from behind one of them and signaled us to move closer. We found cover behind a set of hedgerow bushes only a few yards from the entrance. He parted the branches and peered toward the house.

"You hear that?" he whispered. "She's playing music."

"How do you know that ain't her old man?" I whispered.

"No…It's her. Listen," he said, his voice taking on a familiar air of authority. But this time he was probably right. The music was upbeat and loud, something more suited for a girl about to enter her teens.

"Ronnie told me she always puts on music. It's a signal that it's okay to go in."

"What now?" Mikey asked, moving in to get a peek for himself.

Denny waved us to follow.

"Stay close. This is it."

As we edged forward, the music became more distinct, as if beckoning us to continue.

We stopped to survey the situation. Nothing…. Nobody…. Only the silent night and the line of parked cars just behind us now. And the *music….* In my mind's eye I imagined the joys of Marla's portfolio of sexual favors unfolding in front of me.

Denny carefully opened the wooden fence gate and went up the stone steps leading to the front porch. I was right behind him with Mikey trailing. When we got to the top we half crawled forward getting to within inches of the front door. The wooden porch floor squeaked in protest. From our vantage point the crack in the door was open just wide enough to see inside. Marla was alone, acting like a belly dancer in the middle of the living room. Her rhythmic movements were sensual and inviting. I sensed – no, I knew…she was aware that we were just outside. It was perfect!

Denny glanced at me, and in the dim light I could see his impish smile. Like a cat that finally got the canary and had no intention of apologizing or feeling bad about it. He inched forward, putting his hand on the front door knob, pulling on the door. When he did, the world blew up in our faces.

"What you sons-a-bitches doin' up there, huh? Why you at my house?"

The old man's raspy, booze-laden voice cut into the darkness like a scythe slashing tall grass. I was frozen in place, unsure what to do. I tried to pinpoint where the voice was coming from. In the dim light, I caught the silhouette of someone struggling to get out of the gray Plymouth two-door parked in front of the house.

At first I wanted to laugh. He was so drunk he couldn't pull himself up and out of the front seat, let alone make it to the sidewalk. Every time he tried, he only managed to get half way up, then fell back inside, sprawling on his back.

But that wasn't what got my attention. It was the reflection of the chromium *.38 caliber* snub-nose pistol he was waving around each time he popped into view.

"Ohhhhhh shit! Denny! He's got a gun!"

I should have talked faster. Denny was past me, taking the porch steps in one gulp, high jumping the front yard fence, then disappearing into the darkness. Mikey was several yards ahead of him. That left me holding the bag. I managed to get into my stride just as the old man finally got himself upright and found his balance on the sidewalk. He was spraying the gun barrel around like a fire hose. I knew my only chance now was to bury myself deep into the street's darkness, but he was making progress and building a head of steam in hot pursuit.

"C'mere you little bastards! You boys wanna git yourself a little nookie, do ya! You think this is a whorehouse! I'll shove this gun up your ass! I'll teach you a somethin' about pussy huntin' you'll never forget!"

In the murky light, I saw Denny cut in-between two houses and I instinctively followed. Mikey made it all the way to *10*th *Street* and disappeared. We dove headfirst into a pile of wooden planks stacked against one of the houses. I could feel my heart pounding like a kettledrum.

"What we gonna do, Denny?"

"Nuthin'…we stick. And be quiet."

"You think he saw us?"

"I dunno."

For the first time ever I heard fear in Denny's voice. That scared me even more.

"What if he sees us? Can we get out? Where are we? Denny, shit, he's got a gun.

He punched me in the arm.

"Shut up! I know…Lemme think."

He took a few seconds to collect himself, then looked at me. In the dim light I could see his cool demeanor had magically returned.

"Look, we just lie low for now. Wait...see.... When we get the chance, we run for it."

Neither of us spoke. We were hugging the planks, trying to somehow become part of the woodpile. Then, just as we were beginning to think the danger was over, we spotted the penetrating beam of a flashlight bouncing off the opposite house wall.

"Denny, shit, he's got a flashlight! Where'd he get that? He's gonna see us sure! We're dead meat!"

I tried to get up but he grabbed my shirt collar and yanked me hard to the ground.

"Ssshhh! He'll hear you!"

We both knew we were about to be trapped like rats. If the old man figured out we were in-between the houses, we had little or no chance of getting out. We watched the light beam as it cast about in the darkness, first one way, then another, but always closing in.

Then the beam bounced off the woodpile, coming back again, zeroing in on us.

"You little bastards! I got you now! *Git* out here!"

Denny jumped to his feet.

"Run for it!"

We sprinted in opposite directions. Denny headed for the deepest end of the backyard and I angled toward the back of the house nearer to Tenth Street. Out of the corner of my eye I could see the flashlight beam was pursuing me.

"Git back here! I gotta fuckin' gun and I'm gonna use it if you don't git your asses over here right now!"

Ahead I could just make out a low-standing wooden fence. I had no idea what was beyond it when I went airborne. I landed on a patch of driveway cement and felt the sting on my left knee through the tear in my jeans. It didn't matter. Not more than ten yards further, and just beyond a final row of houses, I saw the 10th Street lights and freedom! There were no fences, or obstructions, just a narrow pathway. I ran toward the light with all my might, praying the old man didn't squeeze the trigger before I turned the corner.

When I finally made it back to familiar territory, I saw Mikey waiting in front of *Hassig's Drug Store.* A few minutes later, Denny casually strolled our way as if he'd just been to a movie.

Mikey looked over my knee and torn jeans.

"You okay?"

"Yeah...."

"Shit, that old man was carrying a big gun," he said.

"Yeah.... I thought he was going to shoot me."

Denny was smiling and looking his confident self again.

Nobody spoke as we walked side-by-side down Central Avenue. I was mainly thinking about what I was going to say to Mom when she saw my torn jeans and the cut on my knee.

Denny broke the silence.

"Hey, you know what...maybe we oughta do this again?" he said. "We almost made it.... Once we got inside, it could have been some real fun. What do you think?"

"Shut up, Denny," Mikey said.

"Yeah," I countered. "Shut up."

Denny laughed. We just kept walking.

###

# Alone...

"How long do you think it's gonna take?" Denny asked, as we worked our way toward *City Park.* The hike we decided on was well out of our range of play. "We can walk alongside the park, then drop down into the gully. I think that's where the track is."

Denny really didn't care. We were about to embark on another adventure, this one along Highway 32. I could have told him that we were about to walk across the Intercity Viaduct, turn right on *Main Street,* and head for the Swope Park Zoo. He wasn't really all that interested in trains. He was an adventure junkie. Anything that remotely suggested getting himself and his buddies close to the edge of the envelope got high marks, and all of his attention.

"Okay," he finally said. He stuck his hands into his jeans pockets and pulled out three shiny quarters.

"You got any?"

I pulled out a shiny fifty-cent piece.

"Good.... We'll go as far as Edwardsville.... We can eat there. Then we hitch-hike back," he said.

I nodded and Denny took his customary lead. We made our way past *Clifton Park.* The old swimming pool bathhouse was just below us. It hadn't been used for years and the empty pool looked battered and spooky.

"Do you think Roger Harlow really *did it* in there just like he bragged?" I asked, glancing at the main door that was now only hanging by a single hinge.

He nodded. It was the kind of response that told me he thought it was no big deal.

"I went down there myself once. Lots of people go there. Used rubbers all over the place."

"Really?"

I wanted to ask him more, but bit my lip. I didn't want to sound too stupid. I never even used a rubber although I'd seen them once or twice. But as we walked by the old building my imagination went wild with images of Roger and the girl he had seduced.

When we finally got to City Park, I was relieved to discover that nobody was around. It was a sultry July afternoon. None of the local kids was on the baseball diamond. The heat had already chased them off to their neighborhood houses. They were probably sucking up tall glasses of homemade lemonade and just hanging out. We walked further. Then, off in the gully and buried in the green sea of weeds and rogue-looking bushes, I spotted the rusted rails of the nearly Kaw Valley trolley line.

"Hey, look at that!" I said, pointing to a spur track that seemed to take off in the opposite direction. It was buried deep inside the hollow, angling south and away from Muncie and the track that I surmised ran parallel to *Highway 32.*

"Let's see where it goes," Denny said, climbing up to the right-of-way. With every step we seemed to go deeper and deeper into a forest of undisciplined foliage. The weeds had grown right up to the edge of the ballast line, then aggressively invaded the inside of the rails between the rotted wooden ties. We looked ahead through the green tunnel and continued around a gentle curve. Ahead, we spotted the entrance to a steel truss bridge.

"C'mon," Denny waved, as he trudged ahead at a faster pace.

I followed behind, watching the bridge unfold in front of me. We stopped at its entrance. Below and to our left was the entrance to the Rock Island and Union Pacific Railroad freight yards. They were side-by-side, but here they funneled together into the two-track main line that ran all the way to Topeka. I vaguely recalled seeing it once when Pops took me to Topeka on a train ride a couple years earlier. It was definitely mystery country. But now, as I picked up on the terrain, I knew I had found something special. This is where it all began! I had discovered the genesis!

We cautiously made our way onto the bridge and stopped about half way across. I looked below and could easily see the well-manicured two-track passenger mainline in the center that formally split the two railroad companies. The track was an extension of the Terminal Junction connection to the Highline a couple of miles east of us. As I studied the layout, I could see the bright glow of a passenger engine approaching from the East. The train was on us in an instant. It was the *Imperial,* the Rock Island's workhorse mail and passenger train on its way to Los Angeles.

Normally, it came through town around 8:30 a.m., but today it was running several hours late. The bright red and silver engines and army green colored cars flashed under the bridge, hugging the northern bluffs as it followed the Kaw's meandering route no more than 500 yards away.

"You think Uncle Fuzzy's inside?" Denny asked.

I shrugged. "Depends…if he's on the Extra Board, he might have caught it. He was home this morning. I saw him cutting the grass out back when I got up."

Denny and I watched as the train rumbled out of sight. On the time card the Imperial was relegated to second-place status with its older equipment and multiple stops picking up and dropping off the mail in small Kansas towns, and beyond. The trip generally took about 48 hours, if all went well.

The Rock's premiere run was the *Golden State Limited* and its time to California was far more respectable, covering the 2,324-mile circuit in around 42 hours. But neither of them could hold a candle to the Santa-Fe's speedsters that bolted out of town on their multiple tracks and specially built elevated line on the South side of the Kaw.  Their premier *Super Chief, Chief* and *El Capitan* name trains were consistently burning up the rails in their 39½-hour jaunts from *Chicago* to *Los Angeles Union Passenger Terminal.*  The Super Chief and Chief were also the so-called *trains of the stars* – the ride of choice of the movie giants of the era.  More than once folks talked about how they had seen *Humphrey Bogart, Clark Gable* or *The Three Stooges* waving from inside their plush private bedrooms as the train changed crews and loaded more passengers at Union Station.  Sometimes during the layovers they would get off and browse through the magazine stands that were wheeled to the train side.  If folks were lucky they would give out a few autographs.

I never saw those runs much, though.  The schedule called for late night and early morning arrivals and departures into Kansas City.  Only the Chief had been scheduled with Kansas in mind.  In fact, the management had been so considerate that they actually routed a portion of the run in Eastern Kansas over their alternate mainline through Lawrence and Topeka. Right neighborly…those Santa-Fe folks.

Both of the Rock Island trains relied on the *Southern Pacific's* route to California that began at *Tucumcari, New Mexico.*  The line cut deep into New Mexico, then into Arizona, sliding to within a few miles of the US-Mexican border.  It was harsh and unforgiving desert – a choice location where lots of cowboy westerns were made by Hollywood's moguls over the years.   The Rock Island promos also noted that their transcontinental route was the *low altitude way* to cross the western US.  The spin here was that some folks were apparently worried about getting high altitude nosebleeds.

The ad writers and promoters had their facts right – at least sort of. Actually, nobody lost too much sleep worrying over bloody noses, but they were right about their lower altitude pitch.  What they didn't say was that there would be a price to pay.  Folks who took this route had to quickly pick up on the joys of *Gin Rummy* in the club car because there was really little to see outside, except hours on end of monotonous desert sage and boring topography.

Yet, as the Imperial weaved through Arizona's copper mining countries, skirting around the barren hills not more than 1,600 feet above sea level, and through mining towns such as   *Bisbee Jct.* and *Douglas,* well that's really when it was right at home with itself, and its purpose.  It was only there to serve, mail cars and all.  The train was really more of a *salt-of-the-earth* kind of offering for the common man.  It trundled here and there in the underbelly of the nation – something that just plain folks would end up taking to avoid the extra fare charges tacked on by its slicker Golden State counterpart.

Still, despite its obvious lack of spit and polish, I always preferred the Imperial over many of the trains that rambled through Kansas City.  Maybe because it was part of the parade of trains I could generally count on when I went down to the Terminal Junction telegrapher's shack to catch the morning action.  Or maybe that I just knew it was still hanging in, valiantly fighting the unstoppable aging process that gnawed at its thirties appearance, and a growing number of head-mail cars that made it look even more unwieldy and unattractive. But it had its place just the same. All those cars and generally fully occupied coaches and Pullmans made me feel that things were *okey-dokey* fine in America. Riding along the line was like getting a peek at somebody taking a bath. You shouldn't be there but there you are, anyway. You learn a lot about small-town America when you see what's going on in the back yards. Kind of like being a voyeur on wheels.

***

We turned and worked our way back across the bridge again.

"I wish I was on that train," I said, as I tried to keep my footing on the loosely spaced ties.

"Why?"

"It's going to California. I hear it's really nice out there."

"Ronnie and Donnie say they like it a lot. They say it never gets cold," Denny added.

To Uncle Fuzzy, having his two sons in the Navy was enough to bust his buttons. When the Korean Conflict began a year earlier, the Navy went looking for officer candidates. They picked the twins. Not only that, both had qualified for aviator's school. That put him over the moon.

We back tracked into the thick foliage and found where the tracks split. The other set of rails angled west, and then disappeared into the afternoon shadows. Light shafts sporadically penetrated the canopy of trees and weeds, and the air felt heavier and wetter the further we walked inside.

"Let's follow it as far as we can," Denny said. "It's heading toward Edwardsville."

We started trotting between the rails.

I didn't like the way it felt as we moved deeper into the darkness. Now the track was snug up against the bluff and outcroppings of limestone began to appear out of the darkness.

"Think there's any snakes?"

"Dunno...but we better keep an eye out. Maybe *Copperheads*. They like to hide in the rocks."

I looked around. I never liked snakes and the idea of one crawling over my flimsy tennis shoes made me nervous. This was ideal snake country for sure. The jagged protrusions seemed to be hiding a lot of things. To our left a sea of green foliage continued to block our view. The mainline was now well below us. Above we heard the muffled sounds of cars on Highway 32.

"How long does it go on like this? Are we heading for Muncie?"

Denny shrugged and then pointed.

"Look, see the tracks curving? After we get there, we'll get a better idea."

Denny looked at me. He was sporting a wry smile.

"You scared?"

"Me? Shoot. I ain't afraid of nuthin'."

He laughed.

"You sound like Emory-Emory."

When we rounded the bend the track opened into the river valley. The ridge had all but given up its ninety-degree angle, blending itself naturally into the widening landscape. Just beyond the clearing, we spotted a wooden trestle spanning a creek, one of many that worked its way from the higher ground and eventually into the Kaw River. And just beyond it there was something else: a dirty yellow Kaw Valley steeple cab electric engine parked under a tree. It was coupled to a couple of cement cars, no more than fifty yards away.

"See that?" I asked.

"Yeah.... What's it doin' there?"

"I dunno. He ain't movin'. Maybe he jumped the tracks."

"Maybe," Denny said, but by then he had already turned his attention to the bridge in front of us.

"So, what do you think? Do we cross?"

"What if it comes this way?"

Denny smirked.

"We can beat it, silly."

He was probably right. But the real problem was that the bridge was no better than the track. There were huge spaces between the ties. Big enough for a little kid to fall through for sure.

"Look," I said pointing toward the creek. "There's lots of rocks down there. We can jump across and maybe not get too wet. The water isn't runnin' that fast.

Denny surveyed the situation, then nodded.

"Okay, follow me."

We stepped off the tracks and slid down the rocky slope. Loose dirt slipped freely under my worn out tennis shoes. Tiny pebbles dug inside my shoes and gnawed at my heels.

Denny stopped by the edge of the water and pointed to the center of the creek bed.

"See those rocks? We'll go that way."

I nodded and watched him take control of the situation. He gracefully negotiated himself half-way across. Then with two more easy jumps he was on the other side. He took a moment to survey his shoes for any telltale water damage then smiled, waving me on.

"C'mon, it's easy."

I managed to get on top of the first two with little trouble. I glanced toward Denny to get my bearings, then jumped. When my right foot landed on the rock, my worn shoe bottom slipped on the watery surface. Before I could catch my balance I was on one knee and my left foot was in the water up to my calf.

I knew I was in big trouble the moment I felt the searing pain in the ball of my foot.  I looked down and saw a pool of blood swirling in the water.

"Denny…I'm bleeding!"

"Hold on!  I'm coming!"  He leaped onto the nearest rock and angled his way toward me, taking a longer but surer route.  He held out his hand.

"C'mon…. I'll pull you up."

I looked down again at the sea of red.

"I'm scared Denny…the blood…. It's comin' out pretty fast."

"Don't look at it.  Just take my hand."

When he pulled me out of the water I could see the bottom of my tennis shoe had been cut almost in half.  Denny kept pulling until I got a foothold on the large rock.  He was holding his own on the edge of his.

"Can you stand?"

"No…it really hurts a lot."

He pointed to the last two rocks.

"Look, we gotta get to the other side.  I'll help you.  Lean on me."

Slowly, we made our way over.  With every step I felt the throbbing pain.  Once on the small embankment, I rested on my back.  Denny carefully pulled off my tennis shoe.  The blood was flowing freely under my left instep.  The cut was jagged and looked deep.  Like it had been sliced with a seared-edge knife.

I felt weak and cold.  I could see in Denny's expression that he was worried.  My teeth were beginning to chatter.  It was as if fall had come to the Kaw Valley in the middle of July.  I grabbed the sides of my skinny arms and rubbed.

He stood up and looked around.

"I'm gonna get some help."

"Where?"

He looked up to the track in the direction of the electric engine.

"There…. Maybe somebody's inside the train.  I'll be back."

"Okay…but hurry…I feel really funny."

He disappeared in a flash, churning up the rocky embankment.  With every dig into the soft earth the pebbles danced over my face.  He topped the ridge and disappeared.  I was totally alone, probably for the first time in my young life.  Nobody to help…. Nobody around…. I looked down at my foot and the blood on my shoe.  It showed no signs of stopping.  I reached inside my jeans pocket, pulled out a handkerchief, and strained to wrap it around my bleeding foot.  It was a painful exercise.  My foot was stinging and I sat up to get the right leverage to somehow ease the throbbing pain.  I wanted to cry but fought back the tears; instead, yanking off my horned-rimmed glasses and rubbing my eyes with a filthy forearm.

When I finally managed to tie the knot, I took a deep breath and lay back down, trying to calm myself.  A patch of fallen leaves and soft clump of earth made a natural pillow.  Through the umbrella of tree branches overhead I saw patches of an azure summer sky.  It seemed to be bluer than I ever recalled it. I wondered if I was going to die. I wanted to go home. Then I shut my eyes.

***

*"There he is!"* a voice thundered as it if came out of a barrel. It was a distinct Southern drawl coming from somewhere behind me. I heard the sound of shoes sliding and felt the dirt pebbles again.

The blue sky overhead disappeared. In its place was a man dressed in faded blue bib overalls. He carefully dropped down on one knee, untied my handkerchief, and made a quick study of my foot. When he did, a big multi-colored tattoo of a bird on left his forearm popped into view just inches from my face. It was a side view of the head of an American eagle etched dead center on his huge upper arm. The writing below it read: *101st Airborne Division – The Screaming Eagles*.

"You okay, boy?" he asked as he took a bright red metal box from another crewman standing alongside.

"Yes sir…. I think so."

"Lemme see…."

Using both hands, he gently lifted my left ankle and surveyed the damage. He put it down again and opened the battered red, emergency medical kit beside him.

"Looks pretty nasty…. Like maybe you cut it on a piece of glass."

I nodded.

"You gotta be careful. People are always throwin' crap in these creeks. Ain't got no respect for the land. No common sense, neither," he said as he removed what was left of my shoe and sock. Then he opened the box, pulled out a fistfull of gauze, and began to swab the open wound. He worked quietly for several seconds. Then he smiled.

"You're bleedin' like a stuffed pig, but it's not as bad as it looks. It ain't all that deep. You're lucky."

He put down the blood-soaked gauze and picked up a small brown bottle and shook it.

"Know what this is?"

I nodded.

"It's gonna sting, but that means it's workin' real good. Just grit your teeth and I'll get it done quick, okay?"

I nodded and looked around. Behind me and to my right up near the track I saw Denny looking on. Another crewman was standing near him. I hated Iodine but I also knew that if I started crying now, I would never live it down. I shut my eyes, grimaced and waited for the inevitable.

"There, that should do it," the tattooed railroad man said, sticking his first-aid supplies back into the case. "The gauze and bandage I put on you should hold until you get home. But you better make sure your folks tend to it. You might need to get a tetanus shot."

He picked up the ripped shoe and studied it.

"That sneaker's for sure done for.  Here…" he said, picking up a piece of cardboard nearby.  "This'll help."  He stuck his huge fist inside the high top Converse and it bulged in protest.

The Kaw Valley man helped me slip on my shoe.  Using just one hand, he lifted me to my feet as if I was a twig.  He toted me the rest of the way up to the track side and then to a footpath leading to the nearby highway.  Sure that we were okay he turned to go.

"You boys be careful now?  Get on home and have your folks tend to that cut proper, hear?" the big man said as he and his partner walked back toward their electric engine.

"And watch out for us.  Hell, we're so fast we'll be on top of you 'fore you know it."

The last thing Denny and I heard was the two crewmen laughing up a storm at a joke only they could really appreciate.

### 

*It's funny about being alone, and afraid.  Decades later in Vietnam, when I sat alone on guard duty, confused and scared like hell in a foxhole – with nothing around me but inky blackness and a million mosquitoes, my imagination took over.  I saw that same railroad man in bib overalls appear over me just as he did that summer day in 1951.  The big eagle tattoo on his forearm was as clear then as it was the day I first saw it.  I was really glad to see him again.  And I wasn't afraid, anymore.*

\*\*\*

# The Experiment...

"**W**hatcha doin'?" AJ asked one lazy August afternoon as I sprawled on the front porch floor drinking a cup of fresh lemonade and browsing through my comics.

She opened the metal gate and hopped on the porch steps, casually slouching on the chair next to me. I looked up. Her spread-eagled legs ended up just inches from my face. I tried not to pay attention but the temptation was too much. I continued to browse through the latest *Terry Lee and the Pirates* comic I had traded with Jenine earlier in the week.

"Want some lemonade?" I said, lifting the glass toward her.

She took it from me and drank, looking around as she did. Then she turned her attention on me.

"Hey, did you see that book Jimmy Fry was showin' everybody...the one with all the dirty pictures."

The question caught me off guard and I felt myself blush. AJ and I had never talked about sex before. All we normally did was fight, and she almost always won.

"Yeah...I guess...."

"Well?"

"Well what?"

Her impatience flared.

"What do you think, dummy?"

"About what, AJ?"

My response was unacceptable. She stood and walked to the front porch rail bending over, looking at nothing. When she did, her behind popped up like a ten-ring target.

"You know what I mean..." she finally said, her voice drifting into nowhere. "And don't say you don't, neither."

She turned and faced me sporting a devilish smile.

"You ever see a girl with no clothes on?"

I tried to stay cool, focusing on the comic book and avoiding her penetrating eyes.

"Well? Have you?"

"No..." I said finally as I nervously threw down the book and picked up another. I was thumbing the pages so fast the characters looked like they were moving.

She sat down alongside me and began to casually thumb through a comic she picked up, intentionally avoiding eye contact with me.

"Me neither…I mean boys…except for my little brother, but he doesn't count."  She put down the comic and looked at me.  Her smile was inviting.

"So…how 'bout it?  You wanna try?  We can do a – well…you know, sort of an experiment?"

The question made me gulp.

"What do you mean, an *experiment,* AJ?"

"Well," she said, blooming her most inviting smile.  "You say you never saw a girl naked, right?  And I've never seen a boy…it might be interesting, don't you think?  We could – well, sort of compare.  How about it?"

I heard the words but I wasn't computing.  The image of AJ standing in front of me buck naked, then me doing the same thing was short-circuiting my mind.  Things were getting out of control.

"Well, what do you say?  I know you wanna do it.  I promise, I won't tell if you won't," she said, bending toward me to make her point.  When she did, I caught a glimpse of her well-formed breasts.  They were a lot bigger than Jenine's.  AJ knew exactly what she was doing.

"Or are you too chicken-shit – just like that Emory-Emory?  Lots of big talk, but no action?"

Her challenge was like a kick in the privates and I felt myself flush.  AJ was always pushing me around.  She liked to see me suffer, but this time I decided to fool her.  She'd pay for her big idea.

"Sure, okay…. Yeah, sure…. Why not?  I'll do it."

My declaration felt great!  I knew that was all it would take to turn the tables on her dumb idea.  No girl in her right mind would do what she suggested.  Especially AJ!  She was so *Catholic* that when she finally did confess to the priest – and she would for sure, he'd have her saying *Novena's* into the next decade.  No way…. She'd never go for that.  And when her pop found out, he'd give her a spanking just for good measure.  I smiled as I watched her stand up, obviously on the retreat.  "You've gone too far this time," I thought to myself.  "I got you now Annie Jean Polanski."

"Good…" she said, surveying the situation like an army field commander.  "Now, the next thing is where?"

She was businesslike and determined.  "She's serious," I thought, fighting off the rush of panic.  "She's gone nuts…lost her trolley pole."

"You mean right now, AJ?" I finally blurted out, still hoping that it was all a well-planned joke.  I was ready to take yet another humiliation from her rather than see this through.

She looked at me in mock disbelief.

"Yeah, now…Dummy…When did you think, next Christmas?  No wonder my dad always calls you *meat head.*"

"But I thought we could have some time before."

She pointed an accusing finger at me.

"See!  I knew you were nuthin' but a chicken-shit…you're no different than Emory-Emory."

"That ain't true".

"Then prove it!"

I was checkmated again and she knew it. AJ knew I was in, whether I wanted to be or not. She turned to the business at hand and walked to the front door, peering through the screen.

"Where's your folks?"

"Pops went with *Tooky*...down on *Sixth Street.* Mom's working overtime today. She won't be home 'till six or even later."

She smiled triumphantly.

"Okay then...."

I sprang to my feet.

"AJ! Are you crazy? If they come home...."

She pulled the door open leading the way.

"You just said they're not around, didn't you? Your pop will be out there yakin' for hours. And you already said your Mom's comin' home late tonight." The impish, sexy smile was back. "You ready?"

"No! Wait a second...lemme think."

I was desperate. One part of me couldn't wait to play *"Doctor"* with AJ but on the other hand if Pops came home.... AJ's patience was running thin as she watched me wrestling with my dilemma.

"Okay, okay, we'll do it...but over there," I finally said in a rush, pointing toward the church. Below it in the basement was the social hall. There was a small stage and a piano at the far end where the choir practiced and the tamburitzas played during festivals. It was perfect.

AJ led the way inside the old storage hall, surveying its insides as if it were a hotel room. She was cool as a clam and looking very experienced. She spotted the stage and pointed.

"We can do sort of a strip show," she suggested, laughing at her own words. But when she turned toward me, I could see her idea was anything but a joke. A girl was turning into a woman in front of my eyes. Her sultry, inviting look cut a hole right through me.

"Okay...who goes first?" she asked.

"You?" I blurted.

She put her hands on the sides of her tight fitting jeans and studied me.

"So...you want me to go first, huh?" Then, she shrugged and nodded, turning toward the stage. "Okay...stay here."

It felt like I was being catapulted into a wet dream. AJ casually stepped up and strutted across the wooden stage, stopping dead center in the stage. She faced me, her expression still sporting that same sultry, inviting look. With her blue eyes riveted on me like lasers, she slowly began to unbutton the top of her simple white blouse.

With every snap my heart pounded even louder. The anticipation of what was coming next felt so good that I wanted to scream. I was having trouble getting my breath. She was down to the last button now and pulled the blouse out of her jeans. Her white bra was in plain view. I could clearly see her milky, soft white shoulders and the outline of her breasts.

She was working me like a pro. "How did she figure all this out?" I thought. Christ, she never missed church. Her mother was a walking library when it came to Catholic teachings, and especially laying down the groundwork of fundamental Catechism everyone had to learn. My mind flashed back to the time all of us went to her church one Friday night. Kids were lined up on the stage and the priest called each one up to a microphone. It was the Catechism final and people were scared shitless. Screw this one up and it meant dropping a year, or worse. Mothers and fathers nervously shifting on cheap wooden chairs in St. Benedict's social hall as they waited for their sons and daughters to get the call from on high. Some of the kids that went up to the priest were shaking so badly you'd have thought they were heading for a life sentence in *Sing-Sing*.

The priest looked down at them, officious…his black attire and white collar declaring that they were being queried by God himself, and that this was judgment day. They stuttered and fought their ways through the answers while the old cleric continued to stand there looking like a stone effigy, peering over the top of his black reading glasses – cupping the small Catechism black book in his hands – waiting…waiting…waiting….

AJ though…she kicked ass. She was unstoppable, rattling off her responses with the ease of a nun who read the *Good Book* every day, and then some. She knew all the ins and outs. She deftly avoided the pitfalls – she knew Satan's games this one did! She saw the light of the Catholic teachings. St. Peter and her were talking things over on a first-name basis. She was a star of the show, even though I didn't understand a thing she was talking about. In fact, she was so damn good that the old priest gave up his customary scowl and nodded, smiling ever so slightly at the little girl with devilish blue eyes who – unlike the others, seemed to relish all the attention. She was a warrior for God.

AJ certainly had to be St. Benedict's pride and joy – the highest example of what it meant to be a good Catholic girl whose family had their priorities right. They *were* the standard. Yet here she was now putting on a top-drawer striptease act. It was as if she were in a world of her own. I was frozen on her every move. I watched in dead silence as she slowly pulled down the zipper of her jeans. Then, she stopped....

"Turn around."

"What?"

She drew a circle in the air.

"I'll tell you when it's okay."

I dumbly obeyed and faced the back of the room. On the far wall was a painting of *Drazha Mihailovich,* a famous WW II Serbian hero – a real *Chetnik.* He was a freedom fighter who the American Serbs saw as the only real resistance to Marshall Tito's *Communist Partisans.* Bespectacled and in his full dress general's uniform, he was sitting on a white stallion. I swore he was looking right at her. Hell, he was leaning forward in the saddle going for a beaver shot!

"Okay, you can turn around."

I tried, but I couldn't move.

"Well…whataya waitin' for?  C'mon…turn around."

I took a deep breath, gulped and forced myself to turn.  AJ was still standing center stage.  Only now, she was holding her blouse over her bust and hips.  The afternoon light streaming through the basement windows painted shadows across her face.  Her hair danced with streaks of golden hues, framing her milky shoulders.  I followed her body contour and could see glimpses of her already well formed thighs and shapely legs.  She was beautiful.

And she knew it.  She knew exactly what I was thinking, and feeling. "You sure you're ready?"  It was more of a tease than a question.

I gulped and nodded.

Then it happened.  The blouse tumbled lazily to her feet revealing her maturing body.  I could see her large black nipples and well formed breasts. My eyes followed her curves like a road map until I stopped and focused on her inner thighs.

"Well, what do you think?"

"Huh?"

"So, tell me, am I really *that much* different?"

I was still riveted on her thighs.

"Yeah…you are."

She laughed, and then nonchalantly picked up her bra and slipped it on, bending again for her blouse.  She was as relaxed as if she was in her own bathroom.  I watched her methodically go through her re-dressing ritual. When she finished she pushed back her shoulder length hair with both hands, making it into a ponytail.  She looked down at me.  The angelic face that had so captivated me just moments earlier had now turned into a business-like frown.

"Okay…your turn…" she declared as she stepped down off the stage.

I heard her command but held fast.

"I dunno, AJ…."

"Hey…you're next…."

"I know what I said, but honest to Pete, I don't know if I can."

"Hey! You know the deal.  Do it!"

I took a couple of steps backward.  AJ leaped toward me, sticking her finger in my face.

"You listen to me, Stevie Milakov…you promised.  You got your show. Now it's my turn!"

"I can't…. Honest."

"What? she shrieked.  "You damn well better or I'll bust you good!"

I held up both hands in a plea.

"Shhh…somebody's gonna hear us…. We ain't even supposed to be down here."

"I don't give a shit!" she snapped.  "You made a deal.  Now get up on that stage and do your part or you'll be sorry!"

That's when I bolted for the door with AJ right on my heels.  I managed to clear it first and sprinted down the street.

"You chicken shit!  You promised…I'm gonna get you for this if it's the last thing I ever do, Stevie Milakov.  You're gonna be sorry!"

I ran like hell until her voice trailed off.  When I found a safe spot near a big oak, I slumped against its sturdy trunk.  I was scared and excited at the same time.  My mind kept re-running the image of that blouse sliding down her body and a never-ending view of her curves and inviting softness.  The electric recollection made me catch my breath.

I got up and dusted off my jeans, looking around.  Then I headed for the nearby alley that ran behind Mrs. Evango's grocery store.  AJ would surely follow up on her threat, I thought.  That, she would do.  I'll pay for sure, someday.

Then I smiled.  It was worth it, though.  Every second…. Really something to see, she was. Then I thought about something else: Maybe someday we might even become – well, *friends*…. I laughed out loud.  Had I gone nuts? AJ was a girl and everybody knows girls *never* make good friends.  They only make lots and lots of trouble.

###

# Shame...

Phillip Fry was alone most of the time. His older brothers, Jimmy and Darrel, were at the age that they didn't have much time for a seven-year-old kid. So, that meant he whittled away most of the hot summer days playing by himself out in the backyard where he had a sand pit full of toy trucks and cars. Still, I liked him, even though he was a year or so younger than me. We sort of made a pact to keep each other entertained, and although I thought he was a little goofy at times, he was generally an okay guy. He was good-natured and seemed to understand his being alone was just part of growing up. Both of us had that in common.

"Hey, Phillip, you wanna go with me? I'm going up to Central Avenue to the five-and-dime," I said one hot Saturday afternoon.

Phillip looked up and sprang to his feet, automatically dusting off his sand covered coveralls and Tee-shirt. Already, the late morning sun promised that it was going to be a sweltering August day. When that happened sanctuaries were few and far between. There were occasional cool glasses of lemonade, or maybe a shady spot under a big tree. Fortunately, our big churchyard had plenty, and on occasion I would fight the hot afternoons with Phillip playing cars around the base of one of them.

Phillip's life centered around his parents, the Lutheran church and the private school he and his brothers attended. Every day they would take the trolley car all the way to Kensington Park over near *State Avenue* where the church and school were located. They were disciplined kids and their pop never once spared the rod when it was called for.

Their dad loved to tinker with their *Hudson Terraplane* he parked out in front of their crickety garage. Actually, he never put the car inside, even in winter. I figured that he thought the termite-ridden, faded white garage with peeling white paint everywhere — and especially its sagging wooden double door, would probably just collapse some day. He wasn't about to take any chances with his fine automobile being inside when that Act of God finally happened.

Deep inside the garage there were lots of interesting things. Jim Fry was good with his hands, and so were his kids. The scattered tools that reflected skilled workers who were in the midst of half-a-dozen jobs were ample evidence that this was a place where a special form of creativity abounded. More than once I tried my hand at shaping or carving something from a piece of old wood and using a vice to grip to hold it. The vice was mounted on the edge of a greasy, thick, wooden workbench along the side of the garage wall.  But I soon discovered that I lacked the skills to go beyond the basics.  I admired others who could use their hands to make or fix things with relative ease.  The Fry family's ability to make something out of nothing seemed to be never ending.  All of them had it – it was a genetic thing, I suspect.

Along the garage's back wall were stacks of used inner tubes to change the car tires or their bikes.  Typically, at least one of the bikes was always under repair.  Pieces were scattered everywhere.  It was chaos on the dirt floor, but they always seemed to know where everything was.  Then one day they would magically roll out a fixed bike, or maybe a wooden *Soap Box Derby* jalopy, ready to conquer the neighborhood hills.  Mechanics are like that.  To others their world is helter-skelter and bordering on the dysfunctional, but to them their pack-rat lifestyles are more like heaven on earth.  Sooner or later their relentless root hogging would find a bolt that fits perfectly in a fender brace, or a cotter pin that safely kept a wheel on an axle.  It was, it seemed to me, a great adventure not much different than unraveling the mysteries of life itself.

It was inside the old garage where they were all total masters of their domain, and their destinies.  Where imagination existed side-by-side: the rubber, metal, bolts, nuts, washers – the tools of their trade – the screwdrivers, wrenches, hammers and saws.  They were there in abundance…like Eden's trees that were full of fruit…or the bounties on Earth that blessed a prosperous Kansas…and a comfortable America in the fifties.

Whenever Jim Fry was out working in his backyard, it seemed to me that life was in order in the neighborhood.  He was a busy man and not one for a lot of talking.  His thick rounded shoulders, broad back, and thin, dark mustache gave me the impression he took life seriously.  He had been involved in his fair share of weathering hard knocks – the kind that relentlessly attacks the spirit of a man, but never quite breaks him.  He had learned to fight off the challenges by imposing a quiet Kansas discipline in whatever he did.

You could just about set your watch to when he came home from his job down in the *Fairfax District.* The old *Terraplane* had a special sound to it – not exactly a rumble, more like a muffled growl, a product of a one-of-a-kind engine design that had a short but colorful life span in American car building.  Its six-cylinder, 145-horsepower engine was something of a novelty to the car markers of the time.  Most were opting for another direction, moving toward birthing eight-cylinder, tail-finned, chromium monsters that were still on the designer's drawing boards in 1952 but destined to become a full-blown transportation revolution by the end of the decade.

By now the obsession for power was well entrenched in the American psyche, and the unlimited supply of gasoline since the war had unleashed a marketing-sales campaign by the auto makers designed to put a car in every household.  Henry Ford's *Model 'T'* assembly line process had long ago made that a reality.

Ironically, Mr. Fry's job as a pump mechanic at a local refinery was helping to make it all happen. But instead of going for a shiny flat-head Ford V-8, the prevailing choice of the day, he settled instead for the six-cylinder Hudson. I figured it was his way of telling all of us that he was an independent thinker.

Still, he was right in other ways about not following the pack. When it came to toughing it out, the Hudson had earned itself a reputation on the Saturday night race car dirt tracks in eastern Kansas. It had made its mark as a dependable machine that invariably ended up in the top three anywhere it was competed. Midwesterners and Kansans are pretty forgiving folks. Their world is one that includes a built-in desire to give the underdog – any underdog, a fair chance. The Hornet proved itself on the tracks, and folks appreciated it. Many paid their respects in hard cash to dealers standing on the Hudson's showroom floors.

The car was unique in other ways. It wasn't a mainstream vehicle, rather an also-ran of the big three carmakers – *General Motors, Ford* and *Chrysler.* It produced its earlier models in Canada, England and Belgium, a process that began in 1911 and continued competitively until the mid-fifties. In its waning years the car was picked up by the little known *American Motors Company* which had produced – among other novelties – the tiny *Metropolitan.* American Motors was a place where innovation ruled. But the heavy-handed marketing and sales that began to define the car making business of the era was not their forte. Not even ingenious thinking could overcome the power of heavy handed sales strategies the *Big Three* imposed at will on an increasingly finicky America.

Actually, the name, *Terraplane,* and especially its sister car, the *Hornet,* was more than appropriate. The cars featured a step-down design. It was low to the ground, wide and extremely well balanced. Its appearance was striking, although a little unorthodox looking for its time. Its wide and rounded exterior looked a little like the torso of a hornet, or maybe a beetle.

I only rode in it once when Mr. Fry took his sons and me fishing at *Lake Quivera.* The lake was noted for its bass stock and we had a full day of catching our share. When Mr. Fry pulled his fishing line from the water to take home his bounty, he discovered a five-foot water moccasin was there, too – and it was just as hungry. He dropped everything and we went home empty handed. We talked about that for months. It was the only time I saw Mr. Fry take off like a rocket. I never knew he had it in him, but snakes have a way of making people do all kinds of things.

At the end of every workday, as soon as he got out of the car the family ritual was on. The boys knew exactly what to do. They dutifully took the dust cloths he pulled out of the trunk and began to wipe the car down. Content the job was finished according to his specifications, Mr. Fry would take his battered metal lunch pail out of the front seat and disappear into the house where he knew supper would almost be ready. He rarely said a word through it all.

On Saturdays, the Fry boys would help him wash their two-toned dark brown and cream sedan. We always knew that was happening because we heard them singing *"On Top of Old Smokey" as* they worked their way around the car. It was a family ritual that had become part of the neighborhood life and it made us feel good about our lives, and our neighbors.

***

The five-and-dime on Central Avenue was a favorite haunt for Phillip and me. Lined on one side of the store wall were several wooden trays full of toys that were sold to the neighborhood kids. Every once in a while they would bring in something new, and when they did, it was hot news.

Not that we had any money to do anything about it to begin with. Phillip and I were mostly contented just to do a little dream shopping. If we spotted something we really wanted, then we'd go into action and that meant collecting empty pop bottles and turning them into Mrs. Evango for cash. It was hard work but we took on the chore willingly enough. I had an old *Radio Flyer* wagon. We'd scour the neighborhood back alleys, checking all the familiar trashcans we thought could yield a bottle or two. *Coke, Pepsi, Royal Crown and Nehi Cola* bottles generally got us two cents each; but with the bigger quart sizes we got as much as a nickel.

The store was nearly empty when Phillip and I went inside and headed straight for the toy section along the far wall. It was still early and the lone clerk was busy attending to a shopper as she mused over a selection of ribbons on the far side of the store. They were both absorbed in the exercise and I figured the clerk didn't even know we came in. Even if she did, it was something she'd long ago adjusted to in the comings and goings of us neighborhood kids perusing her toy collection.

When I saw the new army-green *four-by* troop trucks alongside the wooden display rack, it was love at first sight. I glanced at Phillip who already found a tank made of the same material. His expression told me he was overwhelmed by his own discovery and had no desire to share his excitement. It was a good choice. The tank had realistic looking flexible rubber tracks. We studied the toys in silence, caught up in our own fantasies, fondling them as if they were made of gold.

"I ain't never seen anything like this," I finally said. "Look…the wheels even turn, and they're made of real rubber…and that big star on the side of the door. Just like the real thing, huh?"

Phillip took the truck in his hand and turned it over, inspecting its under carriage, then holding it in front of him with both hands to get a front-on view.

Army toys were a frequent addition to the store's toy line. The conflict in Korea was everyday news, and an opportunity for toy makers to create a market niche they knew had never died. It meant something new was bound to show up. That translated into big dollars with kids like us who were always looking to win any battle that came along, real or imagined.

But these additions were really something special. The combination of carefully crafted cast iron metal dyes and hard rubber put them in a new league of realistic recreations, and we both knew it. I took the tank from him and performed the same thorough inspection – then handed it back.

"How much?" I finally asked, thinking in my mind that it looked like a long day ahead rounding up the empty Coke bottles.

Phillip looked at the glass partition and pointed to the hand-written card stuck just behind it. His expression gave me my answer.

"Two dollars for yours and two fifty for mine! " I gasped. "It's gonna take two weeks to collect enough bottles to get them."

Neither of us spoke. We knew that the problem wasn't time – it was our overwhelming urge to have these toys…*now!*

I looked around. The store clerk was still occupied and her back was completely turned away from us. She and the shopper were bending over and inspecting a wide red ribbon. I stuffed the truck into my front jeans pocket.

"What you doin'?" Phillip gasped, watching on in wide-eyed disbelief.

"Shhh…." I pointed to his tank, cautiously looking again at the clerk who was still preoccupied, and urged him with a hard nod to do the same.

Phillip, hesitated, then swallowed hard, sticking the tank into his pocket, all the while keeping his eyes riveted on me.

"Let's get outta here…" I hissed, as I brushed past him for the door.

With every step toward the entrance my heart raced faster. I was terrified the sales lady would call me back and demand to see what I had in my pocket. But it didn't happen. I put my hand on the door handle and stepped out to Central Avenue, with Phillip right on my heels. We were free!

"Run for it!" I said, bolting down sidewalk, racing side-by-side into the first side street. We had done it!

\*\*\*

Phillip and I sat at the base of the largest Oak tree near the center of the church lawn. Its broad limbs formed a canopy from the hot sun that had set in for the day. But we couldn't care less. We were totally engrossed with the toys in front of us.

"Your tank looks super," I said noting how it rolled effortlessly up the base of the main tree root with Phillip imitating the sound as it fired at an unseen enemy.

"The Marines are coming to give you help…. We'll take out the enemy position with soldiers," I said.

I pushed my stolen truck closer, imitating the sound of soldiers getting out and calling commands to charge. I was so preoccupied with the maneuver that I didn't noticed Phillip's expression. When I looked up he was crying.

"What's the matter…? Is your tank broken?"

"No…."

"Then what is it? You sick or somethin'?"

He stood up and dusted off his thick blue jeans, swiping angrily at his cheeks with a dirty shirtsleeve.

"We did a bad thing...We stole."

His bluntness hit me like a brick. We had stolen and that was something neither of us had ever done before. All we had ever heard was that stealing was wrong. It was a sin. I heard it from my parents; I heard it every Wednesday when I went to Bible study class. I had it drummed into me from every direction. I knew it was wrong and Phillip's crying over it aggravated what I had been trying not to think myself.   Suddenly, the joy of the new toys turned ugly. I looked at the truck and tank and wanted to make them disappear. But they didn't.

"We can't take them back...it's too late," I said, thinking through the realities.

"Look, we'll just hide 'em... nobody will ever know.   Some place just between us...our secret...Okay?"

Phillip' started crying again.

"We gotta do it like that.  If we don't we're gonna get into even bigger trouble."

I was desperate. We had put ourselves into a fine mess and there was only one way out. He slowly nodded, wiping away his tears. He looked at the tank that he was still holding, then meekly handed it to me as if he were surrendering it to the enemy.

"Good," I said, relieved, but now totally focused to follow through on my plan.  In the distance, the *Hudson* appeared in the cinder driveway.

"Your pop's back.  You better go...I'll hide them myself."

"Where you gonna put them?" he asked.

My mind raced through the possibilities.  Then I smiled.

"In Brownie's dog house...nobody will ever think of going in there."

"Won't he chew them up?"

"Naa...he ain't stupid.  He stays in the house.  That's where the food is. I'll put them there...they'll be okay."

Phillip turned to go.

"Remember, nobody finds out what we did...not even your brothers, okay?"

Phillip nodded and ran toward his dad's car as he slowly pulled into the driveway.

*** 

"Why aren't you eating your supper, honey?"  Mom asked as she saw me avoiding the pork chop on my plate.  "It's your favorite...and with mashed potatoes, too."

Pops speared himself another piece and glanced my way, picking up on Mom's cue.

"Why you no eat, Steva?  You sick?"

"He's okay, Dushan," Mom said. "At least have some soup, sweetheart."

I glanced at Pops, then forced a weak smile. I stuck my spoon into the bowl and took some, making sure I concentrated on the bowl in front of me.

Mom had a sixth sense about me, and I knew it. I caught her furtive glances. She was on to me. I knew it.... I swallowed hard knowing the situation was turning worse. But when I heard the knock on the front door I had no idea how bad things had really become.

Mom wiped her mouth using her table napkin and stood up, disappearing into the living room. I tried to eat but swallowing was almost an impossibility now. In the distance I heard the muffled sounds of people talking. Then the sound of the screen door slamming again. When she came into the kitchen her expression said it all.

"Dushan something…terrible has happened."

Pops put down the glass of cold beer he was drinking and looked at Mom, trying to decipher what she meant.

"What you say, Militsa'? Somebody die?"

"No," she said, shaking her head, then looking at me. Her face was full of hurt – the kind that tore you apart from the insides. It was a look that lasts a lifetime.

"What? Tell me?" Pops insisted, sensing that it had something to do with me.

Mom picked up the napkin and began to wipe away the tears that were beginning to build.

"Militsa', what you speak to me?"

Mom looked at me.

"Stevie, do you want to tell your father what you did, or do I?"

The moment of truth had arrived. My own personal *"Come to Jesus"* session had begun. I tried to engage Pops but his pale blue eyes looked like deadly icebergs. I swallowed hard and glanced at Mom, but her expression did nothing to ease the pain. I felt like puking.

"Well?" Mom demanded…her tone now revealing a growing irritation laced with the hurt.

"We saw these toys, Papa…" I finally muttered. "We really liked them – but we had no money. I don't know what happened, Papa…."

It was as if I had somehow managed to leave my body. I saw myself still holding a shaking soupspoon in my hand. My voice was remote, as if I was talking through the far end of a long metal pipe.

"You speak what, Stevo?" Pops demanded.

I threw a glance toward Mom and then straightened myself on the chair, swallowing hard.

"Papa, me and Phillip…we took 'em. We…*stole* some toys from the five-and-dime. Then we got scared and I hid them down in Brownie's dog house."

"Shta ye ovo, Militsa' – shta Stevo kazhe? (What is this, Mildred?…What is Stevie saying?)

"It's true…that was Mrs. Fry at the door. They both stole them," she said.

Pop's face registered the same pain I saw in Mom just seconds earlier. He reached for his half-finished glass of beer and chug-a-lugged the rest, putting it down as he tried to decipher what he'd just heard. When he looked at me his eyes could have cut through diamonds.

"You do that, Stevo? You steal? Why? Why you no ask me – if you want, we always give to you – we never not give anything to you. But you steal? What people will say when they hear this? You do this to your Mama! To me?!"

I hung my head in shame, looking at Mom who had buried her face in her hands and was crying. I needed to say something – anything to find relief.

"Nobody needs to know, Papa…. I never got caught."

"*Chuti!* You talk like criminal! What about you, Stevo? What you think, huh? You know what you do – and God knows."

My tears were unstoppable.

"I'm sorry, Papa…I don't know why I did it. I just wanted it so bad."

I buried my face in my hands and sobbed. When I felt Mom's hand and arm spread over my shoulders, I looked up. She brought me closer to her, wrapping her arms around me as I cried. I was terrified and ashamed.

Her gentle voice blunted the pain.

"Stevie, your father and I know you did something very bad…and you need to ask God for forgiveness. You also need to fix whatever you did the best you can."

I slowly pulled away looking into her forgiving eyes. The love she had always shown me was back. She had already found a way to forgive me.

"But what can I do, Mama?"

Mom looked at Pops. They were speaking to each other, yet not saying a word.

"You must take them back – give them to the store clerk. Tell her you are sorry and that you made a mistake…you must return what you stole and be willing to take your punishment, whatever it is…."

"But I'll go to jail, Mama…I don't want to go to jail."

"It is what you must do, Stevo," Pops echoed. "You go back…you see. Mama will walk with you – wait for you outside…but this you must do, or God can never forgive you."

I looked at both of them and slowly nodded.

"If we go now we can get there before she closes," Mom said.

***

The store clerk held out her hand and took the truck, carefully inspecting it, then wiping it down with a hanky she pulled out of her dress pocket. I meekly stood by searching her expression for any clues to what was coming.

"Well…." she began slowly, her Southern accent sounding serious and no-nonsense, "…It don't look like you broke it none."

She turned and signaled me to follow her into the store, stopping at the toy rack where she lined the truck alongside several others still in the rack.

"You were here earlier today – you and that little feller."

"Yes ma'am…His name is Phillip."

"I know…He was just here."

"Did he go to jail?"

The store clerk fought back the urge to smile, choosing instead to reveal her fiercest scowl.

"Might as well have…his Pop was waitin' for him outside."

She glanced outside where Mom was waiting. She was nervously pacing the sidewalk near the entrance.

"I suspect the same thing's waitin' for you, too."

"Does that mean I won't have to go to jail?"

The store clerk paused as if she was making a life and death decision.

"Well, beins' the truck ain't been damaged or nuthin' – no, not this time. I expect you can go home.  That oughta be punishment enough."

The tidal wave of relief felt like somebody pouring warm oil all over me. I turned to go, holding back the almost uncontrollable urge to sprint out of the store.  Just as I was about to open the front door. I turned and saw her still standing near the toy rack, but now with both hands on her hips.  She looked like a drill sergeant.

"Next time you come here I'm gonna be watchin' – hear?" she said, pointing an accusing finger my way.  "You and your buddies are on my list!"

I felt my face blush, swallowed hard and dumbly nodded, backing myself clumsily through the door and out of her glare.  I knew then for the first time what it was like to be a criminal on parole.  I spun around and saw Mom looking at me.  Her radiant smile was back. She looked like an angel.  I ran toward the light.

###

# Yo-Yo Man

"Hey, look at that…"

Frankie Gibbons pointed to a man standing right in front of the little corner market across from the school. We would often go there to pick up a candy bar or something else on our way. The store was typical for the neighborhood, a bit small, but it had the kinds of candies that every kid liked.

"Look at what he's doing," Frankie said. "He's got two in his hands. Wow! Did you see that? He did a *Loop-de-Loop* with them both at the same time!"

The yo-yo man's performance had a *Pied Piper* effect on us. Kids came from every direction and gathered around the plump little man with dark brown skin. As I watched him *Walk the Dog, Rock the Baby* and do a series of *Around the World* loops, I noticed that his eyes were slightly slanted. I had never seen anyone close up quite like him before.

"Look at his eyes," I whispered to Frankie, who waved me off. He was totally absorbed in the stunts the *yo-yo man* was performing.

"Where do you think he's from?" I persisted.

"Who cares. Look what he can do? He's really good."

When the yo-yo man finished, he bowed and smiled to the applause of the kids, flashing two gold teeth right in front. Now I could see the wooden yo-yos more clearly. They were painted in bright metallic colors, brilliant and almost hypnotic in their blends. Blood reds that billowed into hues of orange and greens covered their wooden exteriors. Blues that gently and effortlessly worked their way into crimson…some of them speckled and exploding into hybrids of still more colors. They were the most beautiful things I had ever seen. Across the yo-yo's face I could clearly see a name: *Duncan*.

"Would you like to hold one," the performer asked picking up on my riveted expression. His speech was punctuated with an accent I had never heard before. It was English, but there was a sort of nasal whininess in the way he pronounced some of the words.

"Can I?"

He nodded and laughed, stooping and picking up a mostly fire red and orange one with speckled bursts of gold out of the box. He handed it to me and it was love at first sight. It was as if a missing link in my life had suddenly been discovered.

Yo-yos are a special kind of toy.  To get the best out of them requires lots of practice. Everyone is different – each has it own distinct feel.  This one was perfect the moment I nestled it into the palm of my hand.  When I flicked it out and down, the freedom of its free-wheeling rotation, how it tugged and bounced a little as it spun on the end of the taut string, told me right then and there that I had to have it.

"How much?"

"One dollar."

I stuck my hand in my jeans pocket but nothing magical happened. The same thin dime that was there earlier hadn't multiplied into a dollar bill.

"I don't have a dollar, sir," I finally replied, too embarrassed to look at him.

"Can you get it?"

His question had a tinge of urgency in it.  I knew I was on a deadline and a mission.

"I think so…But I gotta ask my folks."

The man laughed again.  It was a gentle chuckle that suggested warm tropical breezes and the distinct scent of *jasmine.*

"Okay…I'll be here tomorrow, same time.  If you really want it I'll save it for you, but you have to get it by two o'clock.  That's when I go to Argentine," he said.

The comment brought on a smile.

"I've been invited to give a special performance.... Lots of people are coming."

Frankie pointed to a speckled blue and green Duncan lying inside the box.

"Me too...."

He nodded, then stuck mine back into the box and closed the lid.

I turned to go then stopped and looked again into his friendly eyes.

"Mister, where you from?"

The question caught him off guard.  He looked at me, then smiled.

"It's far from here.  Have you ever heard of the Philippines?"

I nodded, trying to look smart and then vaguely remembered that it was somewhere out in the Pacific Ocean where John Wayne fought the war.  Then I recalled something else: a story about an Army General who had lived there and told the people he would come back and help them out.  It really didn't make much sense but Pops liked him a lot.  He said he might even run for President some day.

We turned to go.

"Tomorrow…same time.  I'll be right here, okay?"

Frankie and I continued walking in silence. Both of us were pre-occupied with the same problem: how to get a dollar out of our folks? By hook or by crook I had to get that yo-yo in my mits.

"You think you can get it?" I finally asked.

"Dunno…" he replied.

I thought about his non-committal response.

"Me too...."

"Who do you ask?" Frankie said.

"Me?  Most times I go to my Pop."

"Why?"

"Dunno.... He's just easier.  If he's got it, he'll give it to me."

We stopped at the corner where we always split up.

"What about you?"

"Same thing…except that Dad's on the road and I don't know if he will be back by tonight."

"Ohh.... That's too bad."

"Yeah," he said, trying to find another angle, but still hitting a mental wall.

Frankie turned and waved as he crossed the street.

"See you tomorrow."

"Yeah," I said, as I headed down the hill.

As I walked alone, the visions of that brightly colored yo-yo danced through my head. I hoped Pops was in a good mood when I got home.  I wanted that yo-yo more than anything in the world. I didn't know it then but it would prove to be the first of a million obsessions that were yet to come.

###

# Black and White...

**G**ramps, Clint Nichols, completely bald, stooped shouldered, and now in his mid-sixties, reached across the large dining room table and deftly speared another ear of corn with his fork. As if on cue, Grams came in from the kitchen carrying yet another plate full of chicken that had been kept warm in the oven. She put the plate on the table nearest her husband, who in turn found himself a plump drumstick and went to work in quiet contentment.

On the other end, identical twins, Ronald and Donald, were busy heaping on seconds of mashed potatoes, gravy, cranberry sauce and garden fresh vegetables.

"*Gadzooks!*...you guys.... Don't they feed you boys on those navy ships," asked Auntie-Mac. She tucked her hand under her chin and studied them with her customary warm, smile. It was the kind of smile that made you want to stay a while and talk some more.

"Not like this they don't," Ronald said, holding up a partially eaten drumstick. "Far as I know there isn't but one place in the world to get chicken like this...52 South Bethany. If I could, I'd have every cook in the navy come down here and take some lessons. That would be government money well spent."

"Ron's right about that. They try their best, but this chicken...it's something special," Donald added. "With meals like these on board the carrier, I bet we could end that war in Korea six months early." Everyone laughed, then went back to the business at hand.

Grams was back inside again, this time carrying in another bowl full of cranberry sauce. Stoutly built, and with silver gray hair pulled tightly into a bun, she wore no make-up and wasn't much for smiling when there was work at hand. And that was exactly how she saw life, a series of work assignments that she took on with boundless dedication and energy. Being married to a railroad man included no-nonsense obligations that she had consigned herself to following decades earlier. Of all of these family rituals, the Sunday afternoon dinner was close to the top of the list.

It had been that way ever since Clint brought his then sixteen-year-old bride from *Hiwassee, Arkansas,* a tiny hamlet of 300 people up in the north end of the state. Over the years, they took the *Kansas City Southern's Flying Crow* to nearby *Gravette, Arkansas,* to see their kin and friends. Because Gramps was a railroad man, he could travel free on the second class train. But the long ride home had its limitations. Back in the fifties, the financially troubled railroad was known as the *haywire* because its operating reliability was, at best, a daily guess along its 870-mile mainline from Kansas City to its two southern links, New Orleans and Port Arthur, Texas. But no matter how much noise people made about its inefficiencies as a reliable people hauler, Gramps refused to join the chorus of gripers. In fact, you could count on him to speak more in protective terms. He was always ready to offer believable excuses over its lackluster performances, even though it had meant more than one delay and frustration for him and Grams. Over the years, when more money was in hand, they enjoyed *sashaying* themselves on down to Union Station to take a *Pullman* ride on the *Southern Belle,* the first class train, and the pride and joy of the Kansas City Southern.

The newly married couple first came to Kansas City around 1903, back when the red brick streets were on Bethany Street. Actually, they lived in a couple of houses, and both of them were on Bethany. Their final purchase was at *52 South,* and that was where the family of six grew up.

Gramps was a believer in a big family. *Uncle Fuzzy* came first, followed by *Leona,* who never married; then sister *Clarice, Vivian* and youngest brother, *Paul* and finally Aunti-Mac. The two oldest children and Aunti-Mac made their homes in Kansas City, but Clarice had moved with her new husband to nearby *Parsons, Kansas.*

Younger brother Paul found work in Dallas and Vivian married and moved to *San Diego.* Of the two boys, only Uncle Fuzzy followed in his father's footsteps and, like Gramps, he loved working on a railroad. That actually began on the Santa Fe but the lure of the Rock Island and working alongside his dad was too strong. He had worked his way up over the years, and was now on the regular Extra Board road service. That meant that on any given day or night he could be inside the cab of one of the scheduled hot-shot freights or passenger trains that ran north, south, east and west from the rail center.

Life at 52 South was typical of what it was like growing up in a large family during the Depression years. Kids spending hours trying to invent inexpensive ways to have fun, punctuated by heavy doses of discipline that Gramps felt obliged to dish out whenever it was needed. More than once, one or more of the brothers and sisters would find themselves standing at the foot of their parents' wooden-post bed wringing their hands as they explained their indiscretions to the Supreme Court. The varnished end railing had long ago been replaced by the oily stain of little hands as they squeezed it, and at the same time fought back the tears at what might be coming next if their explanations didn't work. Gramps, no doubt, was a disciplinarian whose temper could sometimes flash white-hot. But there was also a wide undercurrent of love that ran through him, and that more or less balanced it all out. All his kids felt its presence, and they loved him all the more because of it.

Gramps' career with the Rock Island took some doing. After working around town at odd jobs wherever he could, he finally got a break. The Rock

Island Railroad Master Mechanic gave him a job as a *hostler* (roundhouse engine transfer) trainee. His job was to shuffle around steam engines on the repair tracks and eventually on to the turntable, and into the service stalls that surrounded it. That first job was all the foothold he needed. He loved his work and he sharpened his skills, moving up the ranks from fireman to engineer – and then to a senior engineer. The years of union seniority he had accumulated earned him an eight-to-five, five-day-a-week assignment switching cars in the local yard and transferring loads to the other class-one railroads that collectively made Kansas City one of the nation's most important transportation hubs. Now in the twilight of his career, life had become far more predictable. But railroading was always centermost in his mind. And that meant the *Rock Island Line.*

Those same decades of consistent loyalty to the job had also taken their toll on Grams, but at the same time she had toughened to the challenge. In many ways, Grams' constant attention to business was reminiscent of what one would have expected to see among the wives of earlier pioneers who rode the wagon trains across America. In fact, in the late 1800s her family traveled in the back of a wagon from southern Indiana to Arkansas. She was resilient, resourceful and always, always devoted to her husband. Her pioneer qualities were still very much a part of her life. She believed.

"Mom, sit down and eat some," Aunti-Mac said, as she stood up and took the bowl from her hands. "You've been at this for more than an hour." Her accent was a typical mid-western twang punctuated with a soft, Southern drawl that was light in tone, and captivating to the ear.

Gramps threw a look her way as he picked out another piece of chicken with his fork.

"*Girl,* Maxine's right…sit down an' eat some. There's plenty on the table."

His request was more of a command, but Grams understood. She sighed and nodded, pulling out the empty chair next to her husband. She settled in, running her hands down the front of her apron as she got comfortable.

Leona reached across the table and picked up the chicken platter, placing it nearer to her mother. Using the large fork on the side of the plate, she picked a piece that she knew Grams always enjoyed and put it on the empty dinner plate.

Aunti-Mac joined in from the other side, this time using a spoon to put an assortment of vegetables next to the meat. Then she went for the mashed potatoes.

"You want gravy, right Mom?" she asked, as she scooped a large portion and put it on the side of the dinner plate.

"*Land-a-Goshen* child," Grams exclaimed, "You tryin' to make me heavier than I am already?"

Everyone laughed. Around the Nichols household, Grams' never-ending fear of gaining weight had evolved into a sort of family tradition during every

Sunday afternoon dinner. Truth was, they had all been waiting to hear it, but the twins' arrival and additional food serving had apparently delayed her customary pronouncement. Her comment was greeted with smiles all around. The Sunday dinner at the Nichols clan was officially on.

Aunti-Mac got up when she heard the phone ring in the bedroom hallway but Gramps held up his hand.

"Leave it, Maxine. Fuzzy's up by now. He'll take the call himself."

In the distance they heard the muffled voice of Uncle Fuzzy speaking to the caller. He put the phone down and walked into the dining room, sliding into a vacant chair next to Leona. His bib overalls were starched and pressed crispy clean, the product of Grams' precision on the ironing board. He was wearing a bright red flannel shirt underneath and there was a matching red handkerchief sticking out of his back pocket. He was ready for road service.

Taller and stockier than Gramps, and now into his early forties, Fuzzy had inherited the same thinning hairline as his dad. But other than that, his physical features and demeanor were really a mix of the two, including his serious nature. Fuzzy was a private man, but when he did smile, there was a gentle quality in his ways reminiscent of Grams. He had also inherited that same Nichols *Roy Rogers* kind of clean-cut look that seemed to pop up everywhere in their family tree. Both of his sons had it in spades. So did Denny and even Dee-Dee. The Nichols clan were a handsome lot for sure.

When the twins saw their father come into the room they both offered a respectful smile. He had been sleeping pretty much most of the morning, and although Grams would have much preferred it if he had gone to church, she also understood that being on the road half the night took its toll.

"God wants us to keep our bodies as temples to his glory..." she would say in finding a way to forgive his absence.

The call gave him more than enough time to prepare for the day's work ahead. Working in a railroad home on a twenty-four-hour-a-day, seven-day-a-week basis demanded a mix of horse sense and sensitivity, and Grams was an expert at combining both.

Fuzzy looked over the display of food and started with a couple of chicken thighs.

"I got the *hot shot...3317...*the *zipper* to Los Angeles...five-thirty – track twelve," he said matter-of-factly to everyone, but knowing full well that Gramps was all ears.

He took a bite then looked at Gramps, flashing his soft smile.

"Guess that means green blocks all the way to *Herrington...*unless the Union Pacific holds us up for one of theirs."

"They can't do that..." Gramps replied.

He scooped some mash potatoes out of the bowl and dived in.

"Maybe...but they've been doin' just that lately. We got trackage rights but you'd never know it. *Number three* got in late a couple nights back and they made it sit inside Union Terminal until *69-369* – that UP puddle jumper mail train to Denver got out first."

He took another bite of the chicken and drank the iced tea that Leona had automatically poured.

"Heard the super got pretty hot about that and went to see UP's suits about it, but don't know what good it did, though," he said reaching for a plate of vegetables. "I'm figurin' not much."

Gramps poured himself a glass of iced tea and drank.

"You got good power?"

Fuzzy nodded.

"Three *Alcos,* a cab and two Bs."

"You like 'em?"

"They pull pretty good, I'll give 'em that," he said. "But you know Pops, they're damn temperamental gettin' to the top end."

Grams winced when she heard her son swear. She looked over at Aunti-Mac whose eyes told her that it was nothing to fret about, just man talk.

"You know how many the Rock Island bought?" Gramps said.

"I guess about thirty or so. We got a dozen down in Armourdale. They go all the way to *Tucumcari,* then the *Espee* hooks up for the rest of the way to Los Angeles. I hear they're stickin' for now with their big *cab forwards* and *Lima built Northerns.*"

The comment brought a smile out of the old man.

"That SP bunch knows what they're doin'. Always have. They got a real feel for what steam can do when it's treated right. If you ask me, there ain't nuthin' can beat a properly fired four-eight-four. They can do it all, pull the tonnage and the varnish. Shoot, our five thousand class was the best in the country 'till they started bringin' in those diesels."

Gramps took a drink, then put down the glass.

"They could get the job done proper. The older ones had sixty-nine-inch drivers, but the fifty-one hundreds were bigger. Didn't matter much either way, far as I'm concerned. They could haul the freight, or high step the number three right through town."

The conversation turned into one between father and son with everyone else relegated to the sidelines.

"You're right about that, Pop. I really liked the oil-fired version a lot. There's still a few of those around, but they won't last out the year. *American Locomotive* sure knew how to build a steam engine."

Gramps looked at the group and lifted his right arm above the table as if he were holding on to a steam engine throttle.

"You got to have a feel for your power. Steam lets you do that. It's like a decent woman. Treat her right there ain't nuthin' she can't do."

"Pop, we wouldn't expect you to say anything else," Leona finally said. Her gravelly voice accentuated her father's declaration. Everyone laughed. Through all the rail talk, Grams quietly ate and watched her husband as he made his points. The pride she felt for him was etched on her face.

"Who's your fireman?" Gramps asked.

"LeRoy Johnson."

He put down his glass in mid-drink, swallowing hard.

"You talkin' about the *darkie* holster?  You sayin' he's on road service now?"

Gramps put more iced tea in his glass, then spooned in some sugar. The sound of the spoon banging the side of the glass cut through the afternoon like a church bell on a crisp winter morning.

"I heard somethin' about that goin' on, but I didn't figure on it ever happening.  I swear, sometimes I don't know what the *Brotherhood* is thinkin'."

Fuzzy didn't look at his dad when he spoke.

"LeRoy ain't bad.  He works hard, Pop.  Besides, it's been comin' on for a while.  The union did what they could to hold it back, but they finally had to give up some ground.  At least LeRoy was the one who got picked."

The old man wasn't convinced.  His Southern drawl turned heavier and more intense, a sure sign that he was troubled.

"That ain't the point, Harold.  I know LeRoy and yes, for a darkie he *does* work hard.  It's what's comin' behind it.  That's what worries me.  Next thing you know, they're gonna tell the *Brotherhood* there's no reason to have firemen up in the cabs."

Gramps reached over and dragged a piece of apple pie toward him that Aunti-Mac brought in from the kitchen.

"Back when I was on road service, it wasn't like that, I'll say that. Everybody knew their place and nobody minded, neither."

"They bunk right along with us on the ships now, Gramps," Donald added. It was a half-hearted attempt to open the old man's eyes to the changes going on, but he could tell by the old man's expression that he was sorry he tried.

"Well sir, that may be, and I ain't got no right tellin' the United States Navy how to run its boats, or who should be flyin' their planes.  They're the best in the world.  Look at what they're doin' now?  Hell, those communist fellas don't stand a chance now that the US Navy's over there.  That fight will be over 'fore you know it.  And I don't need to tell any of you sittin' here what they already did to them *Japssss*."

Gramps looked at the group reflecting a look of pride and resolution all over his face.

"But in this house, I'm Uncle Sam...and I still make the rules."

He pointed to the front door.

"And one of them is that there won't never be any of them comin' through that door.  No sir, not as long as I'm payin' the bills around here."

Gramps delved into a piece of the pie and stuffed it into his mouth.  He was still preoccupied with his thoughts.

"Far as I'm concerned, those people are good for just two things – dancin' and singin'...I'll give 'em that for sure.  Nobody in the world can beat 'em at that.  But figure on them doin' anything else?" he said, with a wave of his fork, "...well sir, that's another story.  They're just too damn lazy."

He turned and looked over to Grams.

"Right, girl?"

Grams' face turned reflective, as if she was searching her own buried recollections. When she spoke, her voice was soft and controlled. But her words were laced with steel.

"It's just that God didn't mean them to do too much. They're good people, most of them. God fearin' folks with families and such. But you know, we all have our place. It's just the way the *Lord* made things. It's the natural order. They have their way of livin' and we have ours."

*\*\*\**

From our vantage point out on the front porch, Denny and I were looking at Gramps, and I felt a chill run down my spine. His declaration had the effect of a hammer pounding an anvil.

I looked over at Denny. Hearing Gramps' and Grams' explanations had a powerful impact on me, but still, there were nagging questions I couldn't formulate in my mind. Whenever that happened, I turned to him for help.

"You know any colored people?"

"No.... Just our housekeeper and she doesn't say much."

"Me neither, but I used to see them all the time down in Swope Park. They act pretty mean and loud."

"Yeah, I know what you mean," Denny said.

"You remember that time we got lost and those colored boys chased us?"

"Sure," he replied. There was a tinge of irritation in his voice.

"We were lucky to get away from them, huh?"

"Yeah...."

We turned back to our nearly finished food. I dabbled with my ear of corn, but Gramps' and Grams' words kept banging around in my head.

"Gramps' seen plenty of *them* on the job, huh?" I asked, finally looking at Denny.

He nodded, focusing on the food in front of him.

"Grams knows her *Bible,* too.... She knows what God meant."

He nodded again, still avoiding eye contact.

Our mutual silence told me that something was wrong. Being part of the Sunday family dinner with all the family made me feel secure and wanted. But hearing about coloreds over the dinner table didn't make sense. Yet there it was...and Gramps and Grams standing as one over the matter. Two decent, God-fearing people with views that I was struggling to understand for myself. By the look on Denny's face I could tell without asking that he was trying to work his way through the same thing. It felt like those Indian Summer days of fall that always preceded the coming of a hard, cold winter. Change was in the air....

###

# Harry and Clint...

**A**unti-Mac and Grams were busy washing and wiping the dishes, then putting them in the kitchen cupboards. It was a ritual that all of the sisters shared over the years. But this time it was Aunti-Mac who volunteered for the job. It was a time for some quiet talk.

Grams was doing her best to block out the sounds of *Bluegrass* instrumental music blaring over the radio in the other room, but she wasn't having much luck. Gramps, God bless him, was in violation of the Bible's teachins' about his choice of music. She was also *powerful worried* how he would atone for himself once he reached those *Pearly Gates.* Worse still, there were past indiscretions to account for and the list had gotten pretty long with the passing years. They had been married nearly fifty years, and ever since their first week together, on Saturday and Sunday he took the time to light up. Each time a mark went into the book, but by now nobody really knew whether it was Grams' or God's tallying that carried the most weight.

Aunti-Mac looked at her mother and sensed what was going on. She smiled, then moved a little closer as she wiped the last of the dinner dishes.

"I got a letter from Vivian last week. She and Lester are planning to come to see us week after next."

"Are the children comin', too?" Grams asked.

"Yes."

She wiped her hands down the front of her apron and looked around.

"Then I'd better make sure the back room's ready. They'll be needing a place to sleep, and those old mattresses aren't what they used to be."

"They can stay with us, Mom," Aunti-Mac said. "We've got lots of room in our new house. Besides, Denny and Dee-Dee would have fun. Especially Dee-Dee. She's such a curious sort and doesn't see Vivian's family much these days – all of them living way out there in California and all."

"No child...it's fine.... They can stay with us. The twins will be leavin' in a day or two. Besides, it would be nice seein' that old room used for kids again. That's why we built it."

Aunti-Mac carefully put her wiped dinner plate on the stack inside the overhead cupboard. She paused, choosing her words carefully.

"Mom, I'm real sorry Bob couldn't make it to see the twins. But it was business...you know how that goes. When you're a salesman you have to take care of your customers and that can mean any time. It's just how it is in his kind of business. He asked me to tell you how sorry he was. He really wanted to see the twins."

Grams didn't bother to look up as she put a batch of knives and forks into the kitchen drawer.

"Mom, this job is important to him – to us," she continued, sensing her disappointment. "He's working with *Dell Publishing* and they're a big company. If he makes a good impression, he could go far. He's such a good salesman. Besides, my job at the American Cancer society doesn't pay much and with the kids going to school and doing other things...well, you know, it's expensive."

Grams stopped her work and looked at her daughter. Her face was full of compassion, then quickly clouded with worry.

"I understand, child. I really do. I know Bob works hard. Lord knows he's been a good father to Denny and now Diana. It's just that well, never mind, it's not my affair."

Aunti-Mac stepped toward her mother, gently stroking her on the shoulder.

"What, Mom? What is it? I know you're worried about something. Tell me maybe I can clear up what's bothering you."

Grams sighed, then turned and faced her daughter.

"Well, since you asked...it's your moving around so much, Maxine. Nowadays, it just seems like you are livin' two separate lives. It's not good for the kids. They need roots, like a tree – so they can grow up to be strong. Clint and I lived on Bethany Street all our lives – and for the last thirty-five years right here in this house. We did it mostly for your sake – because we were family. It was just a natural thing to do. Somethin' the Lord expects from all of us when we take on the duties of raisin' young ones."

Aunti-Mac smiled and gave her mother a hug. When she pulled away her face registered the compassion that was a natural part of her makeup.

"Mom, I know you have some pretty strong views about marriage, and I respect them a lot, I really do. But this is 1952. Things are different now. Different than when you and dad were raising all of us kids. These days, if we want to get ahead, you have to make sacrifices. Sometimes that means moving – just like we did when Bob got that job in Memphis. There's so much opportunity out there and he wants to take advantage of whatever he can to earn a good place for himself."

She looked closer into her Mom's face.

"Bob and I are fine, Mom. So stop your worrying, okay?"

Grams studied her daughter's face. Then a smile slowly began to replace her frown. When Aunti-Mac saw it, she hugged her mother again. Secure that she had understood, she turned to finish the balance of the work at hand. Through the open window both of them saw Father Danny Milakov coming out of the back porch door and walking toward the entrance of the church social hall.

"Lord, I feel so guilty," Aunti-Mac said. "I've been just so busy...no time at all to visit with Millie and Danny."

"There's been talk," Grams said. The tone in her statement caught her daughter's attention.

"What kind of talk?"

"Folks' saying' things about all the carryin' on over there at night.  Too much drinkin' goin' on at those socials they're always havin'.  Pastor Danny's been seen too, and not behavin' like a Man of the Cloth."

"I wouldn't pay it any mind, mom.  Folks like to talk and make up stories.  Serbians like to have a good time and sometimes folks don't understand – but they don't mean anything by it."

She wasn't convinced.

"Satan is a very powerful enemy, child.  He can come to anyone – any time.  And he can take any form – the Bible tells it so.  That's why alcohol is bad for folks.  It makes it easier for *HIM* to get inside.  Then to do his evil work."

Aunti-Mac studied her mother's concerned face in silence.  She picked up a couple of wiped glasses and gently put them in the cabinet.

"I know, Mom.  Believe me, I know.... But what we can do is pray for them and be good neighbors.  I love Millie and Danny very much.  She's been such a good friend, and Denny and Stevie are so close, like brothers, really.  Heck, when Bob was off in the Army if it hadn't been for Millie, I don't know how I would have made it.  She never complained, and never even took a penny for her time."

The two women conjured their own memories of the war years.

"It seems like so long ago now," Aunti-Mac said.  Then she laughed.

"Do you remember that time all those soldiers came up Bethany?" Aunti-Mac asked.  The two laughed together at the recollection.

"The boys were barely three years old and playing out on the front porch.  Then along comes that platoon of soldiers marching to a drill sergeant's cadence right up the center of the street," she said.

"Everybody came out and watched.  Some of them even went back inside and came back out waving American flags.  Then Denny and Stevie decided to march right along with them on the sidewalk.  I swear, it was all those soldiers could do to keep their minds on the job."

"Yes, I surely do remember that one," Grams said, adding her gentle laugh and smile.  "Clint and Fuzzy had just come home from the yards after working sixteen hours on the road.  They were plum tired but they stood out on the front porch right along with the rest of us.  Watchin' those boys march made them real proud that they were doin' their share to win the war."

Not that they needed that many reminders.  On the job, both had long ago adjusted to days on the road, getting four hours of sleep a night if they were lucky, then back again on the mainline.  Long drag freights, tanker trains, troop trains, and yards of clogged cars full of war equipment choked Kansas City's web of railroads.  It all had to be moved, and fast.

"Folks banded together.  They worked with one another, because they knew that evil had to be destroyed," Grams said.  "We were God's chosen people to root out this devil.  Us...God fearin' Christian folks, who followed the Bible's teachin's."

Aunti-Mac picked up the last of the glasses and put them away.

"Yes, Mom we *did* prevail, didn't we? "

"Far as I'm concerned, it didn't surprise me one bit to see Mr. Truman show us the way to victory," Grams continued. "Clint always thought he'd be somethin' and he was sure right about that."

Indeed, Aunti-Mac knew there was a special bond between the Nichols family and the President. They had followed his political career for years, and even though there were distant odors suggesting a little chicanery in his background, he always managed to land on both feet in the wild and woolly world of Missouri politics. He was a working man – a *haberdasher* who used his guile, Midwestern common sense, and had a pocketful of luck that eventually elevated him to the pinnacle of the nation's political woodpile.

When FDR died suddenly, Truman showed his mettle. He took over the nation in a crucial period and made the momentous decision to use the *bomb.* That choice saved the lives of hundreds of thousands of Americans readying to invade Japan. Ironically, Truman was a man who came from the heart of the nation where changes were always suspect, and predictability a cherished and fiercely defended way of life. And yet he was the catalyst in ushering the greatest change in global stability the world would ever see.

Grams drifted into a recollection that brought on a soft smile.

"Did you know that Clint met him?"

Aunti-Mac smiled. It was a story she'd heard many times. She could tell by her Mom's expression that she was dying to tell it again.

"It seems that one day your daddy was workin' his switchin' chores over near *Independence.* The way he tells it, he had to push his engine and cars across *Truman Road,* but before he could get all the way clear, he had to stop and wait for his switchman to line up the track inside the factory."

Grams' recollection was so clear it was as if she had been right there in the locomotive cab with him.

"His locomotive was plum in the center and blockin' the cars on the street. 'Fore you know it – here comes this big line of shiny black Cadillacs with their headlights on and American flags a-flyin' everywhere. Clint saw them comin' but there wasn't much he could do."

"What happened?" Aunti-Mac asked, knowing full well what was coming.

"Well, they just sat there because he had everything blocked up. Then, after a while he saw this little man in a white suit and fedora get out of the second car and walking toward him. A couple other fellas were with him but Mr. Truman waved at them and they went back to their car and waited. He kept comin', a-huffin and a-puffin – struttin' like an old  Banti-rooster."

Grams chuckled.

"When the President got to Clint's engine, he looked up and asked him if he knew who he was? And if he did, why was he still blockin' the road? Well sir, he told him he knew who he was for sure…and that he voted for him, too."

"I guess Mr. Truman didn't expect him to answer quite that way," Grams said. "He started cussin' and fumin' – then jumpin' up and down and wavin' his hands in the middle of the street, telling him to move his train, right now."

"What did dad do?"

"Nuthin'.... He just sat there," she said. "Finally, after watchin' him carryin' on for a spell, he leaned out of the cab window. He said: *'Harry, lemme ask you somethin'. You are the President and I respect you for bein' that. It's a real big job.... But I wonder if you still can remember how us workin' folks do things? We do 'em one a time. On top of that, we do 'em right – and real careful, too. We ain't afraid of work, and we're doin' our part to win that fight you got us into in Korea. Just like we did it in the last one. And I expect we'll keep on doin' it – whenever you ask us to. But no matter what – it's always gonna be done right. There's no changin' that, ever.'"*

"That sounds like daddy," Aunti-Mac said.

Grams nodded and laughed. It was a soft, gentle chuckle tempered with the same blush of pride she had shown earlier at the dinner table.

"He told 'em just that, and you know what? Mr. Truman didn't do anything. He just looked at him like he was lost in his mind. Then, all of a sudden he started laughin'. He kept on laughin'. Then he took off his fedora and wiped his brow with his handkerchief and laughed some more.

"Clint didn't know what he was laughin' so hard at, but it tickled his funny bone watchin' him. So he joined in. There they were – plum in the center of Truman Road, the President of the United States and him, laughin' like a couple of hyenas."

"Finally, Mr. Truman caught his breath," Grams continued. "He told him: *'You're right, Mr. Railroad man. I did forget, and I wanna thank you for reminding me. Tell you what, you just keep on doin' your job. I got me some readin' to do back in the car. We'll just sit a spell 'till you're done.'"*

"Then he turned and walked back to his car, still laughin' to himself," Grams said.

"Pop will never forget that, will he?"

"No, I expect he won't, child," Grams said as she put the detergent box under the sink. "And I won't either."

###

# Courage...

Gramps Nichols was worried plenty. Throughout the night he sat by the radio picking up the broadcasts. Then he heard the announcer say the words he didn't want to hear: The dikes east of Kansas City wouldn't be strong enough to hold back the expected flood crest that was closing in fast. Not since the great flood of 1903 had so much water rolled into the Kaw Valley. The crest was projected to top the 35½-foot mark in some places; already it was moving unimpeded toward its natural connection to the Missouri, only a few miles east. Once that occurred the damage was sure to turn from bad to catastrophic. The heart and soul of Kansas City's West and East Bottoms districts lay directly in its path. And that meant major pain for the families who lived in the low-lying Armourdale and Argentine districts.

But that wasn't the only thing that worried him. His Rock Island was in serious trouble, too. The water was working its way into the fringes of the yards on the far east end and there was virtually nothing to stop it. As it gained momentum, the river's strength would surely destroy everything in its path – the tracks, the lines of boxcars, the engine roundhouse and the shops.

The *Rock* had always been a road that survived on its wits and luck. More than once in its colorful history its books had been painted bright red by the accountants who declared it bankrupt. But everytime something came along to breathe new life into the granger road.

But this time the deluge of water promised that it would take more than luck and the clever turn of an accountant's pencil to turn the Kaw River's muddy tide. If they lost this battle, the Rock Island could be submerged, forever.

Gramps leaned forward in his chair and nervously tapped the stem of his pipe on his ashtray, trying to decipher the latest report from the announcer. He glanced through the living room window. Already the clouds were turning dark and ugly – rain was coming in again. He didn't hear the telephone ringing in the hallway.

"It's for Harold," Grams Nichols said, walking into the room.

"He's down in the garage. Who is it?"

"Superintendent Templeton?"

"Bud Templeton...what's he want?"

"He needs to talk to Harold rightaway – says it's important."

The tone in her voice told him more than the words.

Gramps walked to the stairway and peered into the dim light below. He saw his son's stocky frame hunched under the open hood of his sedan.

"Harold, better get up here quick...Bud Templeton wants to talk to you."

Fuzzy pulled himself from under the car hood and looked at his father. He picked up a rag and wiped his hands, wondering to himself what the call was all about. He had come in three days earlier with a hotshot freight for Chicago. No problems or road violations he could think of. In fact, it had been a rough trip – plenty of slow orders and thunderstorms all the way. The roadbed was drenched and swollen; water topping many of the creek bridges didn't make it any easier. He knew it was his last run for a long time. Kansas City was in trouble. There was nothing he could do now except to wait until nature had run its course.

"He say what about?"

"No...just that it's urgent."

Gramps' eldest son tossed the greasy cloth on the car fender and climbed the steeply angled basement steps. He went into the hallway and put the telephone receiver to his ear,

"Yes sir...Harold Nichols here...."

Gramps stood near the hallway entrance straining to pick up the gist of the conversation. He studied his son's face for any clues, but all he saw was a cool, deadpan expression that revealed absolutely nothing. He nervously shifted on his feet for several seconds as he waited for Fuzzy to reply.

"Yes, sir... I'll do that... who's goin' with me? That'll be fine...yes sir... I understand.... When?"

He put the phone to his other ear and pulled out his watch and chain from his pants pocket, popping the cover open and looking at it as he spoke.

"I figure maybe we got an hour to an hour-and-a-half at most, judging by what you say is going on right now."

He shifted on his feet and bent over, ready to end the call.

"Yes sir...I'll be there...fifteen minutes...no more."

He put the phone back in its cradle, stuck the watch back in his pocket, then looked at his father and Grams who joined her husband's side. He forced a smile.

"The water's comin' up real fast, Pop," he said, measuring his words carefully. "Super said the way things are goin', the mainline bridge down at the stockyards is gonna go along with it. If it does it could be big trouble for everybody. This flood's turnin' out to be way more than anybody expected."

"What's he want from you?"

"They got a string of ballast cars sittin' on track eleven – brought up from Tucumcari yesterday."

Gramps put his pipe to his mouth and nervously bit on the tip.

"And?"

"He wants me to run them onto the bridge – cut 'em loose – then get the power to higher ground at Union Station."

Gramps bit down hard on his pipe stem and scowled.

"That ain't good, Harold. That water's movin' in fast. If you're still down at them stockyards you could be sittin' in it right up to the cab, or worse."

"They figure if the bridge don't go it could hold it back some further downstream. Besides," he said, " the Rock Island is in real trouble if we lose that crossing. It could ruin the company."

He stepped into the living room and looked at his dad and mom.

"I'm gonna give it a try."

"Then I'm goin' too!" the old man snapped.

"No need, Pop," Fuzzy said, holding up his hand to make the point. "I already got help."

"Who?"

"The Super...."

"Templeton? He ain't switched a string of cars in near twenty years. He's useless as tits on a mule."

Harold smiled and glanced toward his mom, surprised that her predictable grimace of displeasure at his father's colorful language hadn't appeared.

"He's comin' just the same. Sparky Callahan, too. They'll cut the cars and tie down the first three or four, then get outta there."

Harold turned for the cellar door entrance.

"It's all planned out pop, so don't worry. I gotta go," he said.

"How many cars you talkin' about?"

"About thirty or so…" Fuzzy said, as he made his way quickly down the garage steps.

He slammed the hood of his Ford and headed to open the garage's double doors.

"Full up?" Gramp's continued.

"Yeah…every one. They figure the weight should be enough to keep it from breakin' apart."

Gramps thought the situation over.

"A 1500 class engine and a slug can get it done quick, but if that water gets too high you're gonna be in real trouble. Those diesels will short out for sure."

"He's already fired up the *309* – that old *0-8-0* sittin' on the spur next to the roundhouse…she'll keep movin' – even if the water gets up to the drivers."

The news surprised the old man, but then forced a weak smile.

"You know what to do?"

"Last steam I worked was that old switcher. That's why he asked me…she's reliable…She won't let us down."

He looked up at his father who was still standing half-way down the cellar steps and leaning over the railing. In the dim light Fuzzy saw the worry on his face.

"I'll be back soon as I can. So don't go frettin' about any of this, Pop – things'll be just fine."

He slipped into the sedan and started the engine, then slowly backed the car out of the garage.

"If that water gets rough – git yourself outta there fast, hear?" Gramps yelled over the car's rumbling. Fuzzy stuck a hand through the driver's window and waved as he backed clear of the open garage doors, then reversed and disappeared into the rain which had already begun to fall more heavily now.

When Gramps returned to the living room he saw his wife seated on the family couch. She had a Bible in her lap and was reading, shutting her eyes in prayer after each passage. Her nimble fingers moved from verse to verse as she gently stroked the pages. Gramps sat next to her and gently put his arm around her shoulder.

"Don't you fret now, *girl.* He's gonna be all right. Harold's as good an engineer as you're gonna find anywhere. And that old steamer is strong. She'll get him through all of this just fine...you'll see."

"The *Lord* will guide him to safety, I just know he will."

"Yes girl, *He'll* show him the way."

But the look on her husband's face told her something different. Nature was on an ugly roll, and the worst was yet to come.

***

"Water's comin up damn fast, Super...!" brakeman Sparky Callahan yelled as he leaned away from the engine ladder and peered down the lead track.

The water had slipped into the yard area with an insatiable appetite to devour anything in its path. Already, the switch stands that controlled the connecting yard tracks were partially submerged. But the coal-fired steamer held its ground, pulling hard on the heavy load of ballast. The cars rolled on obediently as Fuzzy gently nursed the throttle, glancing occasionally at the gauges to see that all its vital signs were stable.

"There it is...'bout three hundred yards ahead," Superintendent Templeton said, glancing across to the cab to Fuzzy. "But water's really getting rough.... Looks to be up around the mid flanges down there. We ain't got much time, Harold."

Fuzzy repositioned himself on the engineer's seat and gritted his teeth as Templeton resumed his hand shoveling chores. The steamer's pressure was running steady and true even though the batch of coal being used was wet from days of pelting rain. The work crew managed to fire her up, anyway. Now the boiler heat evaporated anything inside. *She* was making do.

Fuzzy kept his left hand firmly on the throttle, sensing to pick up any sign of trouble. With steamers it was all in the hands and fingertips. The engine could *talk* and Fuzzy was listening.

The lead yard track was relatively flat but they were still pulling tons of dead weight. If the locomotive stumbled and stalled now, there would be no hope. They were too deep into the job to count on any help coming in from behind. The water level was at the point where a diesel has big problems. The switcher was all they had, a relic of the past that had seen better days and was about to be passed to the welder's torch. Alone and disregarded, it sat on the spur track, waiting for its call to oblivion. Incredibly, it was now the star performer in a drama that could save the very railroad that was out to destroy her.

The key was to keep the cars rolling, no matter what. As the engine passed the *Seventh Street Station,* Fuzzy felt the drivers spin on the slippery rails. He yanked hard on the sand bar valve as he looked ahead. The wheels bit hard into the steel rails, jarring the slack ran out of the train. The train lurched forward on its dogged ten-mile-an-hour pace. It was quickly turning into a race of time and test of wills – Fuzzy on one end with his stubby switcher, and foul-tempered Mother Nature ready to rip the heart out of the Rock Island.

From his vantage point on the right side of the cab, Fuzzy saw the bridge's steel girders and the entrance looming ahead. He was moving on blind faith, assuming that the myriad of switches into the lead track had been pre-set by the yard crew. When the switcher passed under the *Highline*, its stack barked in protest, spewing a carpet of thick smoke that swirled around the engine boiler, then found its way inside the cab. Fuzzy gripped the throttle bar tighter, oblivious of his smoky surroundings. The sound of the engine's staccato exhaust echoing under the bridge made him feel good. He would cross that bridge. He would win this battle!

"Christ! Will ya look at that?" yelled brakeman Callahan. "Waters' damn near over the top."

Fuzzy leaned out the cab window into the driving rain. It was as if nature was throwing yet another weapon of resistance in the battle of wills that was unfolding. He pulled himself inside the cab and yanked the throttle open wide. The switcher's bark was sharp and snappy, piercing the air with its defiance. Even though the small grade leading to the bridge entrance wasn't long, it was still dangerous.

He glanced at the speed gauge.

"We're gonna clear the grade and get out there," he said. His statement sounded so cool and composed that the Superintendent stopped his chain shoveling and looked at him in awe.

What worried Fuzzy wasn't so much the water's presence, now less than three-feet below the base of the span. Normally, there was at least twenty feet between it and the placid Kaw. It was what he saw stacked alongside the bridge abutments. Farmhouse frames, bridge pieces from other places, parts of barns, church steeples, and piles of wooden debris were already there. They were all adding pressure to the bridge's infrastructure. If enough of it gathered before it was weighted down properly, it could come apart at the seams.

"We're on!" the Super yelled over the crack of the engine's exhaust. "Keep her pullin'! Once we clear the other side, we'll cut you loose, then tie down the first four cars. Then we get the hell outta here!"

Fuzzy nodded and looked ahead. The rain had become even more intense as the engine inched its way over the Kaw. He looked down into the raging current. In some places the water was already lapping over the bridge's wooden ties and rails. How many times had he crossed this structure over the years – Gramps too – always taking a welcome breather, savoring the cool breezes that aways seemed to hover around the structure. It was like a reliable, trusty friend.

"Shit!  What's that!" Callahan yelled.  "Watch out!"

Fuzzy looked back just in time to see another farmhouse smash against the center abutment.  The force tilted the locomotive slightly.  The groan of steel supports and girders being moved by the force of impact told Fuzzy the bridge was being sorely tested to its design and tolerance limits.  But just as quickly it settled in.  The rock-laden cars were  already starting to  counteract against the current. It was working.

"She'll be okay," Fuzzy yelled as he looked toward the end of the bridge and safety just beyond.  "Just git ready to set us out."

The moment the engine cleared the bridge exit, Fuzzy pulled hard on the brake stand and closed back on the throttle.  The steamer protested, locking its driver wheels and skidding several feet on the slippery rails.  Then it caught itself and began to reverse its spin after Fuzzy pulled the bar again.  The move was nowhere near a standard service stop he had been trained to perform, but he knew the Super wouldn't mind a bit.  His timing was perfect.  The end of the coal tender stopped just a foot or so beyond the bridge exit and on land.  The cars were in perfect position.

Even before the engine stopped, the two railroaders were out of the cab racing toward the ballast cars.  Through the heavy rain Fuzzy saw Callahan disappear, then re-appear again to give him a hand signal to move his locomotive forward.  When he did, he heard the familiar *pop* of the air hose.  Callahan had successfully pulled the first ballast car's *draw bar* open.  The sound of the brake air hose popping was proof that the connecting knuckle couplers opened and separated from one another.  Fuzzy's switcher was now clear of its train.

The switchman was already on the lead ballast car turning the side wheel and hand brake.  The Super, he assumed was on the next car doing the same thing.  With all the river's buffeting that was sure to come, the cars had to be firmly locked down.  Otherwise, they could become a factor to accelerate the bridge's break up under the strain of the gathering debris.  Fuzzy had no choice now but to wait, watch, wonder and listen to the swirling torrent of water rushing under – and now increasingly over the bridge's rail-bed.

When he saw both men reappear through the sheets of rain, he forced a smile of relief.  Callahan was the first to find safety out of the downpour.  The Super was right behind him.

"Get us the hell outta here, Harold!  This place ain't fit for man nor beast!"

The railroad official was drenched.  He reached inside his shirt pocket and pulled out a pack of water logged *Lucky Strikes*.  He stuffed one in his mouth but didn't bother trying to light it. He was smiling like a Cheshire cat.

"But by God I think she's gonna hold. We saved her, boys!"

Fuzzy nodded and opened the throttle, working his way up the lead track. But all he saw now was more and more water climbing up to the engine's driving wheels. The *American Royal* stockyards and auditorium were already falling under the watery siege. He imagined that the stockyard pens a little north of them were suffering the same fate. The smell of death was in the air.

The steamer obediently followed the submerged tracks but the sound of exhaust stack told them the water volume was getting serious. To get to safety meant angling nearly a quarter-mile until they hit the Kansas City Terminal's *Peevine* grade that scooted up the far side of the Highline, leading to higher ground.

"Water's almost over the drivers now," warned Templeton as he leaned out and down into the rain. "We gotta get clear before it reaches the firebox."

Fuzzy wasn't listening. He was having a more critical conversation with *Number 309*. She was telling him something he didn't want to hear. Now she was insisting.

He glanced toward the two railroaders. "I gotta open the throttle all the way…we ain't gonna make the grade up to the station if we don't."

The superintendent grimaced.

"That's a severe curve up there, Harold…even on a good day you could go on the ground."

"I got no choice. She's gonna stall for sure. I can feel it…right here," he said, pointing to his fingers wrapped around the throttle bar.

He looked out into the watery expanse. The lead track that curved up next to the Highline was already in trouble. In a few minutes it would be totally submerged.

"This water is for sure gonna break out of the Bottoms, Super," he continued. "It's goin' all the way to Union Station – maybe not as much as here, but it's gonna get there just the same. I gotta make a run for it now."

Templeton leaned out of the window, then stuck his head back inside, looking at the others. Fuzzy was right, he thought. But if he miscalculated the engine's weight, speed, balance and water resistance – not to mention the severe angle of the curve, they'd end up with tons of water and debris on them, and with no way out.

"Okay, Harold…you're the engineer. High ball 'er!" Templeton ordered.

Fuzzy looked at him and nodded. He readjusted himself in his engineer's seat – then reached for the throttle again. Within seconds the switcher responded. It was now just the 0-8-0 yard goat versus the angry Kaw.

Ahead, the terrain revealed that within seconds they would be in the heart of the curve that would take them to higher ground, or into oblivion. The switcher's exhaust pounded with a determined bark as it hurtled the crew forward.

"Hold on!" Fuzzy yelled, as the switcher shuddered and rocked into the curve.  The locomotive suddenly lurched to the right, then just as quickly righted itself.

"Her flanges went clear off the rails!"  Callahan yelled as he braced himself for a derail he knew was coming.

Fuzzy kept his hand firmly on the throttle, gritting his teeth as he waited for the engine's decision to either stay on the tracks or become a victim of the watery tide.

As quickly at it began, it was over.  The engine balanced itself again and obediently followed the rails until the worst of the rising water was behind them.  Fuzzy eased off the throttle and the locomotive's bark turned mellower and more rhythmic. Tracks and roadbed appeared out of the murky water. Union Station popped into view.

Fuzzy worked his way up the lead and stopped directly across from the station.  Already the water was finding its way into the area.  Within an hour or so it would seep into the terminal sheds tracks.  Only trains going south and away from the river would be able to leave town.  Many had already been held up as far east as the *Sheffield Steel* plant and passengers were bussed to higher elevation in the downtown area.

The engines of other companies were already taking up space around the station's perimeter tracks.  Fuzzy looked out and saw several Kansas City Terminal crewmen running toward them.

"Christ...you boys gone plum crazy?" one of the crewmen yelled into the cab.  "We saw you taking that curve – we thought you were gonners."

"Well we ain't!" barked the Super.  "And we ain't never been better, neither!"

Templeton pulled his soggy pack of Luckies from out of his shirt pocket again. He fished around and finally found one that looked half-dry.  He took out his *Zippo,* snapping at the flint several times, then smiled approvingly when the lighter finally yielded a dull orange flame. He took a drag and exhaled, holding smoke out in front of him, studying it with a jeweler's eye. Then he looked over at Fuzzy who was busy securing his locomotive.

"That was sure somethin' – it really was...." he said.  "You did us all proud, Harold. In fact, both of you were somethin'.  I want you to know the company won't forget about this, neither. I'm gonna personally see to that."

Fuzzy looked up at the two men and smiled.

"No sir...it wasn't me – it was *her....*" he said patting the side of the engine windowsill. "She's the one that deserves the credit.... She's your real hero today."

***

*Number 309 lived out its last days on the spur track next to a roundhouse that gave up half of its walls to the Great Flood of '51.  And when the Rock Island finally got back on its feet, the switcher was sent to the torch.  No one bothered to say goodbye.*

*No one except for Uncle Fuzzy who dropped by late one night when he heard the news.*

*As for the bridge, you can still see it today. It spans the Kaw just as it did back in 1951, but its glory days are over now. Progress.... Sometimes it's hard to figure where it really leads you. This time it's right into a dead end. The bridge's east entrance terminates into the face of a cement floodwall. Just beyond it, the* **Kemper Arena** *parking lot occupies the space where lead tracks once guided highballing freight trains to Chicago and all points east.*

*But the fact the bridge is still there means something, even now. Maybe it's because history reminded the flood control planners that it still has a role to play. Maybe it's all about economics; or maybe it's something legal and best left alone. Whatever...it's there...a monument that tells a unique story about a city's colorful history.*

*The trains that used it are also gone. So are the railroad men who were in the locomotive cab that day. Their real names are perhaps not as important as how they all felt about their jobs: commitment, passion, and pride. This was really a story about all of them.*

*But in the end, it was the accountant's pencil that proved to be more devastating than even nature's ornery ways. By the seventies, the granger road was submerged into a sea of red that proved even more powerful than the mighty Kaw.*

*Still, there are some who say that if you should happen to go down to the old Rock Island bridge late at night just after a hard summer rain, you can hear the hissing, clanking sounds of that old steamer drifting across the bridge with its heavy load of ballast – and the railroaders inside it who were hell bent and determined to save their bridge, and their railroad. I'd like to believe that.... I'd like to believe there are some events in life that never, ever die. I hope this was one of them.*

###

# Part Three

# THE IMMIGRANTS

# The Hunkeys...

T hey came from Europe's backwater countries. They arrived in growing
numbers by ship at the turn of the century, then again during the twenties
and thirties, the era of the second Great Migration. They followed one another
in successive waves, passing through the portals of Ellis Island, and into the land of
many faces.

These newcomers had strange names. Some were dark-eyed and olive-skinned,
angular, mysterious Turkish looking faces. Others were fairer with chestnut hair.
Slavic faces with dancing sea blue and emerald green eyes. Their clothes smelled of
sweat and tobacco stained fingers from smoking too many hand-rolled cigarettes.
Yellowed teeth from spending countless hours sitting in the kafanos, smoking and
drinking Turkish coffee as they dreamed of the day that they too would pass through
the gates of Ellis. They were not very clean, these people of Europe's backwater
world, but they were proud. They were very, very proud.

**Hunkeys**, that's what these newcomers were called as they settled into towns
across America. There they found work; back breaking, thankless jobs that others
shunned. Their hands forged a nation's destiny using steel, cement, and the sweat of
their brows. The power moguls and the captains of industry needed these men and
women from these backwater lands. They were welcomed and crucial additions to a
master plan to expedite America into world dominance. And they did.

America in the late forties and into the early fifties, a time of plenty after the
Great War. A busy, changing America. A thriving, prosperous America, emerging
unscathed from the ravages of war that had engulfed the planet. A triumphant
America that stood up to tyranny and oppression, and came home again after millions
were freed. A heady America caught up in its raw power – preoccupied with itself,
and still adjusting to its new status as the dominant nation in the global community.
Not even the conflict in Korea could deter its internal mission or its sense of self-
importance. Far off and incidental, Korea was just another forum to demonstrate its
invincibility again and the dominance of its superior technology. It was really a
time of looking within. And it was the Serbs of America who shared in the glory of
those achievements.

At first these Serb immigrants were only a tiny current in America's widening
stream of humanity. Despite their numbers they made their marks, settling in working
man's towns: Zanesville, Akron, Gary, Joliet, Chisholm, Butte, and Bisbee. Wherever
they lived they co-mingled, and inevitably it was their Orthodox Churches that
towered above them like a shining star. Gold painted, Byzantine domed with their
wooden crosses, the Church beckoned these Hunkeys to worship and to preserve
their heritage in the new land.

In their social halls they savored the music of their homeland and drank their liquor. The melodies were as varied as the people were. Often it was a staccato, driving rhythm played in haunting minor chords that drew them together to dance hand-in-hand in ever widening circles. They, as one.... They...who snaked across these wooden dance floors, feeling the music deep from within. And then, even if only for a few brief moments, the overwhelming ecstasy of comradeship sharing the beauty and power that resided in recognition of their mutual heritage.

All of this played out in the shadow and protection of the church's dome. It was here that the problems, frustrations, and rejections on the outside were forgotten. Here, in these social halls built by their hands, even the poorest among them could be King; the least educated could lead. This was where the arena of the great and never-ending Serbian debate was held. Here was where they rummaged through old issues and new, and invariably included a litany of life's experiences that had long ago been distorted to impress others, and repeated endlessly through clouds of smoke and drunken fantasies. They were the tales of failed dreams among men who had been battered into submission by the toils of life over time, only to hand their dreams over like a baton to a new generation to run again. The debates and stories were a necessary part of the process; to remember, to try again using new ways, but never to forget the old. To maintain Serbian traditions because that was a Serb's lifeline to identity.

And so it was across America and wherever they worked and lived. In the wine-red summer sunsets of McKeesport and the miles of fiery steel mill furnaces; or on a sparkling spring morning among the grain elevators in Nebraska; or in the open pit mines on a bitterly cold winter day in Minnesota. Wherever there was work to be done these people with their broad shoulders and dancing eyes were willing. It was their investment in America. And when they came together to join hands to share the music of their past, they universally proclaimed their fate:

### Niko nema sto Srbin imade...

**No one has what we Serbs have!** They sang together in their Serbian tongue far into the night. Rich, vibrant voices blending into a natural, full harmony – a gift from God that can only come from deep within the soul. The outsiders who watched on in wide-eyed wonderment couldn't understand what they were saying, but they felt it. There was energy within these walls that told them something powerful was present among these simple people, and it was addictive. It was a current of life that ran rich and deep, a vein of gold that was theirs to enjoy. They were the Serbs.... And they believed.

### ###

# Chapter Five

**B**y 1900 and well into the twenties, Serb families had settled into the West Bottoms neighborhood, just a stone's throw from where most toiled to make a living. They called their neighborhood the *patch*, and the term seemed appropriate enough. It was, in fact, a small piece of green grass and dirt and rutted roads sandwiched between the *Armour* and *Fowler* meat packing plants on its East Side, and the curving Kaw River to the west.

The patch was a foothold for the Serbs, and by all accounts they made the best of it. On the surveyor's map, it looked orderly and typical of any neighborhood in growing America at the turn of the century. It was set up on neat square-shaped block grids. North-south passages were referred to by numbered streets, and familiar American names identifying those that ran east-west: *Lyon, Ohio* and *Riverview Streets* were where the dingy looking shanty homes and boarding houses were built. There was a small movie theater and the *L.K. Wiles Drug Store* had all the basics to keep away the *whooping cough* during the long and dreary winter months. Nearby was a small shoe store and a corner barbershop. The small playground and grade school on *First Street* offered kids plenty of ways to keep themselves busy. It didn't bother them that many were so poor that the dwindling numbers of earlier Irish and Germans immigrants who were leaving the neighborhood for better lives made it a point to give them hand-me-down toys so they could celebrate their own Christmas on January 7th. In the patch you were what you were, and there was no need for pretenses.

On the far south end of the patch, and out of harm's way near Central Avenue, were the pool halls, bars and back room brothels – the quiet, dark places for the lonely men who worked the long, hard hours at barely subsistence wages. The rest of the world paid it no mind. High above the bluffs on Strawberry Hill to the west, there were other interests and new lives to lead. What the Bohunks did down there along the banks of the muddy Kaw was pretty much their business. It was *okey-dokey fine* – unless, of course, one of the bar owners forgot to pay off one of the cops or city officials for turning a blind eye to all the shenanigans going on.

For the Serbs who continued to migrate and settle in, the patch was home, warts and all. By 1910 the unmistakable odor of homemade chicken soup, *sarma (minced pork wrapped in cabbage rolls), gibanitsa (cheese strudel). kupus i grah (sour kraut and beans),* and fresh baked *potitsa (nut bread)* that drifted through the open windows of the tiny homes and boarding houses on Sunday afternoons proved a worthy opponent to the putrid odors filtering out of the nearby packing houses.  Wilson and Armour and Company, it seemed they had finally met their match.

When you came to the patch there was no doubt that you were in Serbian territory…wherever you went the unmistakable *"ich"* tagged to most of the last names on the boarding house mailboxes, front doors and business shingles.

Those who had arrived at the turn of the century scrimped and saved their meager earnings from their packinghouse work, all the while keeping their dreams for a new life close to their hearts.  They were redefining their versions of *freedom* and it was strictly a family affair.  Many had dreams to go into business for themselves and no venture was off limits: *Todor Plecas* and his family opened a dry goods store; immigrant *Vaso Kalinich* and countrymen *Luka Uzelac* saw the grocery business as their way out; *George Bozich* saw the liquor and restaurant business as his path to riches; *Mile Boca* opened a pool hall and restaurant; and *Pete Stepanovich* saw selling liquor as the answer.  Everything was fair game.  If it could turn a dollar, chances were it got somebody's interest and eventually the money it took to give it life.

***

The early settlers who came to the West Bottoms emigrated almost exclusively from the same area of Yugoslavia.  The Serbian province of *Lika*, along the country's northern most frontier, was a desperately barren place that was part of the historic *Krajina* region.  It was an isolated area composed mostly of rural farming carved out of rock-hard land that on a good year yielded a meager existence.  Yugoslavs often joked about it as being the land of *five goats and a shack*…and nothing more to their names.  Lika was a hard place made up of equally hard people who had come to terms with living and embracing the reality of poverty and dying early at every corner.

The Lika region and the villages in and around a regional town, *Plashki*, was a conduit of badly needed unskilled laborers.  Agents from the US were sent to the region to recruit the potential labor.  Over time, the fathers, sons and daughters of those early generations of immigrants wrote back to family members in the old country telling them of the treasures of the new land.  That in turn led to a chain migration that lasted for nearly a quarter century.

Many of their letters were full of unfulfilled dreams, fantasies really, but still vibrant and brimming with optimism.  To those who still toiled the land and waited, they dreamt of images of streets paved with gold.  Yet in truth their lives in America were really not much more than baseline existences, accentuated by brief lulls when the pain associated with the never-ending battle for survival at all costs could be deflected among fellow countrymen who knew what they were all enduring.

Yet, even then in this valley of comradeship, grudges emerged, jealousies percolated…and comparisons and envies were elevated to a fine art among these families. The old adage: *"Everyone wants to keep up with the Joneses..."* or in this case the Jones*ichs,* was alive and well. Under such conditions when the resentments began to mount and then carried over from one year to the next, peaceful coexistence could just as easily flare into bloody clashes. All it took was a spark – too much booze, a bad debt, or a comment or two about someone else's character. These were hard times for hard people who had come to America to find a new beginning, only to discover that what lay ahead first were more years of toil and suffering under the heavy yoke of capitalism.

Still, the spirit that accompanies hope and unshakable belief in the power of the limitless spiritual cup to guide them was never far removed from these Plashki newcomers. In 1906, the first *Saint George's Church* emerged out of the helter-skelter world of the West Bottoms. The tiny church was as much as anything else a sanctuary to the immigrants who worked 18-hour days in the packing houses and other labor-intensive businesses that sprouted in the industrial center.

Saint George was not by even the remotest definition a monument to Christianity that churches sometimes are meant to be. It wasn't the *Notre Dame*, the *Morman Tabernacle*, or even the *First Baptist Church of Dallas*. In fact, the church wasn't really a church at all – it was a *house* at *35 North First Street*, literally within walking distance from the eighty or so families that attended it. Actually, two houses were purchased and remodeled, one that became the church and the other a residence for its first priest, *Reverend Teofil Stefanovich*. Over the years other priests took their turns in building the small parish and each cultural pillar they put in place added to the patch's colorful ethnic history.

No one could dispute that the hearts of these immigrants were well entrenched in the belief of their church teachings. The rural peoples of Lika had always been known for their unbending devotion to the mother Orthodox faith. For countless generations the province had been surrounded by Croatian Catholics as part of the influence of the *Hapsburg Empire*, and to a lesser degree the *Venetian* incursions along the *Adriatic* coast. Both regimes had embraced and touted the Vatican's teachings, and this same commitment continued into the Twentieth Century with the more regional *Austro-Hungarian Empire*.

But even beyond that internal struggle over who was the chosen Christian religion, there was an even more ominous external threat to contend with, and the struggle that followed helped shape Europe in the unfolding century. In the end it took the combined forces of the Austrians and Serbs centuries before they were able to push the *Muslim Turkish Ottoman Empire* out of the land the Serbs saw as theirs alone to rule, and had done so with impunity for centuries.

The Austrians quickly discovered that these stubborn, hardy, and determined people of the Krajina were more than worthy to be called Christianity's official watchdog and, when called upon, a defender against the Muslim incursion. They had proven themselves to be valiant fighters over many decades. Only the tales of heroism of the *Montenegrin* Serb mountain fighters far to the south could equal the bravery they consistently demonstrated against an enemy that had occupied Slav lands for more than five hundred years.

It had, by all historical accounts, been a harsh and brutal occupation that officially began with the near annihilation of Slav nobility on June 28, 1389, at *Kosovo Field.* There, *Prince Lazar* had assembled his army on the *Field of Blackbirds.* And it was there that the Slav army fell, opening the door to centuries of domination and repression.

The Turks were an able fighting force, but they were also corrupt and frequently contentious among themselves. Their dream to establish a vast commerce system and impose their Muslim faith produced only spotty results at best. Among the Serbs in particular the humiliating defeat at the *Field of Blackbirds* had evolved into a symbol of resistance to an occupied people and land. They endured and they waited...and wherever they could, they resisted.

At their zenith the *Ottoman warriors* pushed far beyond the Slav occupied lands they held with an iron fist. At one dark point in history, their army had managed to get to the very outskirts of Vienna itself, only to be eventually pushed back below the Krajina buffer zone. Once there, it was the Serbs of Lika who did their part to hold the line. By 1911, the once vast Turkish intrusion had been reduced to just pockets of influence, mostly concentrating in the regions of *Macedonia,* parts of *Bosnia, Kosovo* and Muslim-dominated *Albania.* For the Serbs, the *Field of Blackbirds* and what followed over the centuries was more than a chronology of Slav history and its fabled war heroes – *it was the saga of their soul.*

All of this was also part of the social baggage the immigrants brought with them to America at the turn of the century. That, along with a willingness to work hard and long hours with little complaint – a fact that soon impressed the capitalist power moguls in search of reliable labor. But beyond their strong backs and iron wills, the fresh memories and the determination that in this new land the Church would once again stand with them was never far removed from their collective thinking.

The patch immigrants, seeing the need for a more dramatic declaration of their faith than the *holy home* they had bought for around a thousand dollars thoughtfully added a church steeple. They installed a church bell that had a single tone that sounded a lot like a steam locomotive's redundant clanging. Nobody really knew, or cared, or asked, where it came from, or even why it sounded that way. It just appeared one day, and it was used. In the patch you made do with what you had.... The bell worked. Its earthy *bong* was calling the faithful to worship and, as was the custom, to stand for the more-than-two-hour church services every Sunday. Perhaps even more important, its powerful tone clanged above the sounds of frenzied capitalism that surrounded life in the patch; and, if even for a brief moment, smothered the shrieks of the hogs as they dangled helplessly by their hind legs. They were traveling down an assembly line of death – instinctively sensing they were living out their final precious moments on earth.

The church offered sanctuary from the agonizing hours on the job with little or no breaks, and incomes that were at best slightly above the subsistence level. Women's clubs were formed and links to other Serbian communities created. The social events became a source of welcomed home-cooked food and the music of their homeland. Enough to reinforce the reality that those who came to this world were building a new life, even if it were on just pennies a day. The husky *clang, clang, clang* they heard on Sunday morning was more than a church bell's ringing – it was the sound of *hope.*

Historians note that two developments – one natural, the other man-made, contributed to pushing the Serbs out of the patch. The first had something to do with the *Great Flood of 1903* and its assault on the low-lying lands. Just as with the rest of the Bottoms, the patch got its share of high water and accompanying misery. The second had more to do with capitalism, prosperity, the *American Dream*, and the sheer number of families that were coming into the region.

The 1900s was a time of growth. Stories compiled by the local *Kansas City Kansan* proudly proclaimed that by 1925 more than five million cattle and hogs were being slaughtered every year in the Bottoms. The original Armour and Fowler packing plants were now competing with seven others. The houses alone employed more than ten thousand workers, making it number two in the meat packing industry in the US. Only Chicago could claim a higher kill rate.

As these businesses grew, the Serbs were also able to improve on their own lives and build families. Social and cultural needs became higher priorities. These fragile dreams were slowly being massaged into realities. America had begun to yield its bounties. It revealed its heart and the Serbs embraced it in the land they now called home. For many, that treasure trove translated into a better life on the bluffs directly above the patch to the west – *Strawberry Hill,* named originally for the fields of wild strawberries that grew there and where the indigenous *Wyandotte Indians* once camped on the bluffs overlooking the Kaw.

Church records indicate that it took no more than forty of the estimated eighty families who originally lived in the patch to usher in a change among all the Serbs that would last until the end of the century. By 1920, some had already left the patch and bought homes in the Strawberry Hill area, settling in a district bordered by *Seventh Street* on the West and *Fifth Street* on the East. By that time the *Hill* was already well occupied by Balkan ethnic groups and their churches were already established. On the northern fringe the *St. John the Baptist Roman Catholic Church* belonged to the Croatians. The Slovenes dominated *Holy Family Roman Catholic Church* to the south. By 1910, their churches, social clubs and schools were busy attending to their ongoing spiritual, social, and educational needs – all the baptisms, weddings and funerals…the ethnic holidays and the musical events unique to their own kind. For the newcomer Serbs, it was a case of being a fifth wheel, so to speak. Only the combined *Russian and Greek Orthodox Church* located some distance south offered any alternatives. Of course, there was always *Saint George's* in the *patch…down there….*

The dilemma on what to do caused some interesting cultural twists to emerge among many of these families. Some actually attended the Catholic churches. The idea that a Serb – especially a Plashki Serb, would be willing to attend a Catholic Church service was in itself a revolutionary change to the new life in America that was emerging. Why some chose this path was anybody's guess. Perhaps it had something to do with simply wanting to be part of the more up-market lifestyle and sharing similar dreams with others, regardless of the religious overtones. To others it may have had more to do with the past: *The patch was where you came from…. And the last time you checked, you didn't leave anything behind.* To others, it was just easier to do.

Yet despite these temporary shifts in religious preferences among some of the Serbs, for the most part the spirit of *Orthodoxy* ran deep among them. The continuing encroachment of industry on the patch and the even greater social needs to re-establish cultural and essentially Serbian oriented ties among these original settlers, were strong and healthy indicators that those early years in the West Bottoms had produced a generation who knew who they were and took accountability in keeping that heritage in clear view. That passion eventually culminated with the purchase of land at the corner of *1119 Lowell Avenue* in Kansas City, Kansas. That was where the second *Saint George's Serbian Orthodox Church* was built and consecrated in May, 1926. A year later they purchased the home at *50 S. Bethany* and for all intents and purposes that was where life began for me.

Interestingly, the parishioners saw no need to change its original church name. *Saint George* for most was the family *Patron Saint* that dominated the Plashki region. He had served them faithfully in the patch – now he would stand tall on Lowell Avenue – spear in hand, ready to slay the evil dragon again. When they shut the West Bottoms church doors for the last time, an era had come to an end. But in their wisdom they also remembered a piece of their colorful history: They brought along *the bell….*

# Chapter Six

In the Serbian community there seemed to be a hierarchy operating about being the best at whatever we did. Among us kids we all knew it was there, and that meant at times we openly competed with one another. This was often played out in sports, but getting high grades was a close second. Among all of us, though, it was *Donald Yovetich* who led the way in both categories. A year ahead of me, he was always doing something that got headlines, be it in sports, or in the classroom. And that meant misery-city for me every time he did.

For a kid just eleven or so, Donald was big...really big.... Husky in build and with a head that was a natural for the flat top haircut styles of the times, he went through life like a Brahma bull that had few, if any, enemies. You couldn't say Donald was the clean-cut type – he looked more like a lumberjack with his ruddy complexion and a pile of zits that thought his face was a five-star resort. No, Donald wasn't a pretty boy. The attraction with him was that everything about his presence was *Triple XXX,* including his wide smile and a voice that boomed over us kids.

Donald liked to debate with people and he generally had a lot to say about lots of things. He seemed to relish on verbal combat, and his heavy handed tactics with us kids almost always won out. We called him *Yogi*...the same nickname of the great Yankees baseball catcher, *Yogi Bera*...the guy who always had something to say about everything, too.

He was seen as a heavy-footed and naturally sloppy, but a generally amiable kid, who came from good stock. The Serbs took note of his stature but didn't say much except making comments among themselves about how fast he had grown compared to the rest of us. You couldn't call him a freak. He was big for sure, but it didn't stop there. Donald definitely had the mental *rpms*, and he learned how to use them in lots of ways. No, Donald was no circus attraction by anybody's yardstick. But he was there just the same – at times in my face, and definitely in my life.

It was during my fifth grade in Prescott that Donald really got things going his way. It began when *Central Junior High School's* head coach and his assistant made a trip to Prescott to see a sixth grade school lad who already stood near six feet and was moving around the school's playground basketball court as if he was the sole owner.

In Kansas City, next to Wyandotte High's starting five, it was the ninth-grade teams throughout the community that commanded nearly the same following. Fans would pack into the small gymnasiums throughout the cold winter months to watch their kids do battle. How Central did against *Turner,* or *Northwest,* or *Argentine*...it all counted. People talked about it.

The idea of the two coaches making a special trip to a grade school to see one kid shot through our school and around the neighborhood like a news bulletin. It was probably newsworthy enough to have a sports reporter for the *Kansas City Kansan* newspaper on hand with us watching on the sidelines. For all I knew, he was right there taking notes.

What they were all really looking for was a *prodigy.* Someone that would rise like the fabled *Phoenix* out of the ashes of the local school system – bring basketball stardom and glory to himself and his family at Wyandotte High...then move on to the ultimate – getting national exposure as a starter with the *Kansas Jayhawks.* This was the engine that drove Kansas basketball. To be a favorite son that validated we were on top of the American game, and that in turn translated into being on top of the game of life.

To say this was *the* dream to Serbian families, or any family in Kansas City for that matter, would have been a gross understatement. It was everything. The prodigy subject, in fact, was closer to being damn near a *spiritual obsession;* private dreams that it would be somebody out of their family's gene pool who would be *the ones* bringing forth a bona fide miracle worker on the hard court. What more could a parent ask for? It was the brass ring every family worked to snatch in the merry-go-round of a life that offered little real diversion to these working class folks.

And now here was the young Mr. Yovetich, as Serbian as you can ever hope to get. *Yogi,* strutting his stuff for the entire world to see. Getting a special visit by the coaching staff just to see *him.* It was a powerful message that maybe *he* was *the chosen one.* The fact that they were at Prescott, even before he checked into Central next year – well, that meant he was being personally invited to register for future stardom.

Their on-court study was clinical and deadly serious. First, the coaches watched him shoot around from the sides at about the six- to ten-foot range, studying his wrist action and shooting mechanics. Next, they had him do a series of dribbling exercises and then lay-ups, moving in closer to get a better look at his footwork.

Then they did something that made us all gasp...they put his back to the basket and dead center in the *lane.* The coaches went out to the point guard slots. They started feeding and cutting to the basket and Donald Yovetich passed off to them as they drove to score. On command, he spun around and took a shot. To me, he looked like a house with shoes, he took up so much space and moved so deliberately. But the coaches obviously saw something else, smiling approvingly, then talking quietly to each other afterwards as we all strained to get the gist at what was being said. No luck. But when it was over everybody agreed: Donald Yovetich was on his way up the basketball *Yellow Brick Road* in Kansas City.

The center slot...the most hallowed of all positions on a Kansas basketball team in the late forties and fifties. The place where the legends of the era were born…the mystical territory of *George Mikan* of the Minneapolis Lakers…*Mr. Basketball* in America…the legend of legends. The legacy of an Indiana farm boy transplant that became a Kansas Jayhawks Center and an All American. *Clyde Lovellette*, the 6′ 9″, 230-pound behemoth who eventually took them all the way to the 1952 NCAA national championship, beating St. Johns easily in the finals, 80– 63.

Lovellette, a native of *Terra Haute*, came to Kansas in 1948. The story had it that basketball coach and icon, *Phog Allen,* had told him that if he chose the Sunflower state, the Jayhawks would get an NCAA championship, and also bring home the gold medal in the 1952 Olympics. He proved right on both counts.

It was an offer Clyde couldn't refuse. The center who had a killer hook shot and soft touch inside the lane, set about the task of becoming the anchor for a quintet that set the standard for a university basketball program that decades later still ranked among the best in the nation.

Old *Terra Haute Clyde* saw that. With his 33-point performance against St. Johns in the finals, Clyde wrote himself into the Kansas history books, not to mention into the hearts and dreams of thousands of us kids he would never see, or know. It didn't matter where he came from. He was one of *us*…a hoop star who made Kansas something more than stories about sunflowers, wheat and poor little *Dorothy* who was scooped up by a tornado to the land of *Oz*. He was the talk of the farming bergs across the prairies, in the bars, after Sunday church, down in the rail yards, and in the back shops of a thousand gas stations. The *Great White Whale*, whose beefy presence in the key promised to clog up the works for even the most well oiled offensive attacks.

And now, here was Donald…picked from *on high* to be the one to occupy that same coveted piece of basketball turf. Like Clyde, he was a formidable presence in his own right. And also in his own way about to become a six-foot, 160-pound lynch pin of a junior high basketball team that had a reputation to uphold. Central Junior was a powerhouse basketball franchise. It consistently took the city crown, although at that time few, if any, games were played among the city's mostly black schools. There the competition was just as tough, and quality of play even more intense.

Clyde and Donald…. Was this a homegrown *prodigy* in the making? It sure looked that way to me. The one that the cheerleaders would look to in their never-ending quest to keep the fans charged up throughout a game, and a long season.

The similarities there were simply too much to ignore. I grimaced as I watched him, jealous, but then again proud as hell when I reminded myself that Donald was a *Serb*, and it was about time that one of us hit the bulls-eye. My thoughts mentally flashed to the Central Junior gym where cheerleaders dressed to the *nines* were going through their routines, passionately calling out his name above the din of the crowd. It was a unique idolization of a local sports star in Heartland America that rivaled the adoration of a *prophet*.

I wanted to puke, but I watched anyway, trying in vain to fight off the sounds of the girls inside my head.  But they just wouldn't go away....

*Yovetich...Yovetich...he's our man...if he can't do it, nobody can!*

But it didn't stop there.  It wasn't enough that Donald was destined to be a kick-ass star on the courts; he was setting the academic records at Prescott, too.  By the time he finished the sixth grade the teachers picked him as the undisputed academic *King* of the grade school.  To prove the point, they paraded him around the playground in a formal ceremony on graduation day.  Naturally, all of us had to hear about the great and wonderful things he had done.  For the second time in less than a month I fought off the urge to dump my cookies.  It was too much too bear.

I was hopelessly trapped again, watching it unfold in front of me like a bad dream.  The *Big Yogi...*who was wearing a stupid looking purple and gold colored cardboard crown perched awkwardly on the side of his huge head.  Then there was the cape that was half-assed draped over his beefy shoulders, and obviously way too small for his already manly frame.  Nobody figured that somebody would get as big as Donald Yovetich by the sixth grade.  But he fooled us all...again.

Then the final touch – the *king's scepter.*  Actually, it was nothing more than a gold-colored wooden stick.  He sat on a chair in front of all of us casually transferring it from one hand to another as the teachers droned on and on about how bright he was, and in the process making me feel even dumber.

He looked ridiculous, but the truth was that I was full of envy.  Worse still, I was feeling real nervous about what this all would lead to in our Serbian enclave.  All of the accolades meant that his accomplishments would spread like wildfire.  And then the real game would begin.  He was setting the pace for kids his age, and it meant everybody had to come up several notches if they wanted to stay in the hunt to be the best among us.  That was how a lot of parents saw it.  As the saying goes, *shit rolls down hill....*

Overall, Donald was really a pretty okay guy.  During the summer, we spent lots of hours together, mostly doing sports things.  He was nuts about sports, any sport.  In the early fall he'd team up with a bunch of guys and play touch football.  I would always be the *lonesome end*, rarely catching a pass, or having much to do with the action.  Donald, though, would be a regular *thunder thighs* on a roll, fearlessly hauling the old pigskin right down the throat of the defense.  He was wonderful.

But basketball was his favorite pursuit and he played at it hard.  Me too...trying like hell to make my mark, but always coming up pathetically short.  Getting the top of my head cracked and my glasses smashed when I tried to go toe-to-toe with him on the boards.  Shooting air balls thanks to his long arms.  Forcing me to arch the old round-ball into oblivion.

I guess you could say I had a classic love-hate relationship that generally leaned more toward the love side when it came to Donald. He had a mind of his own. He really wasn't impacted much by what others thought. He was pretty good at that. I don't think he cared much one way or another about demonstrating the ins and outs of social graces back then. He just went about his own lumbering way, trampling out impressive results. Kind of like a *Clydesdale* who finished a job tilling the south forty. It was only natural...his labors were always expected to produce good results. And they did....

I followed Donald around a lot. When he went to the *Granada Barber Shop* down on Minnesota to get his hair styled into a *flat top,* I tagged along. The Granada sat next to the old *Granada Theater* just west of Tenth Street and both were favorite haunts for him. I remember the first time I went inside the shop with him. There were at least four barbers working pretty hard. They were all wearing smart looking white laboratory jackets. The shop was clean and orderly with lots of chromium trimmed chairs sprucing up the place. There was a radio playing sports news and music. The floor was tiled in stylish looking black and white square-foot linoleum block tile patterns. Sparkling clean mirrors were mounted behind all the chairs. Even the supply of men's hair tonics were stacked neatly in place on clean, white linen.

The buzzing assembly line of cutters chiseled out head after head of perfectly shaped flat tops on kids who patiently waited their turns in chairs covered with bright red vinyl. It was a first-class example of hair removal. The Granada was an *All-American* barbershop.

The only barbershop I'd been to before was up on Central Avenue. Actually, it was just off of Central behind *Schroeder's* fishing and boating supplies. I liked it a lot because it had at least fifty railroad calendars hanging all over the walls. And also a couple of pictures of naked girls on the far end. I mostly paid attention to the train calendars but I casually let my gaze drift the other way, specifically to get a peek at the blond girl with the big boobies. I only glanced at them, though. I was scared that the barber would notice. Once he did and he and all his cronies sitting around had a good laugh.

The shop was dirty and the air was stale and perpetually sticky. It was a blend of cheap hair tonic and body odor that smacked you in the face as soon as you walked inside. It reminded me of *TV* ads I saw years later. Some guy puts after-shave on his face out of a bottle – then he slaps the shit out of himself...the whole idea being that the smell will jolt you into the day. That's what I felt whenever I went inside the barbershop.

The smell made me want to get in and out of the shop as soon as I could. Old men just sitting around doing nothing except puffing on cigars and such...talking rubbish about things I had no idea even existed. They liked to use the corner spittoons as they *chewed* over life's little adversities. They weren't very good shots. And lots and lots of hair on the floor, with no broom in sight. Nobody cared much about that, either.

The first time I went there I climbed on a cracked piece of wood that lay across the chair handles. As the barber cut I'd gaggle at the calendars. Later, when my eyes went *south* all I saw was a blur. It didn't matter too much about the train pictures – but I got to admit the girlie posters were disappointing. Especially now because they replaced them with three new ones. One of the girls had black hair and olive skin. I liked that one a lot.... But at least I didn't need the wooden support anymore. I figured that was progress. The bad news was that between the thick horn-rimmed glasses and the butchered haircut, I looked like a fugitive from *Ringling Brothers* when I went out the door.

But at the Granada, now this was a new deal. Even the barbers were young, not like the two old farts at my shop. Donald went first, of course. Stardom had its privileges. The barbers obviously had heard about his Prescott tryout and his promising Central Junior career. Prodigy news got everybody's attention. When they worked him over, it was an easy job. His hair was coarse and dark, almost black. Great stuff to create a nice, flat surface. He was the perfect specimen in the flat top era.

When it came to me, that was another story. Mine was softer and finer in texture...not much really to work with. My hair color was a lighter brown...not very Serbian looking either, but Mom assured me that was how people looked who came from central Yugoslavia. I only half believed her. She looked exactly the opposite and her parents had come from Lika.

Still, the worst part was that my hair wouldn't stand up like the bristle of a brush the way Donald's did. But at least it was better than what I had in the past. It did something.... When I looked into the mirror, I decided then and there that it was time to make the big jump into the good life. I decided to give up my old barber, nudie new girls and all. Sometimes you hit a turning point in your life and never know it. I went up-market and never looked back.

In the months that followed, I figured out how to get the best of what I had, and I showed Mikey, too. We would go into the bathroom and rub wet bar soap on our front hairlines. When it dried my hair got so stiff that the only way I could break it down was to take a bath – so that meant not very often. I couldn't do it with my entire flat top, but at least it took care of the front edge. First impressions mean a lot. We strutted around the dance hall hoping some girl would notice. But the only one who really did was *Roddy Dodig*, Mikey's uncle. He played the bass in our *tamburitza* group. He was a handsome guy who always had lots of girls chasing him. I figured that was a good sign. Somebody like him would have paid attention to anything that makes you look more appealing. He knew a lot about those things, even though he didn't even wear a flat top. His hair was log and silvery looking.

I told him that my discovery was a special concoction. He asked for more information but I held back. I only gave him a hint that it was something *we all used* – at least most of us, every day. He laughed and told me I was full of shit, then went inside the bar. Roddy never messed around with us kids much. He was too busy chasing his own dreams.

I tried to sell my idea to other kids. Far as I know, though, Mikey was the only one who picked up on its benefits. We never told our secret to anybody, either. Some things should remain buried in the bosom of the past, forever.

On occasions I'd also tag along with Donald when he went to the *Granada Theater*. Donald liked to go to the movies and he had them all down pat. He'd tell anybody within earshot about the plot lines and what worked and what didn't. He had a special penchant for remembering the smallest of details. He was like a *Hoover* vacuum cleaner – sucking up facts and then dumping them out when the bag got too full.

Donald regularly made the long walk all the way from our neighborhood down to Minnesota Avenue. He had this kind of *swagger* – actually it was more like a loping gait. As he walked – most of the time at a near jogging pace, he'd swing his hands wildly while making his points. When a biting arctic wind hit us head-on, he'd respond by cranking up the pace of his hands, arms and legs, and then wave me on to follow. Then he'd start humming some nonsensical tune as he pulled away, drifting rapidly into a world of his own.

"C'mon…you gotta go faster and you'll warm up," he promised. "Just stick with me…it's not far now." But the bitter wind cut through me like a knife and slowed me even more. Not Donald…. He seemed to thrive in it. The colder it got, the more determined he was to turn a bad situation into good. I hated him for that. I hated how he faced any challenge that came along with such positive energy and nauseating optimism. He was so cocky...so confident…so *American*…. I hated his refusal to accept that he was no different than any of us – that he was nothing more than a little leaf floating on the stream of life and he couldn't control anything. The *current* was really in charge. He was just *Donald Yovetich,* a mortal. I wondered if he would ever get a lesson in life that would teach him that.

Donald especially liked comedy films, and in particular the *Dean Martin – Jerry Lewis* series that ran in the fifties. We always sat together, generally only a couple rows from the screen, looking up into the giant figures. Jerry Lewis was acting like a dumb Pfc. in *"At War With the Army"*. Sgt. Dean Martin was always finding creative ways to keep him out of trouble. When Jerry's antics turned ridiculous, Donald would laugh so hard that I wanted to crawl under the seat. It was a thunderous, robust, earthy kind of grown man's laugh that didn't fit with a kid just finishing the sixth grade.

By virtue of fate, Donald was to be a big part of my early years in Kansas City. He and his family had moved into a small little white wood-frame house down on *Twelfth Street* when I was about ten. His mom, *Mary,* was a stalwart of the church, forever volunteering her time to serve on various social committees, and you could always find her in the church kitchen doing yeoman's duties. Her gentleness and inner strength did more than anyone really knew in keeping her family intact – helping her eldest son, Donald, and in the ensuing years his younger brother Gene, keep to the straight and narrow. And also knowing how to support her husband Eli's twenty-four-hour occupation. Eli, who also wasn't afraid to let anyone within earshot know exactly how he felt about things either, and was just as quick to make it known how much he adored his family.

Eli was well known because he was a Kansas City cop, *(he eventually became the Chief of Police)* and maybe even more so because he was a pretty unique kind of person. You either liked him a lot or you didn't like him at all. I fell into the category of the former, but it wasn't always easy.

Indeed, if provoked, Eli's temper could be a sight. Pops managed to do that once after a church social at about 2 a.m. in the center of our living room. Eli came over to the house and blasted him so loud that it woke me up out of a dead sleep. My room was upstairs but he might as well been in there with me. I think they were both tipsy but Eli really didn't need a belly full of booze to get on a roll. It all came on pretty naturally.

Everybody knew about Eli. And Donald only touched on his dad's temperament once in all the years I knew him. "Dad makes a lot of noise, but he doesn't mean anything by it," he said, explaining away an outburst I had stumbled into as I was standing at his front door one hot summer day waiting for him to come out and play.

On rare occasions I went inside his home. If I knew his dad was around, I found myself automatically walking on my tiptoes and whispering. I remember that the house seemed to be perpetually dark. Fans were blowing everywhere, trying their best to keep away the sweltering summer humidity and heat that oozed through the walls at will. Somewhere...*out there*, was Eli who was hopefully sound asleep after working all night catching bad guys. I thought about myself doing something stupid like knocking over a standing ashtray in the murky light, and then waking up a sleeping giant. I shuddered and froze in my tracks. Eli's presence could be intimidating to an adult, but to a ten-year-old kid with an imagination that was perpetually working overtime, the visions he inspired in me were awesome.

Nobody fooled with Eli. He used to talk to everybody the same and his world was black and white, both figuratively and literally. Break the law and you go to jail. It really didn't matter to Eli. If the suspect happened to be black, he was just as willing to wade into a packed bar on a wild Saturday on *Quindaro Boulevard* and haul him out by the scruff of his neck; or stroll into a posh restaurant to hook up a white man in front of stunned onlookers. Both ended up in that great leveler of all mankind: *the pokey.* They sat side-by-side all shackled up nice and neat on the arrest bench pondering their dismal futures. It was also there that they discovered – maybe for the first time ever, how much blacks and whites really do have in common. And it was good old Eli, the social engineer, the *Kansas City Nightstalker*...the no-nonsense peacekeeper, who had made it all possible.

Sometimes, though, Eli and his partner would simply find a quiet place out in the country and *instill* instant understanding on why the person had been arrested. Under the night-time sky they offered a brief course consisting of specialized hands-on instruction that was guaranteed to educate any recipient. After the counseling session had ended, they would turn the violator loose and Eli would go home – on time, and by the way, deftly stepping around the mountain of paperwork that always accompanied any arrest.

Truth was, being a cop in Kansas City was never, ever expected to be a night at the ballet. The only dancing that went on there was somebody's fists and feet thumping on a bare and bloodied head under a frigid winter's moonlight. There was always the never-ending stream of racial undertow that had to be negotiated in handling the calls among the black folks. Sometimes they were resolved by using words, then again there was always the blunt end of a nightstick that could speak volumes.

When it came to getting down and dirty on a sub-zero, dead-of-winter Kansas City night, when the ground was frozen from brick-hard sheets of opaque, dead looking ice blanketing the earth – and when cascades of freezing rain and sleet were crashing down on you, and when somebody's iron fist clubbed your frozen ear so hard that you thought it would sting forever; when you found yourself literally fighting for your life to keep your gun in its holster instead of in some thug's desperate hand, well, that was the official *right of passage* into becoming a Kansas City cop. Get through that and you've earned bragging rights.

In fact, Eli graduated *cum laude* among his peers. He had been there so many times it was damn near a *ho-hum* routine. He was a charter member of the *Kansas City thumper's club.* If you asked them, most folks would have said he also had almost a *divine right* to get a little out-of-round occasionally. And why not? He was on the line when the rest of Kansas City was *beddy-bye* in their warm, cozy and safe little homes. He was the one who kept his finger in the dike and held back a wall of crime – all night long.

Eli could lock and load with the best of them. He had, in fact, evolved into a league of his own. When he strolled into one of Kansas City's *private clubs*, people never, ever had a problem figuring out he was there.

Donald's big-boned status definitely came from Eli's side of the genetic tree, although both sides had their fair share. He took up a lot of real estate. If the barstool he sat on could talk, it would have sued for stool abuse.

Far as I know, though, Donald never picked up his dad's most famous moniker: his patented...*Paaaadnaaahhh*...greeting he'd bellow to any and all. A greeting that was a cross between *John Wayne* and *Zeus.* No matter what went down it always began with that...in an arrest, on patrol, in the station house, down at a church social, or just bumping into someone he knew on the streets. He was in most peoples' view a guy who was born to be a cop. And now here he was with his eldest son, Donald, a basketball prodigy in the making. In-between those countless midnight shifts, he managed to snatch the brass ring from a lot of hopeful fathers. For them it would never be. Maybe what Eli got was a payback from God. Then again, maybe it was just dumb luck and big-ass genes. Either way, Donald Yovetich made the best of it.

# Chapter Seven

**P**ops put the phone down in its cradle and walked into our small living room and looked at Mom who was seated on the couch sewing a patch on my blue jeans. "That was *George Momchilovich*. He called to tell me that Joanne is getting married."

Mom looked up surprised, and obviously pleased.

"Isn't that nice.... When?"

"In October...the twenty-fifth...Saturday...."

"You remember Joanne don't you sweetheart? " she asked, knowing full well that I did.

She shook her head and smiled.

"That family, my, all of those girls are all so beautiful. "

I knew all right...Joanne's sister. *Martha Monchil (the family had later shortened their original name)*, had black hair, dark eyes and was a stunner in anybody's book. Whenever she came around her beauty scared the *BeeJesus* out of me. Even at the tender age of ten when I first laid eyes on her, I felt something special happening inside I couldn't completely understand. But I liked it – and I hated it, too. It was a weird feeling, one second feeling hot all over, the other fighting off an overwhelming compulsion to bolt for anywhere, as long as it was away from her.

She was the one person who drew *it* out of me instantly. And she knew it. If she attended a church function, I'd spend the better part of the afternoon, or night, making sure that I was on one side of the church hall and she was in the another.

But sometimes I miscalculated and before I knew it she was standing in front of me. Martha, looking down and smiling, then bending over to give me a hug. Once she even kissed me! I ran out of the hall so fast that I knocked two tables over. The collision dumped a couple bottle of *Schlitz* on the floor and Pops weren't too pleased about that. One of them belonged to him. Yes, I knew very well who Martha and her family was. Even now when I listened to my folks, her presence seemed to swirl around me. Her perfume...her white skin and long black hair, and her eyes...those beautiful, scary eyes.

"Who is he? That American fellow she's been seeing?"

Pops shrugged.

"Da...same boy she brings to banquets and the dances. George said he wants to convert...take classes."

Mom's face brightened even more.

"Good for her. So many of our young people are being lost to other religions these days. If you ask me, I think it's only right if the man follows the woman when it comes to religion. After all, she will be the one who raises the children and teaches them about such things."

Pops didn't bother to answer. He'd heard it all before. Besides, it was a classic case of the blind leading the blind. Since the war many of the young Serbian men who returned had courted Croatian girls. It was an outgrowth of decades of living side-by-side with one another under the protective cultural umbrella that was part of *Strawberry Hill.* For the most part, it was a peaceful co-existence and despite a war in the old country that had once again pitted the Serbians and Croats against one another.

The horror stories were real enough. Hitler and his alliance – the well-armed and dreaded *Croatian Ustashi,* had systematically murdered more than a million Serbs, Jews and Gypsies as they marched at will through the battered Balkan state. Only the southern most region of *Montenegro* and the neighboring *Kosovo* region had escaped the full fury of the invasion. These brutal lands were so mountainous, so rugged and so remote that not even Hitler and the Allied Italian war machines dared venture too far inside. Here the land was largely controlled by marauding bands of *Chetnik* freedom fighters, para-military vigilantes who fought in the name of freedom. They, along with several other similar groups, were a busy bunch. Not only were they fighting Hitler, but also the *Partisans,* a powerful and more widespread and certainly better equipped guerilla force commanded by *Marshal Yosip Broz. Tito,* as he was more popularly known, was a communist who had been schooled inside the halls of *Mother Russia.* His goal was to bring the region's diverse peoples and cultures under a single banner: *unity and brotherhood for all* was his simple message. Tito played his *pied piper's* tune very well. Millions followed. He would lead them to *Utopia.*

He was also a brilliant strategist and tactical expert who knew how to play off opposing sides to get what he wanted. Despite his communist pedigree, the West saw him as an important ally to counter the Hitler threat in Eastern Europe. His acceptance of the communist doctrine, although worrisome to many, paled in comparison to the Hitler war machine. His philosophical leanings could go on the back burner for now, the allies concluded. It was Tito and his unabashed declaration of resistance at all costs to the *Third Reich* that triggered London to send him arms and whatever else they could supply him against the Germans. As for the rest of the groups who had also picked up the gauntlet to defend freedom, the *King's Free Army,* the *White Eagles,* the *Ljotich Volunteers* and the *Chetniks,* to name a few, it was, as they say *slim pickins'.* So they did what they had always done in centuries past when times were tough and the cause was just; they took the hills and they fought anybody and everybody they saw – the communists, the other para-military groups, and sometimes even the Germans and their Italian comrades.

The story in Yugoslavia was one that had that repulsive, *See, I told you so…it's happening all again…*scent swirling around it. What had begun as a world war for the rest of Europe had predictably disintegrated into an ugly *civil war* there with intimate, deadly and often sub-human reactions. It was, unfortunately for the region, a story that had been repeated countless times over the centuries. Only the names of the heroes and villains had changed. Same thing for the causes that ignited it all.

Still, despite the incoming news of the insanity that had erupted once again between the two major ethnic groups, Kansas City Serb and Croat descendents – many of them first generation, managed to keep their eyes on the big picture: America's commitment to rid the world of the Hitler evil. Sons from both sides stood in line with one another taking their pre-induction physicals as willing volunteers to the US war machine. They fought and many had died, but others finally came home to an America that was eager to forget, and ready to move forward into a new era.

It was a time of taking care of business at home and attending to the natural processes of living. Courtship, marriage, a good job, new family members and a decent future for everyone was just on the horizon. The sweet smell of love in the air floated like the scent of freshly cut strawberries over the *Hill*. Lifetime decisions and commitments were being made inside these small, wood-frame homes, in soda shops after the movies and during long walks in the park.

But there were also prices being paid all around. Changes were also in the wind. One of them, the historic practice of planned marriages – a common occurrence among those who came from the old country, now gave way to a new tide of individualism that flew in the face of these cultural dictates. And not far behind were new ideas on how to put religion in its place, so to speak. Nobody denied it wasn't important and wouldn't prominently figure in the family culture in the coming decades, but the dogma of picking one over the other as a matter of principle was becoming suspect. It was a major sticking point for everybody, young and old alike.

To Pops, the mission in what he had to do about all that, and why, was a bottom line entry in his unwritten job description. As the parish priest, he saw it as his unending task to make sure that everyone who walked into his little church and attended the Sunday school understood the importance of *keeping the faith*. To him, the big issue was always the *Catholics* and his nagging fear that some pretty Croatian girl would attract *one of our fine Serbian boys* and convert him. And that meant not only him, *but all his children, too.*

It was the latter that worried Pops even more. With no children in the church there would be no one to pass on the Serbian traditions. That posed a real danger that the culture would eventually be lost to the wider social mainstream. Children were the insurance policy Pops needed to make sure that the traditions of the past moved forward successfully, and in the face of changes he could see emerging all around him.

The Catholics knew it, too. At least that's how Mom and Pops saw it. According to them what they were up to was all part of a sinister plot to undermine Orthodoxy. The bone of contention had something to do with a so-called religious pledge: Whenever someone converted, as part of the process they were required to sign a *religious contract* pledging all of their as yet unborn children would be baptized Roman Catholics. Without that signature on the dotted line, the marriage could not go forward. No Catholic priest, especially one associated with Croat society, would ever overlook that marital detail. The signed document had to be part of the package. No signature...no wedding.

Pops argued that when someone joined the Serbian Orthodox church nothing like that occurred. What's more, he knew what it all really meant. He could see the underlying intent, and he resented it. Without thinking the problem through, these couples (and the girls were often the more persuasive of the two) would commit – blinded in part by the love bite that had infected them. Children, the prospective groom rationalized, were still some time away, but in fact they often became a reality within months of the wedding day – sometimes even earlier. *Love on Strawberry Hill was a powerful elixir.*

His fears were more truth than fantasy, and the statistics bore him out. In increasing numbers, commitments among the Serb males were being made and the inevitable conversions followed – all this despite his best efforts. When the news got out, no greater event could inspire gossip among the old ladies who kept the rumor circuits abuzz with their daily phone conversations. It seemed that they lived for such episodes in Serbian life. When they happened they worked the phones like media pros. They were the prime conduits to inspire biting criticisms as family heads tried to rationalize their offspring's decisions, and at the same time do whatever they could to duck the volley of sharp-edged barbs that were being launched from unidentifiable sources. *War is hell....*

Within the sanctuary of their homes there were even greater concerns that surpassed these external assaults. Some tried to resolve the decision calmly, while others reacted emotionally – allowing no room for talking and using all the resources at their disposal. That often led to calling in Pops for help to try and turn the tables before it was too late. Unfortunately, his track record of putting *faith* before *passion* pretty much fell on deaf ears. Most listened a little, then generally argued, hollered, cried, and then talked some more – then they went ahead and did what they intended to do in the first place. All that was left was the growing, irritating messages from the old *babas*, which pointed accusing fingers at the families that they had failed to preserve the Serbian way of life. Something had to be terribly wrong inside those houses, they whispered into the telephones across town. Obviously, this latest development was just a long string of problems that had not been visible, until now. But to allow their children to do this? It was tantamount to religious treason.

And yet, as these grumblings echoed throughout the community, there was an irony about all of this that underscored the breaking news.  On one level the Serbs and Croatians had managed to carve themselves a peaceful co-existence in the new land and had discarded their mutual tendencies toward violence that so dominated their historical patterns.  They gave each other respect.  They attended each other's social doings; they went to weddings, they even visited the homes of families to celebrate their patron saint days, and baptisms.  They shared their common ideas and most important, they shared their dreams.  They stood shoulder-to-shoulder fighting America's war.  They did all that, and they did it well.

But when it came to religious preferences and the cultural linkages that inseparably tied them together because of it – well, that was a horse of another color.  Here, those same timeless rigidities re-appeared.  Those same old fears and prejudices plagued the *Hill*....  And the old folks who represented both sides of the street nurtured it.  They relished in turning up the volume, reminding everyone where their real priorities belonged.  Sometimes they succeeded.

Pops, I suspect, understood all of this at a deeper level.  Being Serbian-born he tended to look at religion from the Yugoslav perspective, which made perfect sense.  That meant his religion was inseparably intertwined with his cultural priorities and way of life.  For that matter, it did the same thing for me as well.

But he was also aware that the changes going on in his Serbian-American community fell outside of these traditional perceptions.  While he could never bring himself to understand, or accept, the more relaxed stance toward religion and its influence that began to surface in American society in general, he did recognize that a similar cultural struggle among his own flock was unfolding.  They were Serbians, but they were *Americans*, too.  A new generation was redefining the role of religion. They were willing to make it a part of their lives, yes, but it was not to be the primary institutional instrument in directing how they would live as it had been the case in the past.

Pops recognized all that...and where he could, he vowed to make the adjustments to accommodate what he saw, but it was never, ever easy.  Preserving the centuries old Serbian tradition which included the unshakable commitment to the Orthodox faith, while at the same time trying to find ways to accommodate young Serbs who were living in a changing America – this was the burden that he carried on his shoulders every day.  He would take his hits for sure, no matter what he did.  He was on a cultural tightrope he sensed every priest was walking across America.  Before it was over, that struggle would become deeply personal and would change his life, and mine, forever.

But now, at least this time the Serbs had won one for their side and we all knew what that meant. Everything that followed would be set up to get all the mileage they could get out of it.  First, there would be a traditional wedding in church with Pops officiating.  The wedding itself was an event and one that was bound to impress anyone.  Pops was really good at that. Somehow his voice was even richer than it normally was and I knew that along the way he would deliver his famous, *You are born...you marry...and then you die speech....* He would talk about how life works that way and this part of it was perhaps the most significant since the two people standing before him were about to create a family of their own.  And it was all being sanctioned in the eyes of God and the Holy Church.  When he did that, we all knew these people were married good and proper.  It was the St. George seal of approval, and Pops was the only person who could stamp it.

After the church services, things really started rolling.  Serbian tradition dictated that on his way out the door, the groom performed the act of *Kets Kume*...tossing pockets full of coins into the air on the church steps for us kids to scoop up.

Then throughout the afternoon and late into the night at the church hall next door, everyone toasted the newlyweds and ate the sarma, fried chicken, baked potatoes and a host of other delicacies.  Then there was the music and *kolo* dancing. By the time midnight rolled around the *tamburitza* group would have at least a half-a-dozen ten-dollar bills stuck on the strings of the bass tuner stem.  The dancing of many dwindled to a small group of diehards – men and women who now gathered around the musicians holding drinks in one hand and singing Serbian ballads in rich harmony.  The songs were steeped in Serbian history and about people and places that no one knew or saw, but you'd never have known it.

Of course, by the time the singing had begun, the bride and groom had disappeared.  The cake had been cut and distributed, donations counted and all the speeches finished about promises for prosperous futures. A couple of the merry makers may have gone over the top, but nobody really minded. The combination of food, booze, music, dancing and singing had done its job. The Serbs of Kansas City were at peace with themselves.

###

# Chapter Eight

The main forum where Serbs often erupted into verbal – and even physical conflict was at the church meetings that were generally held on Sunday afternoons. Stories that had percolated out of the mid-twenties and thirties told of how arguments in the small social hall under the church itself got so intense that one of the members allegedly drew a knife and guarded the door rather than let members of the opposition leave before the matter was resolved. Among the West Bottoms and Missouri groups, drawing a line in the sand was serious business. Grudges and gossip rolled through the network and life's ugly little experiences could quickly bring out the best – and worst in all of them.

Most of the time these meetings had little to do with my friends, or me. We generally spent the afternoon playing around the fringes of the activities, sneaking in and out to get a soda, or maybe a pork sandwich that was left over in the kitchen. But now things were becoming more serious and these meetings took on a special significance with my parents.

Ever since the first of the *Displaced Persons (DPs)* had arrived into town, Pops had worked tirelessly to help them settle in. On a couple of occasions I had the chance to go with him to visit these newcomers who were scattered all over the city, many of them living on the fringes of Strawberry Hill. They were friendly enough but also distant in some way. It was as if a dark cloud followed them wherever they went. They seemed confused and disoriented – unaware of the things I had come to naturally accept living in Kansas City. Basics like where to buy food, what streetcar to take, and where, or how to connect with people who didn't speak Serbian.

Some of them were downright nasty – sharp-tongued, and from what I could tell in the rapid-fire Serbian they spoke when Pops went to see them, they criticized everything they saw. Sometimes that made Pops mad but he stuck with it. He worked in concert with one of the church's most successful families, George and Ljubica' (Libby) Zuzich, owners of the prosperous *Zuzich Truck Line* who had taken on several of the DPs and provided them with badly needed jobs almost at the onset of their arrival. They challenged others in the church who were less willing, standing up for the families who had come to the region desperately poor and disorientated, victims of a war that had stolen more than their homes. Someone took their spirits.

For the Zuzich's, the times were especially challenging. Libby's younger brother, *Nick Pavlica,* died tragically in a truck crash northeast of Kansas City in 1949, the same year the first group of more than fifty immigrants were to arrive over the next five years. The accident occurred when he was en-route to Kansas City from Chicago while traveling on *Highway 13* just outside of *Henrietta, Missouri*.   Earlier in the year Nick had married *Milka Plecas* in a typical Serbian wedding. She was expecting…Nick Pavlica died never seeing his son.

The newspaper reports later said Nick had given up his life by intentionally ditching his truck and trailer on the shoulder of a two-lane highway and into a cement culvert, rather than hit a young couple who had drifted in front of him off a country road at the bottom on a long hill.

Well-known for her determined and sometimes overwhelming ways, in the years that followed Libby and George focused their energies equally on preserving the welfare of their church and the company which she and her husband had built from scratch into a successful business.  Some, no doubt, found fault with her hard-nosed approach at times, but no one ever disputed the depth of her commitment and the passion she shared for both. Even more importantly, her husband George's reputation for honesty and character touched anyone who was fortunate to shake his hand in friendship, or in tying up a business deal.  Their two sons, Sammy and Gene, in many ways reflected this same sense of character and determination, although they rarely were part of the church life that their parents so much enjoyed.

I always looked forward to seeing Libby.  Once she gave me an old Kodak box camera that I kept at my bed stand for years.  She had heard I liked to look at pictures and in her creative way, she dropped by the house one day and simply gave it to me, urging me to use it to take pictures of trains. I did.

Her warmth, generosity and concern were always there, and more than once she took the time to demonstrate her affection with trips to *Fairyland Park*, or the *Zoo* – even to her house where she made sure that food and drink were always at my fingertips. Libby and George Zuzich – and for that matter many of the Kansas City Serbs, could tell you a little something about hard times. The arrival of the DPs represented yet another challenge that she and her kind were determined to see through.  Kansas City would extend the open arms of welcome to any and all, and Pops officially led the way.

*** 

By 1952 there were at least thirty single immigrants and a half dozen families who had arrived. Most sought out the church as their anchor in holding their heads above water in a sea of change that at times was choppy and threatening.  But it was not to be the kind of adjustment that everyone had counted on. Increasingly, and with the arrival of still more Displaced Persons, conflict of a very different kind began to emerge.

I saw all of this behind the scenes, mostly in my parent's deteriorating home life that seemed to parallel the pressures Pops was facing with an increasingly unruly congregation.  Inside our home his touch-and-go battle with alcohol was starting to take a downspin and Mom increasingly found herself trying to nurse him back to a functional state when he came home after a drinking bout.  Once, I was alone in the house when AJ's Mom came over and quietly took me to hers.  I knew something was wrong.  AJ's Mom was a nurse and her professional, dispassionate way of bringing me into their home, and then staying with me, told me that something serious had occurred.

Later that night I discovered why.  Mom came by the house and took me by the hand back to ours.  I went inside, not exactly sure what to expect.  Pops was seated in his customary smoking chair.  His face was bruised and his right arm had been wrapped in a sling.  The sight of him in that condition frightened me.

Pops assured me he was okay, but I sensed that below his obvious injuries the telltale sign of drinking was also there.  Mom told me that he had been in an accident.  He stepped off a streetcar on Central Avenue and was hit by a passing car as he tried to make his way to the sidewalk.  They rushed him to Bethany Hospital where he was treated and later released with cuts, bruises, and a sprained arm.

All of this was taking a toll on Mom.  For nearly four years she had worked at the *Simmons Mattress Company*, rising every morning at five to ride with a neighbor to the *Fairfax District*.  The double duties of being a priest's wife, her tireless contribution to the church working in the kitchen and everywhere else, and now the added pressures of church dissension nipped at her from all sides. Pops didn't make it any easier.  For me, the only thing I really knew for sure was how helpless I felt as I watched it all unfold in front of me.

***

Pops stumbled into the bedroom, unsure of where he was.  He was mumbling to himself in Serbian.

Mom sat up in her bed.

"Dushan, go to bed…*ti si napit (You're drunk)*…Tomorrow is church…."

I stood by the bedroom door and watched as my father struggled to gain a perspective, but time and again he bumped into the furniture in the darkness.  Finally, Mom got up and helped him to the side of the bed.

"*Dis novodoshljatsi (Newcomers)*…" he said.  "They want everything. Now they want I take out church organ….They say not for *Crkva (Church)*. Then they say we stand for *sluzhba (Mass)*…and no have organ for choir…. Only Catholics sit in seats.  We have organ!  What they know?  I am priest here!  I know what people in Kansas City need for St. George Church!"

Mom continued to help Pops get his clothes off, taking off his shoes.

"Get some sleep, Dushan.  You have a busy day tomorrow."

He waved her off.

"*Necu!* I go now!  *Natrag (Back)*…. Yugloslavia…to my brothers and sister!" he snapped, trying to get up from the bed, but instead falling across it on his back, and in an instant he was snoring.

Mom looked up and saw me. She gently moved him into a more comfortable position then came to my side.

"What happened to Pops?"

"Go to bed, sweetheart. Papa isn't feeling well," she said, gently guiding me to the stairs leading to my own room.

"Mama, what is it? What's wrong?"

"Nothing, Papa's just very tired.... All the arguing – the DPs making him so unhappy. They want him to make a lot of changes in our church. They're making trouble with lots of the Serbian people. They say communists are here...our Kansas City Serbs, can you believe that? They think we are silly and stupid. Some of them even convinced our best friends that what they say is true. Now they've turned on your father."

I looked at Mom and wondered what was happening, but it was all too complicated. All I knew was that I was afraid.

*** 

St. George Church elder *Steve Docman* was near tears. He was holding a petition in his hand and waving it at the onlookers. The meeting had begun promptly at 1:20 p.m. and there wasn't an empty seat in the church social hall. The cars on Bethany had lined up for blocks.

The night before I heard Mom and Pops talking about what might happen in the living room. Several friends had dropped by to offer Pops moral support. For weeks several DPs along with a growing cadre of disgruntled American Serbs had been circulating a petition to remove my father from his job. They wanted the Bishop in Libertyville, Illinois, to throw him out. The meeting was to consider the merits of these serious accusations.

The charges were in part wild and emotional, but also in part based on fact. They felt he wasn't worthy to be a priest; along with his personal problems and his increasing drinking, he had lost sight of the traditions associated with the *Mother Church*, they charged. He was soft on communism. He was ineffective and insensitive to their needs. He no longer understood how important it was to preserve the historical connection between Yugoslavia and the American Serbians. For all of these reasons and more, Pops had to go.

They even charged my folks weren't legally married. I knew that wasn't true.... Mom had shown me her wedding pictures when she and Pops went down to *Olathe* to see a Justice of the Peace. Pops had been married before, and in the laws of the church a priest could only marry once, and that had to occur before he took his formal vows.

He brought his wife and five-year-old daughter, *Mirjana*, my half-sister, to the United States in 1938 where he took a church in *Joliet, Illinois*. But then something happened back in the old country that made Pops so angry he put them both on a train and boat back to Yugoslavia. The last thing he saw was his daughter's face pressed up against the window. She was crying – mouthing her desperate pleas through the plate glass, wanting only to return to her daddy's arms as the train pulled out of the station. He never saw either of them again.

***

*Years later I managed to complete the circle when I accompanied my cousin, Miodrag, and my wife, Jeanie, to* **Tuzla, Yugoslavia, in Bosnia***... I found my half-sister there living in a small apartment with her mother. On their return she went on to become a hospital nurse, and was tending to her aging mother in her autumn years. She died in an accident two years later and at the onset of the war in Bosnia. But prior to that we both worked hard to bring about closure in the speckled history of a man and those colorful, if not extraordinary times we both had witnessed in very different ways.*

***

After Joliet, Pops went to *Mingo Junction, Ohio,* then on to neighboring *Stubenville.* That was where he met my mother, *Militsa'.* Pops noticed she was barefooted when she showed up one night for choir practice. Priests in those days were expected to demonstrate a variety of skills in leading the flock. Pops qualified...and leading choirs was one of them. When he found out she didn't have a job, the next day he went to see the General Manager at the steel mill across the *Ohio River* in *Weirton, West Virginia.* The Personnel Department gave *Militsa Milivich* a job.

For weeks she never showed up at church. Then one night she was back, and still shoeless. Pops asked her why. She pulled a box out from her simple print dress pocket and handed it to him. It was a watch – a *Bulova*...expensive and elegant. Rather than buy the shoes she so desperately needed, she worked for weeks to save the money to buy *him* that watch. It was a gift for what he'd done for her. Pops knew that Mom was something special. They never left each other again, through the good times and the bad.

They traveled together to *Omaha, Nebraska,* where Pops took on new priest duties, but only for a year. I was born there. A year later Pops came to *Kansas City,* alone at first, worried that Mom's presence might create gossip. He was waiting for dispensation from the Bishop to remarry, and he finally got it. Mom moved in with Pops. I was just a few months old when we arrived. We lived in an apartment on our own for a while, but eventually moved into the parish home at 50 S. Bethany.

Pops and Mom set about doing their duties, with Mom demonstrating her limitless energy and enthusiasm in everything she took on. The socials, the dinners, the customs...as an American-born Serb, her language skills were impressive, even though she herself had barely made it through the eighth grade. Homeless, she grew up going from one home to another in the steel mill communities of *McKeesport* and *Johnstown, Pennsylvania,* then later in *Weirton.* Her father, *Steve Milivich,* a steelworker, had died of a heart attack before she was ten. Her mother died even earlier. Her older sister, *Violet,* had died shortly thereafter, leaving her to fend for herself.

She survived by moving into homes and earning her room and board cleaning houses, or doing other menial chores. She worked anywhere she could, in funeral parlors, in restaurants, and when she was old enough, in the steel mills where so many of the immigrant Serbs had settled and eventually bought homes that sat on the bluffs overlooking these industrial behemoths of Capitalism – where the smell of slag seeped into the houses and the skies were perpetually murky from coal dust. But through it all she still had her *Church*…and, like the DPs who had come to America decades later, it was a life preserver that made life bearable. It kept her hope alive.

*** 

Not all of these new immigrants supported, or encouraged, the revolution of cultural upheaval that began since their arrival three years earlier. In fact, many had taken to Pops and genuinely adored him. They were grateful to the commitment he'd made to find them work. They understood that their lives had been savagely slashed by social forces few in the community would ever totally comprehend. Many openly worked to integrate themselves into the contemporary Serbian society and embraced the shifts in perceptions to what they had known about themselves as a people in their former Yugoslavia. Several married American Serbs and set out on paths that were well on the way to building new lives. They saw Pops as the catalyst to this change, and they were grateful.

But among those who were part of this core group of change, their motivators were very different. They were obsessed with the demons of past memories – and failures that relentlessly nipped at their heels. Fear and anger clouded the present, which in turn put them increasingly at odds in their willingness to assimilate into the new order of an American lifestyle. Rather than integrate, they chose to re-create. They intentionally took on the mantle of the church as the primary institution of importance, committed to preserving the *faith* and Serbian traditions at any cost.

Even before this day had come there had been numerous social events where fights broke out – often involving the original Kansas City Serbs who crossed swords with a DP, generally over some kind of communism scare tactic that neither of them had any business intelligently debating. It was really all about emotions and ignorance. Pops and the other men broke up the fist swinging; then he spent hours – sometimes days trying to patch things up on both sides. It was like bailing the water out of a canoe when one end was already full of water.

So it had come finally, and inevitably to this – a meeting of extraordinary dimensions where my father was put on trial in the very church that he had led for nearly fifteen years. His dirty laundry was out there for everyone to see, and those who didn't were quickly informed through the incessant telephone networking that kept the lines humming. Gossip, innuendoes mixed with few facts, and ignorance – these were the banshees that were tearing the heart out of a once happy, generally peaceful, and energetic sub-cultural community.

***

"What are we doing to this man?" Steve Docman asked the audience. "What about Millie…and little Stevie?"

I stood by the side hall entrance and watched the crowd; some of them feverishly fanning themselves to ward off the tension that was building fast inside. I couldn't understand what had happened – and why they were so mad at Pops. When Steve talked about me I felt myself wanting to cry, but I really didn't know why. I had been a good boy, just like Pops had asked. What had I done wrong? What had *we* done wrong? Why were the people I had come to be so close to saying these things about us or about Pops, Mom and me…?

My parents struggled onward with their disintegrating lives, trying to ward off the charges, the never-ending biting and widening hostilities that got worse with each passing month. He fought as best he could, coping with his private demons as well as those he saw growing all around him. He fought on until at last, the weight of it all was simply too much to support any longer. The cultural sparks that had been fanned for so long by the DPs and others who resurrected old grudges along the way, eventually turned it all into a huge fire that had to run its course. He was a defeated man. Although I didn't know it then, I was about to go on a life's journey that would take decades to complete.

###

**The Immigrants...**

*Sketches from the past...*

# Litany for the Dead...

**T**he smoke hovered low to the ground, blanketing the worn and splintered wooden floor like a thick, dirty fog. It looked like a WWI movie scene after a mustard gas attack. But this wasn't war. This was church. Even so, the parishioners squirmed uncomfortably, fighting their own sweat and the stifling summer heat and humidity with small, really useless, paper fans that had cracked wooden handles. Every one of them had an advertisement written across the thin paper: *Butler Funeral Home...Founded, 1905 – 22 South 18th Street, Kansas City, Kansas, Telephone: Tel: Fairfax, 2222.*

The parishioners were bunched together, standing, then sitting on command along the rows of wooden pews. Occasionally, the pungent odor of BO hitched a ride on the soft morning breeze that drifted through the church's open windows.

Everyone faced the altar and Pops, who was standing with his back to his congregation. Dressed in his flowing, embroidered cleric gown, he turned toward his congregation swinging his copper incense burner. Some of the parishioners automatically transferred their fans from one hand to the other, crossing themselves repeatedly as they reverently bowed their heads. It was not the Roman Catholic left-to-right hand motion beginning at the forehead, then crossing at the chest. It was the three-fingered, right-to-left cross sign of the *Eastern Orthodox Church.*

Directly behind where Pops now stood was a flower-laden casket positioned in front of the Byzantine-styled altar. Seeing the old woman inside dressed in black, her hands, and arms folded across her bosom in a mechanical repose, I knew that Mikey Dodig and I were in for a long day. As acolytes, our job was to keep the symbols of our faith in view to the congregation, and that meant standing our ground directly in front of the casket, candles in hand, as we listened to the chilling wails and choir's chanting gain momentum. We were in the initial stages of a *Litany for the Dead at St. George Serbian Orthodox Church.*

Pop's rich, baritone voice lorded over all as he faced his congregation, holding the holy incense burner out and using its long gold-plated chain to arc the copper burner dangerously close to them. All the while he was reciting the centuries old Cyrillic lyrics for the dead. His act of deliverance and the rhythmic, sweeping motion of the burner spewed still more smoke toward the teary-eyed congregation. Their only answer was to cross themselves feverishly every time he turned their way.

*"Pomiluy nas, Bozhe, po velitsyey milostil Tvoey, molim, Ti sya, uslishi I pomiluy," (Have mercy upon us. O God, according to thy great mercy, we pray unto thee; hear us and have mercy)* Pops chanted. He turned and stopped at the head of the casket, swinging the incense burner just above the old lady's torso. *"Lord have mercy,"* the choir responded, and with it launched a fresh round of sobs and wails throughout the tiny church.

I glanced toward Mikey Dodig who appeared to be holding his own. Mikey didn't like funerals. For that matter, neither did I. For this one we flipped a coin and he lost. Now he was standing directly over the old lady.

It was tough duty, but we both knew we couldn't afford to fool around. This was serious stuff. Pops didn't take kindly to any kind of Tomfoolery, especially in situations like this. Both of us were dressed in our traditional blue altar boy robes. Nobody could see that under it I was shuffling my feet, trying to hold back the *pee* that I urgently needed to take. When you're on the job as an acolyte, there are no potty breaks, no rest breaks, and no food or drink breaks. You just gutted it out.

*"Gospodi pomiluy…"(Lord have Mercy)* Pops chanted, turning again to face the congregation. When he did, I glanced toward Mikey and caught his eye. We were too far from each other to speak, but over the years we sort of perfected our own non-verbal communication code. When it was really important we mouthed our words.

I rolled my eyes toward Pops and Mikey nodded. These were tense times and the escalating humidity and heat weren't making it any easier. I tried to get back into my groove by zeroing in on the candle flame just a few inches from my nose. I had found through trial and error that I could put myself into a trance. I used the dancing flames to trigger my own fantasies about anything I wanted. The procedure was pretty good at shutting out reality.

Today's funeral promised to take my ability to its limit. I glanced at the old lady's ashen, withered face. She was lying in heavenly bliss, oblivious to the commotion going on around her and on her behalf.

"Why don't they just let old people die quietly?" I thought. "What does she care about all this?" To me, Mrs. Martich didn't look any different than she did last night when Pops held mass for her at *Butler's Funeral Home.* For more than three hours I was stuck there – Mikey too, holding the same candlestick. The three Martich sisters, *Bronko,* the eldest son of the family, his wife, and two young children stood next to the coffin as people filed by shaking their hands. It was a big crowd; even the *Marks* family – the King of the *Gypsies* showed up to offer their respects. The St. George choir was there, too, but only half the complement. Pops grimaced every time that *Marie Stoyanovich* shrieked off an unbelievable string of flat notes in her part-time alto voice that cracked and cackled under the slightest strain.

She was at it again today as if she were reading my mind. *Off-Key Marie* was in top form, but now she was turning lethal. All the out-of-sight and out-of-mind measures I had used in the past to insulate myself were caving in fast. Off-key Marie, the heat, the BO, and old Mrs. Martich in peaceful repose – it was all turning into a cacophony of sounds.

I looked over at Mikey who was fixed on the corpse. He looked tired but I knew he was tough. He'd been there before. He'd hold his mud.

I turned my attention to the old lady, this *stara Desa Martich*. I recalled when Pops told *Tooky Carless,* the Church Secretary and Pops' occasional driver, how she had been a pillar of St. George's. She also ruled her home with a typical Serbian iron fist.

Tooky already knew that. Besides, he had a territory of his own to rule and that also took up a lot of time. He was the legally appointed *Falstaff Beer* distributor on the Kansas side, and also the supplier of hard stuff, too.

There was more than one good reason why he got into the business. The hard shell Baptists had decades ago decided to put a stranglehold on the state's local, county and state government. Through the power of the vote, year after year they had managed to keep the state officially *"dry."* No hard stuff allowed except in specially designated package stores. Just the sale of watered down 3.2% alcohol beer at the neighborhood public *beer joints.*

Along the eastern bluffs of Kansas City, Missouri, and near the busy *Sheffield Steel* plant, Serb families who lived in the houses that lined the bluffs had long ago figured out that the way to profitability revolved around opening beer joints, running booze, and keeping gambling tables available for the steel workers and railroaders that proliferated in the area. For whatever reason the dreams that they shared seemed to be bigger and the willingness to pay the price even greater than their patch counterparts who set the pace at the turn of the century. There was a collective drive to succeed among them that would not allow them to settle for the ordinary. Names such as *Zuzich, Trbovich, Pavlica,* and *Petrovich* soon became synonymous for Serbs who were willing and able to squeeze the best out of capitalism.

The Sheffield district was unique in other ways. The small streets that ran on the west side of the plant were reminiscent of the kinds of steel town communities that were commonplace in Western Pennsylvania, northern West Virginia or Eastern Ohio. Yet they were on the fringes of the *Great Plains* region. During cold winter mornings, it was common to see groups of Serbs file into the bars gulping down shooters full of straight whiskey on their way to work. They figured out that the morning booze would jumpstart them into the day and ward off the chilly winds at the same time.

To me, Sheffield was a special zone of wonderment. Here the maze of railroads coming in from the north, south, east and west crossed over and merged with one another. The north and south mainline of the *Kansas City Southern* and *Missouri Pacific* more or less defined the mill's boundary lines. Along with it there was a small *Rock Island* secondary line that ran south, then turned east toward St. Louis. The little line had no distinction other than the fact that during those years it was the route of an old gas-powered two-car *"doddlebug."* In later years, Uncle Fuzzy kept the mystique alive when he more or less retired on a daily run pulling a small drag freight over the line's hilly profile as far as *Belle, Missouri.*

But it was the *Kansas City Terminal's east west mainline* that fascinated me most. Trackside train watching revealed a 24-hour-a-day procession of classy passenger trains that used the trunk line as the entry to Union Station. Among these, the mighty Santa Fe and its parade of high profile trains led the way, but it by no means was the only contributor. If you rode a passenger train in and out of Kansas City, odds were that you would likely pass through the maze in and around Sheffield, and that meant hours of train watching and never knowing what was coming next.

*\*\*\**

Over on the Kansas side, the bounties associated with booze didn't go unnoticed around Strawberry Hill, either. But the truth was that the relationship with the Wyandotte Country citizenry and the state as a whole was never a comfortable one. It was a tug-of-war that created its own unique brand of solutions that included official and unofficial solutions. In a funny kind of way everybody came out a winner. You could, for example, get hard booze out of a paper cup hidden under the bar top counter at virtually any of the public bars. Everybody turned a blind eye to that, including the local cops who often dropped in after work to *listen* to the juke box *music.*

Then there was the licensed *"private clubs."* What went on there was their business. The private clubs were not hard to find; in fact you could spot one on virtually every street corner. In truth, they were nothing more than corner beer joints that had a lock on the front door and a sliding metal hatch in the center to ID people. If you wanted in and were a stranger, it could be arranged...maybe. The rules were basic: if you were white, the door swung open and you walked right in. You paid five bucks or so to join, and that was that. But if you were colored, it wouldn't have mattered if you had a million. The hatch door slammed shut.

Still, folks found other creative ways to satisfy a demand they knew was limitless. The undisputed queen among them was a petite woman in her forties who had a high-pitched voice that sounded as if she belonged in a bible studies class. But *Dragica Boca* was no Bible thumper by anybody's estimation. She was in the *manufacturing* business. Like most of her customers, Dragica immigrated from *Lika,* more specifically from one of the small villages near the town of *Plashki,* a small Serbian outpost buried in the barren hills of Croatia.

Dragica was a special cut of the Plashki cloth. A natural businesswoman whose penchant for fashion included a flare for putting on layers of make-up, people more or less got used to seeing her looking like a painted lady, despite her advancing years.  Most of the time that was fine, but on those sweltering summer days when she showed up for church, by the time the 2½-hour service had ended and she headed for home, little streams of melted make-up were running down her tiny cheeks.  Nobody said a thing.

*Home* for Dragica was a small beer joint and an attached room on *6th Street,* and just a stone's throw from the Strawberry clientele she knew would always drift in for a short beer or shot under the table.  Chances are she would be in the back of the bar putting on the finishing touches of her latest batch of bootleg booze.

Her distribution system to her Strawberry Hill clientele was just as creative.  She had long ago learned how to skirt around trouble with the cops.  Once a week or so she'd *invite* one of the Serb families to join her as she drove around the city and quietly dropped off her customer orders.  No cop would get too excited about seeing a little woman with too much make-up driving her sedan around the neighborhood with a car full of kids.  And even if they did, they didn't pay it much mind, anyway.

*** 

None of that mattered at the moment as much as my aching feet and full bladder.  The service was already two hours old.  I figured that there was at least another hour to go.  Then the long automobile procession to the *Highland Park Cemetery* and another forty-five minutes there.  I sighed at the thought, then crossed my legs to keep my bladder in check.  There wasn't much I could do now except hang in.  I smiled at my own thought.  At least Mrs. Martich could finally rest in peace, and get away from the insanity of the living.

I glanced at her slender, weather-worn face, then turned my attention to the bouncing candle flame in front of me.  She had her good days, I thought.  Her husband, *Vido,* had immigrated from the Serbian province of Lika, just after the turn of the century.  He had originally settled in the West Bottoms, finding work in the packinghouses.  Then, in an arranged marriage that was typical among the Serbian immigrants, *Desa* came into his life, and they eventually bought a little house on Seventh Street, a stone's throw from Providence Hospital.  That was where he died from colon cancer at 48, a premature death that likely was caused more by his meat and potatoes diet than any maverick gene he may have inherited.

After Vido's death, her eldest and only son, Bronko, took on the family chores.  He didn't mind.  He adored his mother.  Desa's three younger daughters also tended to her every whim and need.  She was right where she wanted to be until her death at 83 – dead center in the Martich family circle.

When Bronko married a plain, but wholesome, Serbian farm girl from Newton, Kansas, it had no effect on his commitment to mother Desa.  In fact, *Yelena* willingly accepted her place in the pecking order of a Serbian family.  She happily did her part to keep the old lady's lofty status secure.

Actually, Bronko's marriage to her came as a surprise to the Serbian community. Nobody thought Bronko was the marrying kind. But he fooled us all. After a brief courtship, Pops officially supervised a bigger than average Serbian wedding that led to a lot of dancing and more than enough hard drinking. All par for the course…all in all it was a good wedding.

Bronko was a good man.  Simple as a post, he had an infectious personality that made him refreshing and generally harmless – that is, unless you got him riled up.  Then he could be 260 pounds of thunder and lightning. Fortunately, that only happened once or twice, and Pops was there to keep the peace.  Bronko always listened to Pops, and although nobody ever said it out loud, they really were glad that he did.

Pops thought the world of Bronko.  He was a big-boned, round shouldered and even bigger handed man whose fingers had been broken too many times for him to care anymore. Just one look at his huge frame told even the most casual observer that he was destined to live a semi–skilled laborer's life.

Yet, he still managed his bull-like ways with a particular kind of grace and, yes, a workman's kind of class.  He was also a small businessman of sorts, making a meager living delivering coal with his second-hand dump truck to a dwindling neighborhood clientele that still stubbornly held on to their coal-fired house furnaces built around the turn of the century. By 1951, most families had converted their homes into the city's piped gas system. But for those who didn't, Bronko was available to attend to their needs.

The Martich daughters were another story.  They had their limitations. For one, all three were double ugly.  For another, there were no signs of a future brain surgeon among the lot. They had all stumbled through *Wyandotte High School* and immediately went into the hourly workforce, taking on mostly clerical jobs.  No thought of college and no money even if they had the grades to get in.  One was a customer clerk at *Kresge's* down on Minnesota Avenue. Another worked as a hotel doctor's clerical assistant in downtown Kansas City, Missouri.  The third and oldest, *Maria* had fared a bit better.  She went to work for *Deluxe Check Printers* and after a decade-and-a-half on the job managed to work herself into a midnight-to-eight-shift supervisor's job.  The church folks whispered that she got the promotion because nobody else wanted to work the graveyard shift.  But Bronco was proud of her, just the same.

When it came to the Martich daughters, nobody ever talked about marriage, but if they knew what I did, they might have overlooked nature's heartless cruelties.  If there was one thing the old lady had taught her brood it was how to cook a proper Serbian meal.  I always looked forward to going with Pops when he made his yearly visits during the holiday season to bless the houses.  He had a mission: to chase away the *Demons* that found refuge in the attic, basement, or some other corner of their skinny little abodes. Whenever we showed up, Mrs. Martich always singled me out.  She'd start off by offering me a big bowl of *chip potatoes…*then quickly graduate into the traditional Serbian delicacies that seemed to be never-ending. The three Martich sisters were on kitchen duty and the pork-filled cabbage leaves, *Sarma*, had a special aroma that drifted throughout the house and melted into the wallpaper. To the Martich clan, having Pops drop by was the event of a year. Everything had to be perfect, and it was.

But it was the roast pig that sat in the middle of the dining room table that got to me. While Pops went from room-to-room throwing holy water around like a fireman, I sat in the chair and patiently waited. Just me and that pig. It had certainly seen better days. The roasted apple lodged in its open mouth took away the last remnant of dignity it might have had.

To Serbians, roast pig is more than a delicacy. It's a culinary statement! Only roast lamb came close. But the *prasa* still won out. During the summer, the church social club would roast a pig over a pit behind the church hall. *Nick Legino,* the church butcher, would see me coming and always cut off a piece of the skin and give it to me. I loved to suck the fat off, then chew the gristle, washing it all down with a bottle of *Nehi Cola.*

But going one-on-one with this pig was different. It was the centerpiece attraction, surrounded by frilly lace, and all the side trimmings. I sat and patiently waited, but the pig was winning the stare-down. Above me, I could hear the sounds of footsteps and creaking wood as Pops moved into another room. His baritone voice was pounding the walls. The *Devil* didn't have a prayer of a chance today.

Blessing the house was an important ritual to Serbians. Aside from its symbolic Biblical cleansing, it was also a signal that the long, dreary winter days were at the halfway point. In a few weeks the traditional *Lenten* season that culminated with Easter and Spring, would begin. It meant the frigid temperatures and unforgiving wind, snow, sleet and slush that made working out-of-doors a sub-zero hell in Kansas City was on the mend.

To Pops, these visits to the parishioner homes also meant an added income, a few hundred dollars donated to him personally for his services. Once in a while one of the family heads would slip a couple of dollars my way. For both of us the season was seen as a family bonanza month. *Both Christmases....*

American Serbs had long ago adjusted to the reality that every year there was going to be double holidays. The reason was that our faith had opted to follow the older *Gregorian Calendar,* whereas the Roman Catholics respected the more recent *Julian Calendar.* Their Christmas fell December 25. Ours was always two weeks later, on *January 7.*

Easter was a different matter and bounced around from year to year. But that didn't matter much to me, anyway. It was Christmas where the prospects of getting a little cash were most promising. Not only that, I was born the day after Serbian Christmas, which meant an even bigger payday. A few people always remembered, and old Mrs. Martich was one of them.

\*\*\*

Off-Key Marie's siren wailing did its job. She brought me back to reality and I looked around. Mikey was sending me a signal. He looked like he had a nervous twitch, snapping his head repeatedly toward the coffin. I squinted hard, trying to decipher his non-verbal message. Finally, I cautiously turned my head and looked for Pops. His back was still to us. The oldest Martich girl had fainted and was lying on her back in the front church pew. Her sisters and Bronko's wife were attending to her using their accordion fans and massaging her neck.

The choir launched into another thundering crescendo and Pop's full, rich voice stood above it with towering strength and determination. It was a musical war being played out in minor chords, and Off-Key Marie seemed to be pushing for dominance again. I glanced again toward Mikey. His expression had turned a pale green.

Slowly, I inched toward him, trying not to draw Pop's attention.

"What is it...what's the matter?"

Mikey tried to reply, but the words stuck in his mouth.

"You sick? You gonna puke?"

He shook his head and swallowed hard.

"I was watchin' her...I saw her eyebrow twitch!" he finally sputtered above the din.

"She's alive! She ain't dead, Stevie!

"You're nuts. She's dead. Dead people don't move."

"Oh yeah, then you look! Just watch her," he said, pointing the way with his finger.

Mrs. Martich's weathered face was tranquil looking, but from my perspective, she looked to me now as if she were frowning. I looked down at her hands. The tiny gold ring was in clear view on her right hand. Behind me, the choir was at its climax. The heat, the sobbing, the wailing, Off-Key Marie and Pops – it was all boiling over. I held my gaze on that tiny gold ring until I saw it.

At first I refused to believe it. But when it happened again my heart climbed into my throat. Her ring finger twitched! Mikey was right. She was alive!

My head whirled with the discovery. Flashes of the movie, *Frankenstein* got in the way. The doctor's discovery when he saw his monster's hand twitch. *"He's alive! He's alive!"*

"See! I told you!" Mikey blurted from somewhere in the distance. "She ain't dead! Her hand moved. I saw it! You did, too!"

I tried to move, but couldn't. I was terrified, and with it a rush of other recollections of dead people coming to life paraded in front of me. Once Pops had taken me to Butler's Funeral Home. Without thinking, he brought me into the embalming area. He was looking for the funeral home owner, *Harry Butler.* But instead of me staying by his side, he left me to wait in a cold, dark room. I tried to orient myself. When my eyes finally adjusted to the light, I discovered I was standing in the middle of half-a-dozen corpses that were in various stages of embalming preparation. Most were under white sheet except for an old man who was propped on a high-backed wooden chair seated just behind me. He was naked as a *Jaybird*. When I looked at his face, he was sporting a weird smile on his craggy face. It was the kind of grin that looked as if he just cracked the joke of the century, but I didn't hear a thing.

I ran for the door. But in the murky light and in my confused state of mind, I turned the wrong way. I was desperate to find Pops, but he was nowhere in sight. Suddenly, I heard a *groan* coming from under a gurney sheet directly in front of me. A human form began to rise. When it did, the white sheet slipped off revealing a woman's torso. Even in the dim light I could see that she was a stunning beauty, and probably no more than twenty years old. She had the biggest tits I had ever seen! But what really sent me into a panic was that she was looking directly at me! Her round, dark eyes and full head of raven black hair was only inches from me.

For a second I thought about AJ's *T-shirt* and how it had slipped off her the same way. But her nipples couldn't compare to these. Then suddenly, the reality of where I was and who *she* was exploded in my brain. I was comparing *AJ* to a corpse! I bolted for the same direction I came from. I grabbed the door handle and pulled it with all my might. But nothing happened! I pulled at it again, but the door still wouldn't give. I could feel her closing in on me!

"Pops get me oughta here! Pops where are you?"

She was almost on me. No time left! That's when I felt the hand on my shoulder.

"Stevie, why you so scared?"

I wheeled around to see Pops looking down at me. Harry Butler was standing next to him. A thin man with a long, narrow face, he was wearing a thick, black rubber apron and long gloves. There was a syringe in his hand and I could smell the *Formaldehyde*. I wanted to puke.

"I wanna get oughta here, now Pops! I wanna go home!"

Harry looked around and quickly put together what had happened. He went over to the corpse and readjusted it on the gurney. Then he glanced toward me revealing an understanding smile. But I wanted no part of him, or his business.

"It's okay now, Father," he said. "He's had a bit of a scare. We'll talk later."

Pops opened the door and I charged through it, running full bore through the funeral parlor's front door entrance, finally stopping on the front steps. The playback of what I had just seen was spinning inside my head. A dead woman with the most beautiful tits I had ever seen had just made a pass at me. And I loved it!

\*\*\*

"Stevie, I'm scared!" Mikey's voice punched through the fog of my funeral home recollection.

"Shut up," I hissed. "Lemme think! This ain't real! Somethin's screwy."

Mikey wanted no part of being patient. All he wanted was out. I could see the flood of tears welling in his eyes. He was terrified and depending on me to figure out what to do next.

I looked down at Mrs. Martich again, and that was my second mistake. Her frown had now turned into a full-blown smile! I glanced toward Mikey. He saw it, too and now there was no holding back the torrent of terror that was crashing down on both of us. Behind us, the choir, Pops, and the *Litany for the Dead* had gone over the top.

Suddenly Pop's voice was booming in my ear. I glanced to one side. He had turned and walked to the head of the casket. We were trapped! Her smile turned even wider!

*"Oh God of spirits and of all corporal beings..."* he chanted, swinging the incense burner over the body. I looked at Mikey who by now was out of control. He was holding his candlestick in a death grip, eyes shut tight and gritting his teeth.

Then it happened. I felt the warm urine running down the inside of my thigh, rolling down my leg, and dripping onto the church floor. Try as I might, I couldn't stop it. I looked around in desperation, and then at Pops. His glare cut through me. He knew! The *pee* was out there for everyone to see, and old Mrs. Martich knew it. She left this world having the last laugh.

###

# Bostich and the Bell...

**M**ile Bostich took his time shuffling the deck of cards in front of him. His nimble fingers and the clever way he merged them into the deck was already a well known trademark among the players who watched him doing his magic. Content he had shown the deck of fifty-two who was boss, he deftly flicked them one at a time to the three players seated around the green felt table. But before he picked up his own, he eyed the full whiskey shooter sitting on the table. He picked it up and offered a salute to his friends.

"Zhiveli...(*Cheers...*)" he said taking in a hurried gulp. The booze cut through him like a hot flame and Mile shook his head in protest as he fought the urge to cough.

*Bogamu (By God)...*'dis whiskey...damn good, you know..." he said, his voice still cracking from the struggle to master its bite.

"Where you get it?" the tall man on the end of the table asked.

"From the *Italiani....*"

Mile's answer was characteristically blunt. There wasn't much need for anything else. Everybody at the table knew that he had been wired to the Kansas City mob for years. They more or less formed a business alliance over in Missouri that had since produced mutual benefits on both sides of the state borders.

For Mile, making friends was something he wasn't good at. In fact he was a disaster. He had a white-hot temper and was quick with his fists. When it came to dealing with Mile Bostich, it was always a good idea to remember never, ever to con a con man. Those who tried it always paid a heavy price.

The Italians more or less adopted the Serb and maybe it was because nature gave him a little help. With his dark hair, dark eyes and swarthy complexion, he looked like he would have been right at home sitting in a patio chair drinking a morning *Expresso* in front of a bungalow in sunny Sicily. So Mile Bostich, the independent businessman, and the Kansas City mob talked – and then they talked some more. Then they went off and made a truck load of money with Bostich picking up a mob distributorship selling hard stuff to the thirsty citizens of Wyandotte Country and all points west – in fact, anywhere on the Kansas prairie he thought he could cut a deal with the local police and officials. Mile Bostich knew how to work with the laws...and the one he liked best was the one that made Kansas a dry state – no hard booze allowed. It was truly a gift from heaven.

The war on booze seemed to be a never-ending issue among the rural oriented and religious Kansans.  Decades before the nation adopted *Prohibition* in 1919, Kansas had already shown them the way, at least sort of…. By 1880, the battle lines were drawn between the prohibitioners and the saloonkeepers who had routinely found loopholes to keep their shops open. It was a game that lasted another decade, even though it was the law of the land.  The facts were that many local officials *(probably due to their fears of losing lucrative private incomes)* had refused to enforce the law until the state's Governor, Edward Hoch, and the Attorney General, Fred S. Jackson, finally became directly involved at the local level.   Their political weight apparently did a fair bit of damage.  By 1906, the more than 256 saloons that dotted the region had been closed.  But despite that, the relentless pursuit of libations refused to die.  Within months new outlets began to reappear, masked in different ways and in different locations.  Kansans, it appeared, were exercising their right to *Home Rule.*

Among the Serbs who simply could not comprehend a normal life without having booze around, the entire matter was non-negotiable.  So they quite naturally set off to invent their own solutions.  Whenever the patch residents learned of the arrival of trains coming in from the South bearing carloads of fresh grapes, they made it a point to be on hand to *greet* the crews.  Using one means or another, they toted home bushels full of grapes where they were later either kept or sold outright to others in the neighborhood.  Inside their houses they went about the business of brewing their own spirits.  These homemade wines were never intended to be part of a five-star dining experience.  They were hundred proof and better replacements…potent booze at the baseline level – and it worked just fine.

*"Dai mi dve…"* (Give me two) *Petar Stepanovich* said, as he gently stroked the three cards left in his hands.  For a big man standing well over six-five, Petar's face and the metal-framed glasses he always wore made him look more like a school teacher than the *King of the Serbs* moniker he earned among his countrymen.  Yet, everyone at that table knew he was every bit the businessman that Bostich was and then some.

Easy going *Petar S…*loved to go fishing almost as much as he did getting the best of people who really had it coming.  He was anything but one-dimensional and he was the antithesis of Mile.  He was the type of loveable sort you couldn't help but respect and like at the same time.  But you always knew that when you dealt with him something was surely coming down the pipe and you would probably end up regretting it.  You knew it, but you stuck around, anyway.  It was just business. No, Petar was just somebody people just liked to be around.  He was a natural politician.

He also knew how to size up anybody who had well-honed Mediterranean instincts – *cunning* some might call it.  His got his lessons growing up in Plashki and seeing folks wheel and deal with each other – watching how *sixes* could be magically turned into *nines*…and seeing people get out of long jail sentences simply by using the perfect choice of words.

When Petar saw Mr. Bostich arrive in the *patch* and make his early moves, he decided early on that if ever anybody deserved to be his business partner, it had to be him. In many ways they were made for each other. Mile, running on a perpetual red line and Petar calmly keeping things ship-shape and orderly. Using his knack of moving to the edge of the envelope but never, ever going over it. Letting smiles and handshakes get the job done instead of knuckles and fists. Petar was a negotiator, and a damn good one at that.

Still, facts were facts, and in this instance they told him that Mile's natural instincts were a cut above the rest, even though he consistently knee-jerked himself into demonstrating his talents in sometimes-brutal ways. But when he put his mind to it he could really be something special. Mile could snatch the gold fillings out of your mouth before you smacked your lips. Some people did things that took an eternity – Mile did it in a heartbeat.

It didn't take long before his mental *rpms* started generating a string of green backs for the both of them. That took some doing in the unforgiving world of the West Bottoms, so *Gospodin Petar*, the consummate politician that he was, made it a point to make sure that Mile's talent was kept right where it would do the most good: next to him. So they talked, and then they also talked some more…and when it was over the two of them agreed that they would have a good time pulling the strings in the state of Kansas pushing hard booze and rolling dice games. In fact, providing all the creature comforts that put life in perspective. *God Bless America….*

But none of that mattered to either of them at the moment. When it came to these poker sessions, friendships and business partnerships were left outside. The pool hall was a place mostly for men with time to kill and a little money to spend, except, of course, when a hooker happened to drop by for a short-neck *Falstaff* before hitting the bricks on a busy Saturday night.

The pool tables for rent always had somebody trying to lift a *sawbuck* off some unsuspecting yokel who stumbled inside. Once in a while Mile had to pull out his *.38 caliber Smith & Wesson* from under the bar to remind customers where the limit lines were. That nearly always worked because folks knew Mile had no hesitation about squeezing the trigger. He was once arrested and jailed when he shot dead a man over money. It was later ruled as self-defense.

No, this backroom gathering among *friends* wasn't about making money at all. It was about getting the *edge* on anybody who happened to get in the way and *five-card draw poker* was the way to sort out who really had the goods.

"*Nhista za mene…*" *(None for me)* Bostich said, keeping his voice flat and low as if trying to get the message through without anybody noticing. Everybody did.

"*Kuratz…(Penis…)* You get more luck, eh? How much more you want tonight?" grumbled patch storeowner *George Bozich* as he nervously shuffled the three new cards he picked up, then studied them along with the two he kept.

George was high strung and prone to squirming around whenever he got bad news. Whenever he did, his wooden chair squeaked. It might as well have been a news bulletin to the others. Mile always made it a point to give George that old chair. Nobody ever complained.

Worse still, George's face was as easy to read as a roadmap to Omaha. No matter how hard he tried, between the chair and his face, he was always the one who gave up the most cash when they called it a night. Ironically, he was also the most punctual of the lot. He was never late, not once in the more than five years the Saturday night card ritual began.

Not only that, he always showed up dressed in style. He looked the real *Dapper Dan* in his black denim trousers and a nicely starched long sleeve white shirt and bow tie. When he sat down he promptly rolled up his sleeves, taking care to make sure each turn was exactly even on both arms. His wide, always black suspenders had become a symbol of his meticulous ways as he went about his business in the small corner grocery store he and his wife and five children ran. By patch standards George Bozich was a man of substance, although admittedly his occasional eccentricities rippled through the Serb rumor network. To tell the truth, there were times when he could be a little...well psycho.... Like a compass that suddenly goes haywire, then returns to normal just as quickly. No rhyme or reason to it...it just happened. Then it was back to the grindstone and living life like a family man he was.

"I open..." Mile said in response, tossing out two red chips into the center of the table. One of the chips temporarily mesmerized them as it spun on its edge, then finally fell to one side. Nature's ever-present power over all had asserted its dominance once again.

"Call," said *Ilija Vusich,* tossing in his chips and then settling back in his chair as he studied the competition. A man whose thin mustache and piercing dark eyes suggested that the real stories about his quiet nature best belonged in the past, Iliya was also the most skilled among the group. As a youngster living in the small village of *Divoselo Gospic (county)* in the Krajina, he apprenticed in the carpentry trade from his father. The years of learning paid off almost immediately on his arrival to the US at the turn of the century. He soon found himself doing odd jobs around the patch, and then elsewhere. Now his small company was growing nicely thanks to the expanding bottoms industry and the good times that seemed to be coming their way in 1910. Iliya, among other things, was a man who possessed a handshake grip of steel as part of his command presence, but the trait also carried over into his life. When he shook your hand you could rest assured that his word was every bit as firm as his grip.

Yet among them all, everyone deferred to Mile when it came to five-card draw. He was a gambler in more ways than one and a unique *provider* of services of all kinds. He just knew what to do, and when. And it was that instinct that was more a matter of good genes than anything he had really learned. His partnership with Petar S...had turned into everything he had hoped it would be in coming to the new land.  It was certainly a far cry from the endless days of back breaking work when he helped his father work the small plot of farmland just outside of Plashki.  When the agent from America came to call one morning offering him a chance for a new life, he grabbed it.

He knew it meant leaving his elderly parents and his younger brother and sister to work the farm that had been in the family since the Turks were finally pushed out of the *Ogulun* region a hundred years earlier.  He knew all that, and he saw it in their saddened faces the day he hopped aboard the back of an old flatbed truck heading into an uncertain a future.  That made Mile uncomfortable…*but not sad*.  Mile never, ever felt sad about anything.  What he was thinking about was that he had found a way out of the barren hills and the poverty.  Staying on the farm was a road that terminated in the bosom of misery.  When he left, he never looked back.  If he had, he would have seen the tears streaming down his father's cheeks.

All of the men who sat around the poker table with Mile had similar stories.  They were, one could say, veterans of the *Industrial Revolution's* Atlantic crossing.  And all except the more skilled Iliya had been baptized in the hip deep tide of animal waste they spent hours sweeping and mopping the packing house killing treadmill and wooden floors.  They had, in fact, embraced the challenge.  They followed the *ritual of the packing house* to the letter holding high a dingy tin cup full of cow's blood, then chug-a-lugging it as others stood by and cheered.  They had willingly given up their *virginity* to support America's moguls.  The red juice of life ran down their stubble chins, and on their heavy bib overalls, trickling through the cracked wooden floor, disappearing forever.

Yes, they were all veterans of a very different sort.  They had long ago adjusted to the feel of the biting Kansas winter winds as they knifed through the packinghouse walls and ceilings, adding to the numbness of their near frozen hands.  Fighting the sting in their eyes as they worked hour upon agonizing hour throughout the night as they tended to the mechanized slaughter; turning off the terrified sounds of the animals in their heads as they blindly stumbled into termination; then coming home to sleep three-in-a-bed, or on the cold wooden floor in one of the patch's dingy boarding houses.

"Okay *brat moj, kazhi ti mene…shta imash? (Okay, brother mine…tell me what you have.)"* big Pete challenged as he tossed in his chips and stuck yet another *Camel* in his mouth and lit it with his gold-plated lighter.  He studied his adversary through the flickering orange flame, looking for any clue, any weakness...that told him he might be too close to the edge.

Mile caressed his cards, shuffling them one under the other, once, twice, and then a third time as he waited.  It was a tactic used when he sensed he was on top.  He looked at them and flashed a sinister grin that would have rattled the *Devil* himself.

"*Evo…"(Here…)* he said, picking up five more red chips and intentionally lining them up side-by-side like warriors across the table's green felt top.

*"Opet ti sve dobiyash…" (Again you get everything)* grumbled George who underscored his bitching with a toss of his cards on one side of the chips. "Lady luck…she makes love to you really good tonight, ehh Mile…?"

Mile shrugged and looked at the group.

*"Shta ya tu mogu…? (What can I do?)* She likes me."

He turned his attention on Iliya who sat in stony silence, oblivious to his antics. He was focused on the cards in front of him. The collecting smoke from Petar's cigarette rolled lazily above him in the humid summer air and mixed with the heavy layers of the pool hall's cigar haze that had already collected under the table's lamp shade. For an instant it looked as if there was a halo hovering directly over his head. But the illusion was short lived. When he looked up, his glare at Mile was a very different message. What was unfolding was anything but a spiritual experience. It was more like: *God helps those who help themselves.*

"How much you win tonight, ehh Mile…?" he asked, his voice controlled and guttural. Among the Serbs, Iliya was often described as having a *crn glas, a black man's voice* because it was so gravely sounding. It got your attention.

"Why?"

Iliya shrugged.

"Nothing…I just ask…."

Mile laughed. It was a patterned response that really signaled he was on the alert for something deeper, maybe even a growing threat.

He pointed to the several stacks next to his left elbow.

*"Vidi…pogledaj ti sam…(Here…see for yourself)* I got 'dese chips here…'dat's my winnings…. Maybe…what…? Two hundred…*ne mnogo." (Not much)*

Petar studied both men. There had always been an undertow of hostility between Iliya and Mile, and it came from dark places on both sides. They sensed each other's weaknesses, but something deeper always urged them to probe further than they needed to. It was a competitive instinct coupled with a very Serbian version of *machismo* that both were generally able to impose on others at will. But when it surfaced between them the result was always a *push*…and that was where the danger resided.

*"Ajde, Iliya (C'mon, Iliya…)* what you want to do now, *brat?"* Petar asked, breaking the chain.

Iliya's building glare on Mile softened. He glanced at Petar then concentrated on his cards again, putting them face down on the table.

*"Dobro*…I'm in," Petar countered, tossing his chips every which way on the table.

*"Ajde, Mile! Pokazhi mi tvoye gace," (C'mon, Mile, show me your underwear),* Petar commanded.

Mile laid the cards on the table in front of him face down and began turning them over one at a time. The first was a *nine* of diamonds, next a *ten* of clubs, then the *Jack* of spades followed by a *Queen* of hearts; finally came the *King* of diamonds.

"*Evo...pogledaj sam... (Here...see for yourself)* I get 'dis...first round..."

Petar studied the cards and laughed. It was a soft, warm response that belied the steel that was just below the surface. He snuffed out his cigarette in the ashtray next to him and flicked his cards on the table. He had two pairs. There were times that talking did no good. This was one of them.

Iliya kept his cool. A slow smile began to appear. When it did, it got all of Mile's attention.

He spread the cards in fan-like fashion for all to see. It was a *Full House, Aces High....*

"This time you pay back a little, *brat* – to me...." His smile turned into a quiet laugh as he reached out with both hands and scooped in the chips.

For an instant Mile's eyes flashed, but just as quickly his guarded smile reappeared.

"*Svaka chast, Iliya...*" *(You lucky tonight for sure)*, Petar said. "Maybe lady luck want to sleep with you now...ehh?"

Petar reached for the *Jim Beam* bottle on the table and poured himself a shooter full of whiskey. Then he looked at the group. A mischievous grin came out of nowhere as he gulped down the booze.

"No...I don't think she go to you Iliya. She stays with him.... *Ona njega strashno voli...(She likes him very much)* Maybe it's his eyes, what do you think?" He took a drink and put the shooter down glass hard on the felt table.

"No.... It's his *kuratz...(Penis...)* That's what she loves," he continued, pointing to Mile's groin. "Everybody knows that...ask Dolly...she tell you...."

"Petar, you got big mouth...you know..." Mile countered holding his hands up to make a sign of a clown's wide smile. "Anybody got three daughters already and no sons got cotton balls...."

"*To je istina, Bogamu...(That's true, by God...)* I never thought about it like that," George said.

"See...*is* true..." Mile added pointing to George. "All those stories about the King of the Serbs...maybe if they think about his *kuratz...*they change their minds."

Petar's long silence was as good as an admission. He smiled as he fumbled with the gold lighter in his hand.

"I admit to nothing," he finally said.

George started squirming in his seat.

"*Ajde*...we play some more...it's late...I gotta work tomorrow...doin' inventory."

Mile pushed the cards his way and clumsily began to shuffle the deck. As he passed them out, the mood around the table changed.

"*Iliya, hochu neshto da te pitam,*"*(I have something to ask you...)* Petar said.

"What you want to know?" Iliya replied.

He took a swig of the long neck *Schlitz* that replaced the empty shooter glass.

"You been on church board long time now.... You also built that steeple...very nice one, too."

Mile rolled his eyes and laughed when he heard his partner talk about the church.

"You mean 'dat one that ain't go no bell?"

Pete looked at his partner and smiled, reaching for yet another cigarette. This time he took a long metal filter from out of his shirt pocket and stuck the *Camel* inside it. He lit it and took a puff, studying the smoke as it drifted into the evening light.

*"Shta to pitash, Petar?" (What are you asking?)* Iliya said.

"It's what Mile said.... Why we Serb people still no have bell for our St. George Church? Four years now and nothing."

Iliya picked up his cards and studied them. He thought to himself how many times he had tried to get the job done, but somehow it just didn't happen. Bells of quality weren't cheap...in fact they were works of art. Besides, there were other priorities and over time they had more or less learned to live with it. Still, Petar was right. No bell...it wasn't right.

A lot of that delay also had something to do with plain old Serbian stubbornness. Whenever the idea of getting one was brought up to the people, they insisted it came from Plashki and no place else. For centuries Plashki had been a regional headquarters of the church in the Krajina. Its church bells were a symbol of their Orthodox faith. They wanted a Plashki bell or nothing at all. Until then, they would wait.

That was how it stayed until Iliya had built a nice steeple and belfry, and that made some of the parishioners uneasy. There was a slight but still visible chink developing in the congregation. A nice church steeple with no bell...it was like roast beef and no potatoes. The steeple and belfry was a strong and proper looking one at that.

"How you build a church steeple then forget bell?" Mile chided.

"Then maybe you do something, too, ehh Mile? Maybe *Boga (God)* will see who you are and change his mind about you," Iliya said his gravely voice revealing the edge.

He tossed his cards onto the table.

"Gotovo...."(Done)

*"Iliya, Nemoj da budesh takav," (Iliya, don't be like that)* Petar said, picking up on the irritation. "We know you do your best.... But Mile ask good question, and I want to know, too.... I went to church last week and saw the Pope on the steps ringing small bell he holds in his hand."

"You went to church, Petar?" George Bozich asked, his eyes bulging in astonishment. "You sure you don't cave in roof? Iliya maybe you go check.... I go to church tomorrow. I don't want no trouble."

Petar laughed and studied his cards. He threw in two chips.

"I call...*dai mi dve....*" *(Give me two.)*

George was about to deal him the cards when the pool hall back door flung open. *Miss Dolly Dunda* walked through it, and in the process took up every inch of the available space. She was a big-boned women whose figure had seen better days, despite the fact that she was dressed to the nines in a strapless, full length blue satin Victorian dress that emphasized her butt and her more than ample cleavage. Her peroxide blond hair was rolled on the top of her head like a cow paddy.

Dolly's make-up was as heavy as it was liberally splashed across her face. It was well supported by fake three-inch long earrings and a rhinestone necklace that was long enough to allow a teardrop-shaped stone to wedge itself between her boobs.

"Mile, what the hell you doin, huh? You go crazy?" she said pointing her finger to her head and making a *cuckoo* sign.... Her Polish-born accent turned heavy and thick, a sure sign that she was revved up and looking for trouble.

She rumbled toward him. With every step she took the poker table rattled even more. She stopped in front of them all, putting her hands on her hips like a DI.

"Well?" she said leveling a steely glare at the players.

"What you speak. *Danica*? "

"Christ Mile...you sit there and tell me you know nuthin' about It?"

"Chuti! Shta hochesh, jebem li ti!" (Shut up! What do you want? Fuck you!)

Petar pointed his empty cigarette filter at her.

"Dolly...what you speak here? We play cards...that's all.... We know nothing."

She turned her glare on him but Petar's cool response calmed her – but only for a moment.

"So all of you say same thing.... You know nothing...you see nothing," she said with a sweep of her beefy arm.

"What you speak about?" Mile protested. "*Zashto toliko vichesh ovde?*" *(Why are you yelling so much here?)*

"To hell with you, Mile," she snapped. "To hell with all of you!"

"Maybe you tell us why you so angry – maybe we can help..." George said. But the moment the words left his mouth, he knew he made a mistake.

Dolly glared at him.

"Okay.... You help me? I show you..." she said. "All of you get up off your *dupete (Butts)* and see...now!"

She turned and headed for the door. Despite her hippo proportions, she was surprisingly nimble on her high-heeled shoes. When she reached the doorway she turned again and looked at the group.

"Well? What you *gentlemen* wait for...? Come on.... Dolly shows all of you."

The players' bewildered looks only got worse as they tried to figure out what had sent her temper into overdrive. Not that it was anything new. Since taking over the brothel, she had more than once single-handedly thrown out an overzealous customer who tried to take his sexual fantasies too far on one of her girls. Mile liked that side of her personality. It meant that he got a two-for-one deal that saved him money – part brothel manager, part bouncer....

She was good, too. She took pride in keeping the house ship-shape, hiring and firing the endless string of girls who drifted into town looking for temporary work, and keeping a watchful eye on the regulars who lived in the five-bedroom Victorian home, arguably the best groomed piece of property in the patch.

Dolly knew what the folks thought of her occupation and although she couldn't do anything about it, she made Mile promise that her *office* would be a model showcase in the community. Naturally, Mile bitched at the cost of the frequent lawn trimmings, building the useless white picket fence, and all the touch-up house painting. He grumbled that it took out too big a chunk out of his bottom line. But when the Mayor came a-calling one night and told him how he thought his *home* was the showcase of Kansas City, Mile decided then and there that it was money well spent. He congratulated Dolly for demonstrating her outstanding business acumen, then promptly bought him a fifth of *Jim Beam* as he personally escorted him into the VIP suite where *His Honor* had requested he get *sandwiched* by two of the cat house's best. Mile said it was on the house and all in the name of PR. Dolly Dunda got status....

Her book keeping expertise was almost as legendary as her bedroom bouncing. She monitored each and every transaction to the penny, and when things went awry as they occasionally did, she engineered an endless hunt to find out why. Clothes and suitcases flew out of windows and people were tossed out the front and back doors. Dolly hated to be cheated and that was just fine by Mile. There were, after all, bills to be paid for the price of doing business. Especially the weekly rituals of shoving a wad full of dough in the cops' pockets when they showed up for cash and free servicing.

But there was more to Dolly than good management and a temper that could turn wood into flames. There was the unmistakable scent of *love*...between her and Mile, and their combined torches frequently flamed into new heights.

Dolly's secret was her girth, but it was Mile's obsession with it that created the chemical reaction. The rolling layers of fat-on-fat were simply irresistible to Mile. It rocketed his sexual fantasies to new heights. So Dolly did what came natural – she ate even more, and they bounced even better.

It was a *bonafide* bonfire obsession. Ironically Mile, in fact, publicly courted a girl who was nothing like that at all. *Christina Jaich's* high-pitched, bird-like chirpy voice and petite size made her more a candidate to marry an undertaker rather than a hard-nosed gambler and man of the streets. But still she had shape, that one. What she missed in girth she more than made up for in guile. She had long ago learned to put up with Mile's antics and, in fact, had a few of her own that were uniquely hers. Christina also knew how to turn a dollar and she didn't mind God knowing about it, either.  Mile had a hard time remembering where the church was, but Christina found the front door almost every Sunday.

\*\*\*

Dolly was the first to walk into the ornately decorated waiting lounge.  The motif was deluged with heavy red satin curtains with gold tassels.  No one was inside seated on the gold braided, high back couch, but the night was still young.  Two other similar chairs sat on each side of the room.  There was a *Victrola* player placed on the mahogany table between one of the armchairs and the couch.  This was the greeting area where the men callers met their dates for the night.  From there they went up a flight of wide, carpeted steps into private rooms.

Dolly waited until all four cleared the double doors.  What they saw dead center in the living room drew stares of disbelief.  It was a *bell*...a filthy, muddy, dull black looking bell somebody plunked down in all its sludgy, greasy, glory – leaving a circular imprint in the center of the expensive Persian rug that graced the room.

"Look at that," Dolly demanded.  "Who the hell put that there?"

She pointed an accusing finger at Mile.

"Mile, are you nuts...what the hell do we need a bell for in this place?  I got bells ringing everywhere.  You don't believe?  Go upstairs...hear."

Mile shrugged and looked at Petar, who in turn shrugged and looked at Iliya, who in turn shrugged and looked at George.  He stepped closer to her, trying to muffle his voice.

*"Zlato....ya nez nam."* (Sweetheart, I don't know...)" He pointed to the rug.  "Why you think I do something like 'dis?  I pay plenty for 'dis...for you...."

"Don't give me that bullshit, Mile," she snapped.  "You put here because you got some kind crazy idea.... God knows what.... And now it don't work right...and you don't say you wrong."

Mile stood in silence as he studied the bell.  Petar stepped onto the rug and next to it.  He carefully looked it over, peering over the top of his glasses at the words etched in the metal near its top.

*"Pogledaj! (Look!)"* he said.  "It says something...here...near top."

He bent over and took out his handkerchief, rubbing some of the grease off it.

*"U-N-I-O-N.... Shta je Union?"* (What is Union?) he asked looking up from his hunched position.

Iliya came to his side and read for himself.  Then he turned to Dolly.

"How did the bell get here?"

She laughed so hard her big boobs bounced nearly out of their halter.

"How?  I tell you...two *niggers* put it there, that's how.  They put on trolley and dump it right there...on my beautiful Persian rug!"

The recollection brought on tears of frustration.

"I was in back and heard noise.  When I get here it was too late.*"

She pointed to the spot.  "They told me man who gave them money say where to go.  Put it here…no place else."

"The *tsrntsi (Blacks)* say that?"  Mile asked.

"*Yesi gluv, Mile? (Are you hard of hearing, Mile?)* They say right there…" Dolly snapped, on the verge of balling again.

"Did they know him?"  Iliya countered.

"No…only that he was a *beltsi (Whites)*.  They saw him down on 7th Street.  He talked while they were loading furniture from a warehouse."

"*P-A-C-I-F-I-C…*" Petar continued…"Union…Pacific….That's what it say here for sure…."

"It's a *railroad* bell," George Bozich concluded.  "That's what it is…by God….  They musta got it from the roundhouse.  It's near the Seventh Street Bridge…."

"Got it…you mean *stole* it," Dolly snapped.  "No railroad ever give up one of these.  They need to call everybody for working. "

"Somebody steals a bell…then put it in my beautiful home!" she wailed as she tried to bury her big-boned face into a dainty lace handkerchief she pulled from somewhere out from her bra.

But her breakdown was short-lived.  It quickly was replaced by the fury of a 220-pound woman looking to settle the score.

"Okay…you assholes…all 'dis very funny… now who did it?  Nobody lie to Dolly Dunda!" she bellowed, pointing a closed fist at them all.  "I want truth!"

Mile looked at his partner.  He had seen her lose her cool in the past but never like this.  This was a real red-light situation.

"You were down on 7th Street today, *brate moj. (My brother)*."

"So were you…*brat*." Petar said, falling victim to a sarcastic reply.

The men looked at each other trying to pick up any clues as they listened to Dolly weep into her tiny handkerchief.

"*Mile…shta ti znash za ovo? (Mile, what do you know about this?)* You can tell me…we're partners."

"I ask you same thing, too, Petar. You like to make joke...sometimes… maybe this time, eh?"

Petar shook his head.

"*Nisam ja, brate…(It wasn't me…)* This time I know nothing."

Petar looked at Iliya who was standing with George as they continued to inspect the bell.

"*Ovo (This)* bell," Illiya said, breaking into Dolly's rhythmic sobbing…" I look at it….  It's okay, you know.  Nothing broken….  Maybe we take to church – put inside."

Dolly caught her breath.  She slowly dropped the tiny hanky covering her face, peering over the lace fringes.  She looked like a little girl who had just been told her favorite toy could be fixed after all.

"You...do that?" she asked between lingering sniffs. "You take to church...put inside?"

"This bell will be loud and strong one," Iliya said. "Maybe *narod (People)* will say okay until we get Plashki one we want."

"You on church board...you can do that, Iliya...*molim te...*"*(Please...)* Mile said. The request sounded strangely sincere and definitely out of character.

Iliya thought it over...studying his adversary's face, then Dolly's who was still peeking over the top of her handkerchief, anxiously waiting.

"*Mozhe...(Can...)* First I move it to my shop and clean it...then I talk to Pope.... Maybe I tell him it's a gift from you, Mile...or Dolly...even...."

Mile sighed and nodded, relieved that maybe now they could get back to their card game.

"*To nije dobra idea...*" *(That's not such a good idea)* Petar suggested. "Pope knows Mile and Dolly.... He won't like, no matter what he give...."

The group pondered the downside of the suggestion. Then Petar smiled.

"Maybe you can, *Juro...Ti to uradi za Mile...(Do this for Mile...)* You say you get it for trade and you give it to church, *za badava...(Free...)* They respect you, *Juro*...they listen to you good," Pete countered.

George Bozich thought over the request, then nodded.

Before he could move, Dolly was on him.

"*Dobro*! *Juro...*! *(Good George...)* she said, hugging and holding him with both arms in her vice grip. His face was perfectly stuck against her generous cleavage with nowhere to go.

Petar walked over to the filthy bell and looked it over as if it were a diamond in the rough.

"Now *Saint George* got bell," he said." And good one, too."

"We got bell, yes, but where it came from? Who give it?" George asked.

"*Ne znam brate*," *(I don't know, brother)* he replied."Maybe we just say it came from *Boga....*"

The four men looked at each other and smiled. Yes, this was definitely God's gift. That had to be the answer. The bell would go into the church. But how and who got it there would forever be locked in the vaults of the patch's history.

###

# Us Versus Them...

I went straight for the kitchen, threw a quick glance toward Mom, the opened battered, white *Crosley* fridge. I was in luck. It was still there – that single lonely-looking piece of apple pie still in its metal tin. I took it out and sat at the small table. Mom had already anticipated the move. A fork and napkin were waiting for me. I was ready for my bedtime snack.

She didn't bother to look up as she worked. She had her hands full, half ironing, and half wrestling with Pop's white shirt and black vestment. She had made some headway, but the shirt had scored a few hits, too. Sweat streamed off her forehead and down her narrow, Slavic-looking face. Her black hair was wet from the physical workout and the uncompromising humidity of a warm August night. Unconsciously, she used her forearm to wipe away the perspiration from her almost pitch-black eyes, then cut a new path on the shirt using the steel iron's blunt nose. Her strokes were grand and determined, a veteran campaigner at work.

Mom was just where she was expected to be on a Saturday night. The ironing board was also positioned near an open window, and already several shirts were on hangers arranged along the top of the kitchenette's narrow windowsill. They were crisp, white merit badges of earlier hard fought campaigns in her never-ending quest to achieve perfection in the categories of neat and clean in the Milakov household. It was, in the end, more than a chore, the ironing, washing, cleaning and scrubbing. It was a ritual of life, and Mom pursued it with a tenaciousness that even the most veteran campaigners would have admired.

"Where's Pops?"

"He went over to Mr. Supica's house for a little while, honey," she said. She threw a glance of displeasure my way.

"You know it's impolite to talk with your mouth full, Stevie."

I paused in the middle of a second bite, then looked toward the open window.

Mom smiled and picked up the vestment she'd been ironing and gave it a once over. Satisfied the war had been won, she draped it on a wooden hangar, then hooked it on the leading edge over the window top. For an instant, it looked like Pops standing there.

"When will he be back?"

"I don't know...maybe in a couple of hours."

She stopped her ironing and looked at me. Her face was clouded with worry. Mom worried a lot. Worrying about others and things she couldn't control was her passion. Over the years, I had learned to decipher her full stable of concerned expressions. This one was near the top.

"Pappy got a call from Tooky. He said that Roddy was mad at him. He went over to his house to talk."

"Why? What did Pops do now?"

She reached for another white shirt and began a new campaign with the iron.

"It's silly," she said. "Something about not pouring wine on his mother's body before they closed the casket. Some Serbs believe that you can't get into heaven unless the priest does that."

"I never saw Pops do that before."

"Not for a long time, sweetheart," she said, as she continued her ironing.

"They used to do it a lot back east. I remember they did it in *Weirton,* but not out here. Papa discouraged it. He just didn't think it was right."

I listened, then shrugged, and ate the final piece of the pie.

"What's the difference? She's dead."

I pondered my own statement as I studied the fork in my hand.

"What did Mrs. Supica die from?"

"Cancer...."

"How does it kill you?"

Mom stopped her work and looked at me. Her dark eyes were filled with tears. She put the iron upright on the wooden board and wiped her hands on her apron.

"It eats up your insides, that's what it does. If you ask me, the moment the doctors open you up and the air hits it, that's what really kills you."

She sighed and turned back to her ironing.

"At least she didn't suffer too much. Sometimes people have it for years. They just dry up. I'm sure Roddy was at least grateful that she didn't have much pain at the end."

Mom looked up again, this time with her patented hurt look.

"I wonder what God is thinking when he makes people suffer from such terrible diseases?"

"Granny Nichols says all the answers to questions like that are in the Bible. She says there's no reason to ever question anything God does. He just does it."

"Baptists have their way – and we've got ours, Stevie. That's what makes America such a wonderful country. Everybody can do whatever they want...as long as they don't break the laws."

I was still unconvinced.

"Why are we so different from everybody else?"

Mom fumbled with the shirt collar and shot a glance toward me. She was prepared. She'd dealt with this issue before and her responses were laced with passion.

"I guess it's because we're the oldest religion. We were there from the start. Everything came after us."

"I thought the *Catholics* were."

She quickly put down the shirt and looked toward the heavens, making the sign of the cross across her bosom.

"Stevie Milakov!  If your father ever heard you…who told you that?"

"AJ."

"Well, she's wrong.  Catholics always say that because they just don't know the truth," she snapped, crossing herself again for good measure.  "God help us.  You must always be careful what you say about *us… and them….*"

She pointed an accusing finger at me.

"You must also never forget that you are the son of a *Serbian Orthodox* priest.  You will embarrass us all."

I stood and walked toward the refrigerator again.  Just as quickly as her temper boiled, it disappeared.  She returned to her ironing.  Besides, her cautions were all too familiar.  I greeted them as a sign of warmth and caring.  It was a signal that life was in order.  It was her job to always keep me well aware of my role and duties as St. George's parish priest's son. I knew she meant well.

Mom was devoted to Pops.  She couldn't abide by anything that remotely suggested he was anything less than a pinnacle of leadership when it came to the expected roles we all had to play and especially how it all had to do with Serbian history.  It was her mission in life to stamp out everything that could put her family and her husband into harm's way.  A comment like that bordered on treason and it was no surprise to me that she flared up. She had passion.

Through the open kitchen window the sound of an outbound passenger train caught my attention.

"Stevie, did you hear me?"

"Yes, Mom, I heard you," I said, turning and looking at her again.

"But honestly, I can't see what's so wrong with the Catholics.  I know lots of them.  AJ's a Catholic.  And she's no different than me…except she's a lot meaner. But she's a girl, so I forgive her for that."

Mom put the iron back on its cradle and walked around the board.  She reached for the priest's vest and collar, caressing it as she spoke.

"It's very complicated, sweetheart.  You're too young to understand what it all means.  It's got something to do with the *stari krai.*  You must trust me on this.  It's something we *Serbs* all know.  It's our heritage.  There are good reasons why we can't have too much to do with them."

"It's always got something to do with the old country," I thought. It was always written off to some mysterious decision that occurred in Yugoslavia.  Hell, I had never even been to Yugoslavia.  Neither had Mom.  She was born in West Virginia.  Yet it always seemed that whatever went on *there* meant it had to be re-lived *here*, in modern America, circa 1950.

"It's time for you to go to bed.  You've got church tomorrow, so I want you to take your bath tonight," she said.  "I don't want the neighbors to think we're dirty people.  God only knows what they say about us already."

I got up from the kitchen table chair and headed for the doorway, then turned around. She was on the job again, sorting out still more clothes for ironing. Her forehead and brow glistened from the labor at hand.

"I still think all these rules are silly. Maybe some day we'll all be together and we can do whatever we want. That's America, too. People can be whatever they want to be. Anything's possible. Even President of the United States."

The simplicity of my childlike defense brought on a smile.

"Maybe, honey, we'll see.... Now, it's time for your bath."

Militsa Milakov watched her only son disappear through the doorway. She sighed and rubbed her hands across her apron, then started ironing again.

"God help us all if he's right," she muttered. "If we vote in a Catholic the Pope will tell us all what to do for sure. What will happen to America?"

###

# Dead *Boy* Walking...

"**T**his is a big day for you...sweetheart," Mom said as she bent over to check that my baggy jeans and flannel shirt were lined up neatly. "You know the way...Mommie showed you how to get there already, remember? Just go down to *12*th *Street* and walk past Chica' Milovan's house...follow the road around the corner and then up to the top to *Valley Street*. From there the patrol boy will take you across the street. You'll see the playground from there."

She stood up and put her hands on her hips and studied me with her smile. "There...now...don't your forget lunch box. Mommy put your favorite inside – peanut butter and jelly. There's a hard-boiled egg and apple, too. Promise me you'll eat it all during recess and lunch."

I took the lunchbox from her and gave it the once over. It was a classic *Hopalong Cassidy.* The decision on what lunch box to buy had been a big one. We had been up and down Minnesota Avenue looking at all the back-to-school goodies. On top of the list was the all important lunch box. The search was kind of exciting in its own way. Already I could feel the early nip of fall hovering around us we walked from one store to another. Talk of football was everywhere. Summer was over but not far in the distance was Christmas and those first winter days when the snow fell fresh on the eastern Kansas hills. When the earth tone browns and orange colors of Fall replaced the deep greens of Summer, kids were everywhere pretty much doing what we were. Pencils, tablets, lunch pails and a full line of fall clothes dressed the window displays. We were moving along with our lives and nature was showing us the way. Now, standing in front of Mom, I knew it was time to deliver. For days my parents had been talking about the school year with the rest of the parishioners. It seemed they were all playing a kind of Serbian *one-upmanship*...noting how they expected their kids to be at the top of their classes, just as they were the year before.

As for me, I had no real track record one way or another. In fact, the whole thing was a bit embarrassing. The problem had to do with my birthday. The cutoff to get into Kindergarten was to be five by the middle of December. Since I was born on January 8th, it meant that I either had to go into school a year early, or a year late. Mom and Pops opted for the latter.

For whatever reason the church people talked about that, too. It was as if I were handicapped in some mysterious way and my folks were more defensive than they really needed to when they explained the circumstances. Mom and Pops weren't that bad, but there was this never-ending stream of avocations at being *perfect* and not ever forgetting about who I was in the Serbian community.  This *special identity* at times gave me almost celebrity status.  Then again it was the root cause for a lot of emotional pain that popped years later.

That's why *Hoppy* was so important.  He stood for something…a real American hero and an individualist who did it all with style.  Someone who never worried about what other people thought.  He set the pace.  Ready to help the oppressed, and always looking so *chic*…with his all black cowboy duds and his dazzling white ten-gallon hat, and that shiny, silver studded belt, and a pair of silver plated pistols tucked smartly in black holsters that were cinched with matching black leather straps around his thighs.  And when he sat on his snorting white stallion – well, I just knew he had his priorities right.  As I started down the street, I purposely swung my *Hoppy* lunch box a little higher, hoping that somebody would make the connection.  Nobody did….

What I later learned about this school thing would have made even *Hoppy* go bad.  The red brick school loomed in the distance like a fortress out of the dark side as I crested the hill.  I felt like a prisoner of war when the patrol boy escorted me across the street, pointing officially to the sidewalk ahead which by now had plenty of neighborhood kids who were also on the way to their own destinies.  In the distance I heard the growling sounds of an outbound freight heading out of town.  The wind direction picked up the rumbling diesels and its flat air horn as it gathered speed.  I wished I were in the cab going someplace…any place but where I was headed.

###

# Kets Kume...

"**H**ey, you ready?" Mikey Dodig called as he found his spot near the base of the church front steps. "He's comin' out any second." I felt a rush of adrenaline as I ran to the other side, snuggling up against one of the stone supports. Any minute the groom would pop through the church's front door.

I looked around and re-assessed my tactical situation. Three other kids were on hand but I didn't know them very well. They generally came around only for special events like these. I figured they were real amateurs and probably more curious than anything else. All three positioned themselves further back, and more in the center of the sidewalk. Mikey and I knew better. We'd already learned that the majority of the coins generally ended up either on one side or the other of the entryway. There were some benefits to being altar boys, and this was one of them. We were ready.

How did they figure it out? I wondered who squealed...and especially to these nobodies? Not every Serbian wedding had a Kets Kume celebration; even though it was a long-standing Serbian tradition. Pops said it was common back in Yugoslavia, but in recent years the tradition was less popular.

But not the idea of a *best man.* That was still a big item. In Serbian weddings he was more than somebody who kept the ring and gave it away at the right time. To us, it was an honor that really meant a lifetime commitment. That in turn meant his entire family, even though they weren't blood related, was connected for life. The bloodlines of church and Serbian tradition are what did it. In hard times it was the *Kum* who would even take on the heavy burdens, and that sometimes took precedence even over his own family. It might mean taking and rearing the groom's children as if they were their own. There was nothing he wasn't empowered to do if the situation warranted it.

The Kum was an important person. He had to show what he could do and Kets Kume was just one of many ways he could demonstrate his worthiness. He was supposed to be the *Ace* card in the deck *(Kets)* a provider – a man of substance who was committed to take on the weighty responsibilities handed to him. Even before the marriage ceremony began, other men stood around the fringes of the church steps and passed around a jug of *Jim Beam,* a gift from Kum and yet another token of his generosity. It was also a precursor of the celebration that was to follow. Some preferred to stay outside for the entire service, enjoying the camaraderie of each other and *John Barley Corn* as opposed to the formal proceedings going on. Nobody minded a bit.

Now, the guests had already settled inside the church hall while the bride and groom posed with Pops for the formal wedding pictures.  Soon they would join the waiting audience.  But before they did, Kum would come out first, and on command pull coins out of both his pockets, throwing them high into the air.  Whatever we found was ours to keep.  And good old *Ace* would make sure we got enough for our time.  Just another signal of how powerful he really was as the couple's designated protectorate.

When I saw the door open I inched forward, then cupped my hands over my mouth.  "Kets Kume!"

In a flash, the bridegroom, who was dressed in his tux, reached into his pockets and used both hands tossing the coins into the air.  We were being rained on with money and when the jingling coins skipped and spun all around the sidewalk, it was our cue to move fast.

"There...over there," I yelled.  When I bent down to pick up the quarter that fell near my feet somebody snatched it right out from under me.

I wheeled around and spotted a fifty-cent piece.  Again, one of the kids I didn't know beat me to the punch.  Only this time he did it with a shoulder block.

"Hey! What you doin'?"

He didn't bother to answer; he and his two partners were working the sidewalk like street sweepers.  When I went for another coin, one of them pulled me away while the other snatched it up.  They were starting to do a lot of damage.  I tried to pick up another one, only this time I was greeted with a punch in my side.  I grabbed it and faced the bigger kid who was smiling at me.

"Hey! That ain't fair. You guys can't do that! Gimme that coin!" I snapped, trying to pull it out of his hands.

"Beat it!" When I stepped toward him he pushed me again and I landed on my behind. He laughed again.

I felt humiliated.  This was my turf!  I worked for this opportunity.  I scrambled to my feet and bolted for another loose coin but ran into yet another roadblock that put me flat on my back.  The rage inside me was boiling.  Kets Kume had been going on for more than ten minutes but I hadn't picked up a single coin.

The strangers kept up the pressure, edging me out at every turn.  My rage suddenly turned into tears of desperation.  I glared at the boys who by this time managed to pick up a big pile of coins.  Mikey had his back to me and was stuffing change into his pocket. There was nothing left except to sit down on the steps and cry.

As quickly as it had begun it was all over.  The kids had picked clean every inch of the sidewalk and then disappeared into the hall.  I sat by myself, fighting back the sobs.

"What's the matter?  What's wrong?" Mikey asked.  His voice sounded as if it was a thousand miles away.

I looked up at him.

"Why you cryin'?"

"Nuthin'! I wanna go, okay!"

Mikey patiently stood by looking as he looked down me, still trying to understand what had happened, but not having much luck.

"How much did you get?" he finally asked.

"I didn't'...."

"Huh?"

"Yeah, zero...those guys...they got in my territory. They pushed me around. Every time I tried to pick up something one of them pushed me out of the way and his buddy took it. Who are they, anyway?"

"I think they're cousins of Ronnie Chambers...they don't come around much. They're *Croatians.* I seen 'em before down at *Polaski's Dance Hall* down near 7th Street."

"Damn Catholics! Why don't they stay where they belong and do their own Kets Kume? Why they have to beat up on me? "

"Do they do that?" Mikey asked.

"What?"

"Who cares! All I know is that they took my money. All of it...and now they're gone."

Mikey stood quietly as he watched me fight back a new surge of tears.

"No wonder we don't like them. I bet they wouldn't like it one bit if we came to their church and did that to them," I mumbled as I dusted off my trousers.

Mikey considered the point then shrugged it off. Having people take things away from him was a regular occurrence. Living over on Strawberry Hill meant having to hold your mud almost on a daily basis. Sometimes you made out okay...then there were times you weren't so lucky.

"C'mon...let's go inside. I need a *Nehi,"* he finally said. The idea made sense. There was nothing left here, anyway. I stood and walked toward the church hall entrance.

Mikey stopped and looked at me.

"What?"

"Here..." he said, stuffing his right hand into his pants pocket. He opened his palm revealing several fifty-cent and quarter pieces. "Take 'em... I want you to."

"No, I can't...it ain't right."

"It's okay.... Those guys beat you out of it.... They didn't play fair and square. Go on...I got plenty."

His determined expression told me he wasn't going to take no for an answer. I held out my hand and took the coins.

"Thanks...." They felt good as I stuffed them in my pants pocket.

Mikey smiled as he opened the hall door.

"Heck...we're buddies...ain't we?"

"Yeah...buddies for sure...for life."

Mikey slapped me on the shoulder as we went inside and took the steps two at a time into the hall.

"And those Croatians…they can go to hell," he said.

"Yeah," I said.  "They deserve it…straight there, and they don't get to collect no two hundred dollars neither for passing '*Go*', neither."

We both laughed, drawn to the sounds of the tamburitzas.

###

# My Finest Hour…

"**S**tevie… Help… Get him off me…"

I looked around to see where the call for help was coming from. There, under a tree and on the front lawn of a house on *Valley Street,* I saw Donald. Somebody…I couldn't make out whom exactly, was on top of him.

I ran to get a closer look and couldn't believe my eyes. It was some kid named *Harold Parrish.* He was from the Ozarks…and already well into becoming a professional drifter at twelve or so. He was a stocky, incredibly strong predator who sported carrot red hair. It was an ugly kind of red orange shade with blotchy patches of dishwater blond hanging sloppily around the nape of his neck. He would show up unannounced in a neighborhood and deal grief to anybody that caught his fancy. Harold was an indiscriminate hunter, attacking for no real reason, or provocation. Already, he had dropped out of school and now had nothing to do except make other people's lives miserable. But he was mean as hell, too, and that meant giving somebody like him a wide berth.

"Get him off me…I'm choking," Donald pleaded again, but this time his voice sounded coarse and distant. Harold's knees were on Donald's back with his right arm wrapped around his neck in a chokehold. He was pulling on him hard using his other hand to form a deadly vice grip. He was in trouble.

I thought about the situation. Was this my fight? Did I want to hurt myself? But when I saw the blood starting to ooze out of his nose – a dark almost purple color I had never seen before, I knew the answers. I ran hard as I could and dove headfirst at him, grabbing one of the straps to his bib overalls as I flew over him. It was just enough to tilt him to his side and allow Donald enough leverage to get back on his feet.

I could see the ugly colored blood still running freely down his nose. As he tried to regain his composure his legs wobbled from the strain, but he was holding on. He took his shots for sure. His left eye was already turning into a purple-colored shiner. Donald instinctively knew that his bigger size was all the leverage he had. He had already figured out that he was far too slow to duke it out toe-to-toe, and too clumsy to hold his own wrestling. His only real chance was to get one clear shot where he could really *T-off.* Once the lithe-built and agile redhead got him off his feet, then it was all to his advantage.

"What do you want? I never did anything to you," Donald said, as he backed up in a defensive maneuver, with Parrish stalking him, moving in to cut off the yard space like a fighter cuts off an opponent in the ring.

Parrish didn't answer.  He just smiled.  It was more of an ugly sneer that revealed a couple of front teeth had already rotted.

"I don't want any trouble from you," he said.  "Leave me alone."

I watched as the two of them continued to circle, Donald backing up and Harold closing in.  I wondered when he would make his move.  Donald's fists were clinched and white knuckles tight.  His face was a roadmap of his thoughts.  It was covered with the look of fear that told him he was in a situation beyond his control.  Donald was quickly becoming the helpless leaf on a current of water right in front of my eyes.  He was in virgin territory and quickly learning an important lesson in life.  He was losing and there wasn't a thing he could do about it.

Harold feigned a couple of false charges, but backed off.  I stood on the sidelines wondering, what if anything, I should do to help.  It was as if I was invisible.  Even my lightweight, *Bonsai* charge didn't get the attacker's attention.  His total focus and hatred was directed only at Donald.

"What you boys doin'?  You better go off my lawn before I call the cops!"

I looked toward the house front porch and saw an old man standing at the screen door.

He stepped outside.

"Get outta here, right now, you hear me?  You wanna be roughnecks, then do it somewhere else.  Git!"

Parrish looked at Donald.  His sneer had become even more sinister.  Then he looked toward the man.  The intervention worked.

He turned to leave, running backwards down the sidewalk and pointing an accusing finger at Donald.

"I better not catch you again," he said, his accent laden with a Southern drawl that was laced with arsenic.  "I'll kick your Hunkey ass from here to St. Louis – big time basketball hero."  He turned and sprinted down the street toward the yards, disappearing over a small rise.

I ran up to Donald who by now had pulled out a handkerchief and was wiping his still bleeding nose.

"You okay?"

"Yeah," he said, dusting himself off, then picking up his schoolbooks and papers that were scattered everywhere on the ground.

We started walking toward home down *Lowell Avenue.*  Donald's customary gait was gone – so was his booming voice.  He looked like he'd just been in a war...and he had.

"Why'd he pick on you?  You know him?"

"I saw him a long time ago.... He said he didn't like *Hunkeys.*"

"What's a Hunkey?"

Donald glanced down at me, still wiping his nose.  The blood had now turned into more familiar looking cherry red.

*"Us...."*

"You mean Serbian people?"

He nodded.

"And for that he tried to beat you up?"

He nodded again.

"Why?"

"How should I know?" he snapped. "He just doesn't like us – I don't know why…."

We walked in silence. I looked up at Donald. His battered face and bruised pride made me realize something I never recognized before: *he was a friend*…more than that, he was my *Serbian* friend. Being called something like that for no reason. Who was he, this white trash to speak to him that way? Or about me for that matter? I wanted to punch Harold Parrish in the nose.

Donald turned toward his house. When he did, he stopped and looked at me. His expression said it all.

"Thanks…."

"For what?"

"For what you did. Getting him off me."

"Heck that was nuthin'…."

"Thanks anyway."

He turned and I watched him walk the last few steps and disappear into his house. For the first time ever, I was glad as hell to see the Yovetich *swagger* had returned.

I turned and began the climb *Lowell Avenue* for Bethany and home. As I walked I picked up my pace. First it was a quick jog, then I broke into an all out sprint. It was uncontrollable. I felt great. A sense of pride and exhilaration I had never experienced before. I knew I had made a big discovery about myself. I knew that no matter what, I could deliver. I could be counted on. I knew that now. *Best of all, Donald Yovetich knew it, too.*

###

# The Junction...

**P**ops stood up from the stack of railroad ties he used as a temporary seat as soon as he saw the powerful locomotive headlight in the distance. I stood too, then threw a quick glance down at Brownie, my mutt, to make sure that he wasn't doing anything stupid. When the train came by it would surely make a racket, and I didn't want my dog to panic. But Brownie couldn't care less. It was a sultry late August night and Brownie was catching up on welcomed snooze, thanks to the cooling breezes that had popped up from nowhere and cooled the railroad yards.

The passenger train was still some distance away, but in the darkness I could tell that it was already making its way off the Highline. It had briefly stopped to pick up passengers at the 7th Street Station that was attached to the bridge crossing both the Union Pacific and Rock Island's freight yards. I nervously shifted on my feet anticipating what I knew was going to happen next.

It was a ritual I had seen a hundred times but somehow I could never get my fill. Watching a train and imagining what the string of passenger cars would look like once they got here – then listening to the big diesels cranking up for their appointed schedules, going to anywhere.

It was just me and Pops, and good old Brownie. The trip to the end of Bethany came up unexpectedly. I was playing in the living room when Pops suddenly came in and waved for me to follow. Earlier I saw him talking to AJ's Mom out near the gate and he learned that the whole family was going to Houston tonight to see their dad who had been put on a special job down with the truck company he worked for a few months. They had decided to take the train. It was the Rock Island's *Twin Star Rocket.*

Pops said he would see them off and told them to sit on the right hand side of their car when they left town. If we were lucky we might be able to give them a trackside send off.

Going to Terminal Junction was something I hadn't done with Pops for a long time. It seemed like forever, actually. With all the goings on in church lately he wasn't around much. His decision to go now was a surprise, and especially this time of night.

Pops generally liked to go down to the yards around sunset, when it was still light enough to see the tracks and surrounding yards. Generally that meant no passenger trains were due in or out, unless they were really late. But there were always the freights. These days you never knew what was coming out of the UP yards – a giant (4-12-2), 9000 class steamer on rare occasions still plied the rails west of Kansas City in 1952, or maybe one of those bright yellow Alco diesels that were taking over slowly but surely.

Once we got there we settled in, listening to the sounds of cars being switched on the Rock Island side of the yards.  The Terminal Junction telegrapher came out to have himself a smoke and Pops chatted with him about nothing special.  He didn't like to bother him much, but in truth I think the railroad man was kind of glad to see us.  Sometimes his work got pretty lonely.

Terminal Junction was a working man's zone for sure.  The constant sound of the telegrapher's key echoing inside on the loudspeaker up and down the line to Topeka, plus all the phone calls and typing train orders inbetween – they all generated a sense of urgency that things were happening in places I couldn't see, but that were still connected to us.  Sooner or later we'd be involved.

The command center for everything was located dead center in his desk.  It was the big brass telegrapher's key with its black plastic key button where he used *Morse Code* to talk to other telegraphers along the line.  There was a yellow Kansas City Terminal train orders pad that had perfectly cut sheets of carbon neatly slipped in-between each sheet.  And on the other, a set of pads where he would scratch out the order by hand as he listened to the code signal and then responded.

Within arm's reach and stacked neatly on one another were three *Book of Rules* – the *Kansas City Terminal, Union Pacific and Rock Island Railroads.* I rarely saw him use any of them, though.  The telegraphers had long ago memorized the important rule numbers and routinely used them in virtually all of the train movements they authorized.

Gracing the perimeter, along the top of the desk were several sharpened *Number 2* pencils neatly lined up like a yellow picket fence.  Off to his left and resting on a metal stand all to itself was an old *Smith-Corona* typewriter.  All the margins had been preset to accept the stack of three orders he slipped under the roll bar and locked into place with the paper holder.  Using a two-finger technique, the telegrapher whacked out the train orders in simple, declarative sentences.

### First Subdivision – Speed Restriction: Rule 14c
**All Westbound trains must slow to 25 miles-per-hour, Milepost 33.2 to Milepost 34.2 for track repairs, Linwood**

### First Subdivision — Work Extra: Rule 422
**Work Extra 292 has right over all trains on eastward track, or both tracks, between Mileposts 21.4 to Milepost 25.3, Loring**

Sometimes when it got really busy he'd put on an old pair of headsets with frayed wiring, then work the telegrapher's key and telephone simultaneously. That was impressive. When he was in that mode, he was ready for anything the UP and Rock Island threw his way.

When the telegrapher finished typing the train movement orders on the yellow-colored *flimsies,* he attached several to a row of V-shaped wooden sticks that were lined up against the far wall near the screen door. He deftly used a piece of string, stretching and tying each end across its widest part at the top, and also making a loop in the center to hold the folded train orders. Then he sat down and bided his time until he heard it...the intrusive *buzz* and *click* of the emerald green warning light that popped on inside a battered wooden receiver sitting on a small desk next to the windowsill. A passenger train was arriving from the West and heading for the Highline. It had just passed *Kaw Junction.* Action stations....

He got up out of his squeaky wooden chair that had a soft cushion lined on the back. His gait had a bounce to it as he picked up the three-train order sticks he had already prepared as he headed through the screen door. Once trackside he patiently waited until the train's headlight popped into view as it passed under the *18th Street* overpass. The train closed in but he held his ground, like a matador waiting for a charging bull.

When the locomotive glided by he lifted the first of the order sticks high in the air to the engine crew – then again to the brakeman in the center of the train and the conductor standing on the vestibule on the last car. After performing a visual safety check, he'd turn and go back into his telegrapher's shack, ready to build a new set of orders for the next train.

It was an orderly routine. Knowing this gave me a sense of power...of understanding that some things in life remain the same and that made me feel safe and secure. I could somehow *predict* the future. Railroads are like that – life isn't.

*** 

Pops dusted off the side of his dark blue pants as he continued to peer down the track at the headlight. Locomotive headlights are different from regular ones. They're more yellow looking, actually, kind of a cross between an orange and banana color. They're brighter, too, and they seem to me to signal a friend is approaching – a very big friend. I stepped closer to him, looking in the same direction. By now the headlight was flooding the track and casting its beam on the rails in front of it. They shimmered a steel reflection, growing brighter as the train neared. Through the stream of oncoming light, I could detect the train's snake-like movement as it drifted off the Highline lead track and crossed several switches as it approached us. It was an unstoppable event that had only one outcome.

"Is that it?" Poppa.

He looked down at me, and in the light's growing luster I could see the same look of excitement in his expression. He nodded and smiled. I grabbed his hand and it felt good. Pops and me…together, we could figure out just about anything.

Now just yards away, two sleek red, maroon and silver painted diesels approached, their sides bathed only slightly by a lonely street light standing along the side of the old dirt road. The light had no real place in the master plan to keep Kansas City brightly lit at night. In fact, it offered nothing of the sort. It was there, I suspect, more as a matter of satisfying a bureaucrat's regulatory penchant to have lights placed at specific intervals and locations throughout the city. Its dull glow barely reached the perimeter of the Terminal Junction property line. But it still managed to perform an unexpected service: Thanks to its indirect light, I caught my first glimpse of the shimmering stainless steel passenger cars that were following obediently behind the engines.

I glanced toward the railroad shack, and in the growing light I saw the telegrapher standing next to the main line. He was challenging the *bull* yet again, holding one of the train order sticks in his right hand, and storing the balance in the other. The ritual was about to begin.

"Is he on time Pops?" I asked, trying to recall if it had made its customary 9:45 p.m. departure out of Union Station. Pops glanced at his watch and nodded, focusing his attention on the approaching streamliner.

"Da…Stevo.... He comes now. We see."

"Will we see AJ?" I asked, then mumbling to myself why I even bothered to want to see some silly girl in the first place.

"We watch close, maybe."

Now I could clearly hear the diesel's steady rumbling. Without warning, the locomotive's melodious chimes cut through the night air. They were typical of the Rock Island's whistles – distinctly soft but set in a close harmony that allowed the sound to glide on the airwaves, warning others of its approach. The chimes were warm sounding, a lot like the railroad that ran the daily streamliner every night down the spine of the nation, and deep into the heart of Texas.

As trains came and went, this one was pretty unique. The *Twin Start Rocket* actually began its run in *Minneapolis* and cut a north-south route through Iowa, then into Missouri, and finally into Kansas, the halfway point on its 1,363-mile journey.

After rolling on Union Pacific rails to Topeka, it found its way to the Rock Island right-of-way and to its division point at *Herrington.* Then it continued southwest and eventually due south through Wichita, into Oklahoma, and then into Texas where it stopped in Dallas, and terminated in Houston – hence that's how it got its name…the *Twin Star Rocket.…*

Not more than ten minutes earlier the UP's *City of St. Louis* had passed us on its straight arrow, no-nonsense run West to Denver, and on to Los Angeles. Brownie slept through that one, too, a veteran of train movements and all the railroad hoopla.

Now it was the Rock Island's turn to strut their stuff, following on the heels of its yellow-colored competitor. It was a ritual of predictable sound I heard from my house on countless nights, but up until now it had always been too late to see for myself how all of this came about.

"Watch, Stevo," Pops warned. "She come close now."

I looked into the blinding light and saw the telegrapher was now totally awash in its brilliance. He deftly hoisted one of the bamboo sticks high into the air. Then, just as the engine was almost directly in front of him, the headlight dimmed.

I rubbed my eyes behind my thick glasses, trying to adjust to the change of light and the scene unfolding in front of me. But already I detected the silhouette of a man hanging gracefully outside of the engine cab door, his arm extended fully outward, ready to snatch the train orders in his forearm.

I inched closer as the locomotive fireman and telegrapher performed a railroad ballet, each involved in a perfectly sequenced choreography of man and machinery working in harmony. Then, with one graceful swoop of his hand and arm, the fireman ran his arm under the taut string, holding his forearm up and close to his chest like somebody who just gave a pint of blood. The train orders were with him snug and safe – their roadmap to the track conditions ahead.

"Pops! Look! It's Uncle Fuzzy. He's on the Twin Star! See?"

Somehow, in the midst of all the action and above the din of the growling units that were now free to sprint West, Uncle Fuzzy had figured us out, too. As the engine flashed by he looked back and waved. I saw his wide, warm smile as he thundered into the night.

I was still watching him when Pops tugged at my arm.

"Watch now…Stevo…. See windows…look."

The fluted stainless steel cars looked as if they were gilding on a magic carpet, the passenger car trucks painted an identical silver color and muffling the contact the wheels were making with the rails. The cars were moving faster by the second now. The diesels stepped up their growl as I held my focus on the sides of the passing train, trying to capture glimpses of the people who were inside. For an instant I thought I saw them in the lounge car, then in one of the coaches, but before I could tell for sure the car flashed by.

All that was left now were the three trailing Pullman cars, and as the train gathered speed, I strained to see who might be inside. Many of the passengers had already turned off their bedroom lights and pulled down the car's window blinds, indifferent to what Kansas City had to offer. But when the last car approached by I spotted a single light still on, almost at the end.

I was beginning to think that seeing Uncle Fuzzy was the only surprise I would get tonight. But then I saw AJ's face flush against the car window. Next to her were her brother, Jeffrey, and little sister, Linda. Her Mom was standing behind them and waving.

"There they are, Pops!" I shouted, waving my arms and jumping as they flashed by. In the blur I saw AJ smiling and waving back, pushing her face against the glass even more as they rolled into the blackness past the telegrapher's shack. Then, they were gone.

I watched the streamliner's oscillating red rear-car warning light twisting slowly in the dark getting smaller and turning into a pinpoint of light as the darkness swallowed it. In the distance I heard the melodious chimes sounding again, and for all the world I wished I were on that train with her. I didn't care...AJ could tease me...kick me in the shins like she always liked to do...or even make me play *Old Maid* all night and listen to her stupid little girl stories. Heck, she could even win for all I cared. I just wanted to be on that train going somewhere...anywhere.

*** 

Pops and I walked in silence, both of us basking over what we'd seen together as we made our way up Bethany Street toward home. Brownie was there too, trotting along a few yards behind; no doubt not pleased that we jarred him out of his well-disciplined snooze for the hike up the hill.

Pops pulled out the pack of *Chesterfields* from his shirt pocket, pausing for a moment to light up. He took a long drag and smiled, looking over at me.

"Stevo, you tell Papa what your favorite train is? You have favorite, right?"

"You already know that, Pops."

He laughed and resumed walking.

*"Da...I know, Stevo...but you tell me again, okay?"*

"The *Zephers...Burlington Route*...Silver...black and really fast! And they've got dome cars...you can see everything."

Pops stopped and flashed a mock look of surprise.

"You no like *Eagle*? How about *Eagle*? We take it to Omaha...*ide kao zmia!*...in the hills...Beautiful...."

"It's okay, Pops...blue and white is a nice color for a train," I said matter-of-factly.

Pops took another drag off his cigarette as he thought over the comment. He had the kind of mind that could be thorough once he zeroed in on something that really interested him. He could intellectually peel an onion on any subject. When it came to train talk I didn't mind. But when it came to why I didn't do well in my arithmetic class – well, that was another story.

"Zepher...no come here to Kansas City?"

"No, Pops, it does...*The Silver Streak*...it's the only one, though. It goes to Omaha."

"Then*?*"

"Then to California...the *California Zepher*...and the *Denver Zepher,* but it don't have any domes. It's just really fast."

"Okay..." Pops said, nodding to himself approvingly over the deal he just made in his head.

"Pops? What is it?"

He looked at me and smiled.

"Next year we go to Omaha...then Colorado, you pick train...you pick, Burlington, okay?  You pick Eagle, also okay."

The news overwhelmed me.  I ran toward Pops and wrapped my arms around his waist, then looked up into his smiling face.

"You mean it?  You mean we can take the California Zepher and go through the Moffat tunnel."

"*Da*...but you must do something for me, first okay?"

I pulled away, giddy with joy and eager to please.

"You have long time before we go next year."

"What Papa, what do I have to do?"

"You remember who you are – you are son of the Serbian Orthodox priest.  People watch how you are.  You make mistake – *they* talk.  Then they tell me – and hurt Mama."

Pops started walking again, slowly making his way onto the brick sidewalks that led to our house.

"You are different.... You never forget."

"Have the people said I was bad, Pops?"

He smiled and gently patted me on the top of my head.

"No...nobody speak nothing.  But you must always be...*perfect,* always."

I looked into my father's eyes.  I was determined that he would never have to worry, ever, about anything I ever did.

"I promise, Pops...honest... I can do it...and I will."

We resumed our walk in silence again, preoccupied with our own thoughts.  I thought about all the planning and decisions I had to make.  Studying the various railroad time tables, scouring over the arrival and departure times...checking out the towns along the way...looking over the equipment for every train I had in mind...figuring out what I wanted in what had to be the longest train ride I would ever take.  Then I slipped my hand into Pops' and began to swing it gently back and forth as we continued walking.

"Pops...what's a *DP*?"

In the dim light I could see his smile had suddenly faded.

"Who teach that word, Stevo?"

"Nobody, I just hear lots of people use it.  What does it mean?"

"It means someone who has no *kucha (house)*."

"You mean those people who come to church now?  They have no homes?"

"*Da*...they come from war...now live here with us and try to make new lives.  They are very poor."

"And we help them?"

"*Da*...because...they like us, Stevo...they need help, so we help."

"Then why is everybody fighting in the hall all the time?"

The question caught him off guard.

"What you mean...*fighting*...Stevo?"

"Lots of folks…I see them. I even saw you getting mad at one of them…"

Pops stopped and glared at me.

"*Sednitsas (meetings)* no for children…why you watch?  Why you no go play with your friends?"

His sudden irritation frightened me a little.

"I was just watching, Pops…like I like to do sometimes.  I didn't mean nuthin', honest."

Pop's expression turned softer again.  He put his arm around me and we began to walk.

"These people…they come from the old country…they see war, Stevo.  They see how communists throw God away.  They don't like…they want it like before."

"Then why are they angry here…we didn't throw God away."

The question forced him to nod his head slowly and smile.

"God lives here…yes.  So we try and show them okay?  Maybe soon they see everything and we all be happy.  We look…and see…we try."

"Maybe…" I thought to myself as we stepped through the small gate leading to our front porch.  But I was having a lot of trouble believing it.  There was something not right. Not much laughing and happiness any more. People were mad at each other.  Every night I heard Mom and Pops talk about it…the phone calls in the middle of the night and Pops leaving, sometimes not coming back until the morning.  Ever since they arrived things were different, and I didn't like it.  I didn't like it one bit.

###

# Epilogue

## *Home*

*T*here are voices in the wind that welcome me every time I visit Bethany Street...I think they are the Spirits of Kansas City, Kansas. Maybe I'm the only one who can hear them, but I don't think so. They are there all right, and they speak with clarity. All you need to do is to listen.... They want to talk – they demand to be heard. They are the clarions of our past. They will not be denied.

They tell me how it was – of the men and women who toiled on Bethany and in the surrounding neighborhoods to elevate America to the leading edge of the community of nations. They speak proudly of the strong backs and callused hands that made it so. They talk of family pride, of educating their young, and a handshake that was a man's word, or at what can be achieved when men and women come together from all walks of life to support a common cause. They speak to me about all of these things. But every time they do I can also hear the numbing sobs of sadness at what it has become today.

***

I can see for myself the source of their pain. The battered homes...the posted, handwritten placards nailed to wooden lamp posts by residents coping with the invasion of drug dealers and hustlers roaming their streets. These are rag-tag protests at best, but they come from the soul. The decay that always accompanies neglect and abandonment is everywhere. It's the new trademark of Bethany entering a New Millennium.

Bethany Street's always been a sanctuary for the immigrant. The Highland Park Cemetery tombstone epitaphs proclaim the names of those who prospered in this new land, living lives of modest achievement, then moving on as it is inevitable with all living creatures. Yet in doing so, forging a cycle of tradition that's still evolving today. The events that marked their presence on earth have long passed. Only our fading memories remind us they were here at all.

Mr. Danowski and Mr. Schnyder are both gone now, but I wonder if they've finally found a way to mend their differences, thanks to Divine Intervention and God's gentle hand. I hope so...it was such a silly, man-made concern. Decades later during a visit to St. George Church I watched two Hispanics square off on the corner of Lowell and Bethany. The argument over a fender bender began in the mid-afternoon. The men were standing nose-to-nose, heatedly making their points in Spanish. With my hit-and-miss ability to translate the facts, it sounded like a going-

*nowhere event. Hours later when I left the church and the late afternoon sun was finally cooling off the day, they were still there, and pretty much in the same state of mind. Finally, a cop car showed up and moved things along.*

*It was all pretty funny, watching those men in their mid-thirties wildly waving their arms and pointing accusing fingers at one another – neither willing to give an inch. I dismissed it with a laugh, writing off their antics as nothing more than a couple of silly immigrants whose ignorance got in the way of their common sense, and in doing so letting their emotions take over. I saw it as typical of what you would expect from those foreigners. But then I thought about Mr. Danowski and Mr. Schnyder way back in 1949. They did the same thing, except they took theirs all the way to the Pearly Gates. False pride and blind faith…powerful forces that can drive us all to the pinnacle at what we are capable of achieving for the good of others, and ironically are also the seeds of our own destruction.*

*So many of those early immigrants are Highland Park Cemetery residents now. They never made it into the New Millennium, but I don't think they were really counting on it. Germans, Italians, Irish, Polish, Croatians and Serbs – on earth they all had one thing in common: The undeniable look of hope in their eyes. A belief that this new land would help them turn their dreams into realities. And with it burning desires to pay whatever price necessary to pass it all to the next generation to enjoy.*

*But among today's newcomers all I really see are the dull, lifeless expressions that invariably accompany extraordinarily hard times. Their futile undertaking to find a way to survive in a new economy world where increasingly everybody needs a high-tech driver's license to get along. Where* dot.com *savvy is tantamount to reading, writing and 'rithmetic. As a result, these new ground rules choke the breath out of new life, covering the light of hope with darkness. Repeated failure and the inability to compete nurtures negativity in a world that in turn systematically destroys dreams, punches holes in our passion to achieve excellence, and ushers in the darkest sides of the human condition. It invades the soul and ultimately leaches into the very land itself. It's everywhere, and we call it many names: ignorance, poverty, desperation, agony, emptiness, rejection, segregation and prejudice. Bethany Street today is a mirror of all these – its streets have been turned into a social report card of the "haves and have-nots."*

***

*Yet, despite the ugly symbols of sadness I see today on every corner, buried deep within the soil of Bethany one can still hear the faint chimes of hope ringing their distant defiance. It begins during the late afternoon when shafts of soft light give way to the approaching blanket of night. When the smell of cut grass greets the dusk. When crickets serenade the neighborhoods with their continual vvvreeeee…vvvreeeee…vvvreeeees of their nightly mating calls. The chimes of our spirits of the past are buried in all of this, far removed yes, but not silenced. They are ringing for their right to be reborn again, and they find sanctuary among the shapes and forms from out of our past that are still standing. These structures are the soldiers of another time standing guard today, only now they're surrounded by scenes of poverty and social decay. Yet, incredibly, they protect it all as if it were gold, giving no quarter. They tell us about our proud past, but they aren't what they once were; they've been mutated into the world we have today. But they are here with us anyway, and wherever they can, they continue to serve us faithfully.*

*The old A&P grocery store on Central Avenue that rang in modern living among the blue collar workers in 1950 has given way to a cheap odds-and-ends store today. Its role may have changed, yes, but the building still serves a purpose. It is needed.*

*Hassig's Drug Store is in a lot of ways just as it was, standing guard at its 10th and Central location just as it did more than five decades ago, or even longer. But gone is the marble soda fountain and high back metal stools where the soda jerk cheerfully made vanilla, cherry and chocolate Cokes for kids coming home from school. The pharmacy is the main attraction now. Just as it was decades ago, it's still a haven to bring relief to this new society of immigrants. It stands for something.*

*The Fidelity Bank on 10th and Central is a pawnshop in today's world – the ultimate symbol of a neighborhood's decay. Ironically, for these immigrants it's a source of cash, and sometimes a final, often desperate, last resort to survival. Not a bank...but a kind of financial institution all the same. It is necessary.*

*Mrs. Evango's little corner store is boarded up now, but the brick building is still sturdy and strong, waiting for an assignment in a new world that probably will never come. She's there, too – standing over her big, black cash register. I know...I felt her presence when I dropped by one day for a social call. She said she was glad to see me...*honey please look*...she said. The "ching-ching" of her metal plated NCR register never sounded better.*

*Prescott grade school is gone, too – but today it's a park where sounds of children at play still float on gentle neighborhood breezes, just as they did decades ago.*

*Our parish house is no more, as is Gramps and Grams' – demolished to put in an asphalt parking lot for my church. When I stand on the spot where my home once was, I can see it as clearly today as if I was looking at it in 1949. I see my folks sitting on the simple front porch, or Mom alongside the low standing, silver-colored cyclone fence talking to Aunti-Mac about this and that...about fear...frustration...and life. No different than the knots of Hispanics today who find time to talk over their parched and battered hedgerow fences that survived, even though nobody cared.*

***

*The rutted dirt road at the base of Bethany Street that once led to the wooden Terminal Junction telegrapher's office is gone, replaced now by the I-70 turnpike. Only a silver-coated metal signal shack that houses electronic gear next to the tracks serves as a reminder that there are memories still hanging around here. It also blandly declares man to be redundant in this increasingly automated world. No more rat-a-*

tat-tats *of the telegrapher's* Morse Code *key echoing inside the room where the smell of cigarettes and cigars never, ever leaves.*

*Still, the shed's location tugs at my memories – it's just a few yards from where the telegraphers endured a 24-hour-a-day railroad challenge, and also where Pops, me, and Brownie watched the sleek streamliners roar into the sunset. They're all gone...but the mainline is still a pulsating two-track steel ribbon that today supports more than 100 trains a day, and with even more planned – piggyback trailer trains, coalers, freights with Chinese sounding company names on the sides of container cars going to Asian ports across the Pacific.*

*Muncie, Edwardsville, Bonner Springs...Turner and Olathe...they are all there, too. But instead of fields of corn and plowed farmland separating one from the other, now it's warehouses, trailer parks and drive in convenience stores that pepper the Kaw Valley landscape.*

*Bonner Springs is on the map as the new home of a* NASCAR *racetrack. Speed and Americans...inseparable as mother and apple pie...a genuine red, white and blue addiction. I worry that old, reliable, Bonner will go Hollywood on me once those TV cameras zero in. I don't think so.... The seed store is still boss around these parts. Always been that way – always will be. Farmland has its own cadre of followers. It's a deeper relationship than all those screaming fans watching 400+ horsepower cars going 'round and 'round an asphalt circle.*

***

Minnesota Avenue *is no longer the heart of local shopping it once was, and it hasn't been that for a very long time. Its meandering, neither here nor there mall road looks like it lost its way. Maybe it's more to do with politics, passion, and egos pulling it every which way than the road design, I really don't know. But the library is still there, which means that kids from all of the community's ethnic and racial groups can reach out for knowledge, if they want it. They can see beyond the horizon by simply taking a moment to go inside. Some do...and they are always greeted by courteous smiles and warmth that is so unique to Midwestern folks.*

*The old* Huron Building *– once touted as the tallest in Kansas, was imploded; the* Town House Hotel *overlooking the Bottoms is now a home for old folks, but here again it's fulfilling a mission of a kind – offering shelter and comfort to someone who may need it more today than back in the days when businessmen sat around in the lounge and cut their deals; or when a stray husband cautiously picked up a room key and quickly disappeared into an elevator; or when tired travelers and their children held up for the night on their way to California to find work in the defense industry; or for the dreamers going the same way who were convinced that stardom was their divine destiny. It was there for all of them, an oasis overlooking the Kaw – the last stop before plunging into a sea of flowing wheat fields.*

*The former* Katz Drug *store on 10th and Minnesota is still something of its historic self, only now there's a new name taking it into the Millennium. Like the city it serves, it has evolved – first it became* Skaggs, *and today the* Osco Drugstore *and building. What's in a name? To lawyers hell bent on writing the perfect contract, it's a legal best seller.  To Kansas Cityans, it's just a ripple reflecting a gentle change in the pond of life.*

*Another historic and personal milestone of a much smaller scale is the discovery in a Bonner Springs giant supermarket that* Valomilks *are still around.  The Merriam, Kansas, company has somehow found a way to keep its chocolaty, marshmellowy sticky filling out there on the front lines in the high volume, supermarket wars that defines America's eating habits today.  The candy's adhesive quality is so damn good it gives* Super Glue *a run for its money.  And here it is today, stacked in piles inside in its own display box in front of the registers – positioned to hook yet another generation.  I dived right and picked up an armful, waving at other shoppers to join me.  They thought I was nuts, but they obviously didn't have a clue about its "original flowering center" promo copy written on its silver-white wrappers, plain as day.  They weren't kidding.  Folks who come from Merriam never lie, cheat and steal. What you see is really what you get.  Valomilks are proof positive.*

***

*Over at 18th and Minnesota you can still see the remnants of the old Kaw Valley interurban line.  The streets are pretty much as they were five decades ago – only now, well-worn dirt paths and cement parking lots cover the fading signs that something important once passed through here that was an intimate part of a city and a region's unique history.  Beyond the intersection, the railway right-of-way widens into a gully just below* Wyandotte High School.  *If you happen to chat with some of the old timers who still live there and ask them about the line, they'll think it over a spell.  Then they smile.  It's a kind of reaction you'd expect when somebody remembers an old friend who passed on, but is not forgotten.*

*I spotted a lone female officer sitting in a patrol unit in a vacant lot.  I introduced myself.  She flashed a familiar Midwestern smile that overshadowed the big service revolver and nightstick on her hips when she got out to chat a while.  I pointed to the high school, remembering names such as* Coach Walt Shublom *and his powerhouse basketball teams.  She was too young to remember those years first hand, but she nodded as if she knew all about it anyway – stories, no doubt, that drifted in and out of the station over the years, comparing the then to now where Kansas basketball stood, and where it was heading.  When it came to that, time stood still.*

*As we talked about those times, I sensed she wished that she could somehow go back in time instead of what she was doing today, patrolling the neighborhoods for burglars, armed robbers, drug dealers, and resolving family disputes.  A time when folks considered it a lifetime embarrassment if ever a police car parked in front of their house and officers knocked on the front door intent to deal with whatever went terribly wrong inside.*

*The officer pulled a card from her uniform shirt pocket and invited me to drop by the station to take a personal "ride along" some night in circa 1999.  A chance to see for myself what Kansas City was all about, and what she and her partners were living every time they went out for a night on the town.*

*Later, I looked over the card. It was more than a PR ploy. She meant it. Not only that, I sensed that she qualified every bit as good as Eli Yovetich and his badge brothers during their time. She was a full-fledged member of the Kansas City Thumper's Club, all right.*

*As a former LAPD reserve officer, I saw first hand how far people were willing to go to enter the gates of Hell. I remembered the gurneys lined alongside the morgue wall and the three autopsy rooms going full blast at LA County General following a routine, typically violent Saturday night in the City of Angels. And how I fought to keep my breakfast down as a more experienced officer pushed me to my limit in a guided tour set up especially for rookies. Later, as we stood at a corner burrito stand in East LA, it was the seasoned cop that ended up heaving his guts into the gutter. And when I offered him some of my beef and beans burrito, telling him, of course, that it looked a lot like the innards of the guy we just saw on the cutting table, he heaved some more. Never mind…I knew then and there I had qualified. I got my membership card into the Brotherhood of the Bell. You know, the kind that lasts a lifetime, and where no diplomas and certificates are ever awarded. But it's yours, anyway. It's stamped in your memory banks…forever.*

*Flashes of recollections came up with the Hispanics who lived in East LA. How they sauntered, stumbled, and even attacked my desk at Hollenbeck station with their never-ending stories of violence and insanity and fears of bodily harm – and of my trying to apply reason and order to lives that had long ago turned into chaotic, dysfunctional, booze and drug laden existences with no end in sight. I thought about all that and I decided to keep my memories about where I grew up in a safe place – in my head, rather than come face-to-face with the realities I knew would overwhelm me once I got into the backseat of a patrol car on a hot, muggy August Saturday night in Kansas City. I stuffed the card into my wallet. It's still there…I hope she is, too.*

***

*Strawberry Hill has given up much of its heritage to progress, a victim of highway engineers who carved out part of its east-facing bluff for I-70 and all points East & West. The engineers knew what we had figured out decades earlier: folks still want to get out of town in a hurry. That hasn't changed. There are dreams beyond the horizon that need tending to. Ours could wait.*

*But like a defiant soldier who lost a limb in battle, what's left of the "Hill" has been put to good use. There's been adjustments for sure, but it's here where the voices of the past ring their harmonious clarity. The homes and those who live in them are now the second, third and even fourth generations of those early Croatian, Serbian and Slovenian immigrants who came to America. St. Anthony and St. Mary's church stand as guardians of the faith just as they did decades ago. Strawberry Hill is not just a neighborhood – it's an act of defiance that not everything in this world operates at light speed through microwave and telecoms links and then up to satellites flitting around the planet. It hasn't succumbed to the "delete", "insert", default", "e-mail", and faster-faster-faster dot.com lifestyle that has evolved our kids into speaking a foreign tongue that promises to "bits and bytes" us all into cyberspace oblivion. Where electronic viruses created in a Third-World country can bring technically superior nation to its knees…when people chewed their fingernails over something that sounds more like ET, the extraterrestrial, rather than a fixable techie problem on terra firma – Y2K, and the doomsday scenario that made the world hold its breath, only to gush in global relief as we all rolled into the New Millennium without a hitch. No…Strawberry Hill is more than that: it's the official keeper of Kansas City's Spirits. People there know exactly where their priorities lie. Maybe somebody should put a sign on the side of the hill just to sort of set the record straight. Make it big enough so the folks whizzing by at 70-plus will understand just how important this place really is. Maybe it should say:*

**Attention, all you New Millennium people…you are now rocketing past Strawberry Hill…. We want you to know that we're different. And that's just fine with us…in fact, we love it! We know exactly where we came from, who we are, and where we're going….**
**Do you?**

**Thank you**
**A Public Service Advertisement Proudly Brought to you by the**
**The Spirits of Kansas City, Kansas….**

*\*\*\**

*But it's the West Bottoms where these changes have been most dramatic and here again the Spirits of our past are being redefined to respond to a new order. Unlike Bethany Street, however, these new economy dollars are surfacing in a very old place.*

*A mound of dirt – a tiny island – with metal outlines of cows that look as if they are stuck on the ends of giant cocktail stir sticks randomly pop out of the foliage. New bridges ease motorists into an area where it was once a challenge to find the way inside the heart of the West Bottoms and the still standing* Golden Ox *Restaurant adjacent to the* Kansas City Livestock Exchange Building *on* Genessee Street.

*There's no sign around telling us why this knot of land is where it is, or what it's intended to do. The answer, I think, lies in its proximity to what's around it. It's the entrance of the old stockyards area – the immigration point, mostly for cattle, but also pigs and other animals that completed their long rail journey on the* Katy Railroad, *and who were all eventually herded to their collective fates inside the slaughter houses. It was here where the cowboys, the dozens of wooden pens, the heavy, harsh smell of animals, and the long cattle trains came together. It was the economy of the times working in a fluid, systematic, and yes, deadly fashion.*

*Today, the same area is the home of yet another new example of orderliness and precision: It's the sprawling, surgically clean exterior of* Gateway Computers *that now dominates. As if drawn by the magnet of commerce that defined this part of the*

*Bottoms since its earliest beginnings, this spot again reflects a new frontier of growth and prosperity. It has become the place where the single most necessary tool in ushering in America's new dot.com economy is being mass assembled and shipped around the nation, just as cattle were gathered, slaughtered and then put on racks and in boxes in decades past. The distinctive black and white patches on the sides of their Gateway computer shipping boxes look like the hide of a Holstein cow. History does repeat itself...well, sort of....*

*Gone...but not totally. Only the dismantled, decaying pieces and stacked remnants of wooden pens in an open parking lot between the Stock Exchange building and the Gateway computer plant validated for what had been a growing concern that my memories were fading fast. History was still hanging around. The dull red bricks that dipped in harmony with the shifting soil beneath them — the very place where millions of cattle hooves passed en-route to their eventual oblivion, confirmed that this was the beginning of the process that eventually put steaks on the table for a nation. I stood next to an abandoned railroad siding where the offloading probably occurred. The tracks were rusted and all but gone now, buried under patches of unruly weeds. Yet it was precisely here that I sensed the Spirits were close to me again. Riding on the soft spring afternoon breezes I heard the distant, muffled sounds of terrified cattle calling to one another and the clash of steel when the slack ran out of a long string of cars that reached its destination. Then the sounds of men at work, urging their quarter horses to herd the confused animals into the waiting pens.*

*"They're still here...everything...just like before," I told my son, Tim, who was busy picking up on the benchmarks that define today's landmarks. He couldn't see into my mind, but I could tell by his expression that he was feeling something. He knew.... Spirits can talk to lots of people...if only they care to listen.*

\*\*\*

*Elsewhere in the Bottoms, the changing of the guard is not as dramatic, nor as contrasting. In fact, one could argue an uneasy truce of sorts exists between the old and new. Near Wyoming and St. Louis Streets a cluster of old red brick buildings still serve useful purposes, but mostly as places to store things. Across the street the symbols that transportation still rules the Bottoms are everywhere. Shingles and logos are mounted on newly prefabricated steel blue and grey, single-story warehouses that allow ample parking space for the big rigs using them. The Wagner Warehouses and Kansas City Shipper's Association – corporations today doing a job that's always been the heart of the Bottoms' working lifestyle. Only now the rusted rails that carried goods to all points are gone, replaced by rubber tires and Teamsters who keep America rolling.*

*It's all a testimony to the West Bottoms and what it took to put it on the map in the first place – the struggle against nature battling three major floods over the past 100 years; the changing economies; and, yes, in its own way the creative shifts to survive – to hold its own in a changing America.*

*There's been plenty of hits along the way, casualties that stood their ground, but in the end were pounded into brick dust obscurity under the weight of the steel ball and chain. Falling in the name of progress:* The Standard Seed Company, Faultless Starch...Rudy Patrick Seeds. *What's left, though, is what counts in the long-term campaign for survival: It's the land...that good old Bottoms earth, ready to support another business, regional commerce and yes, life itself in today's middle America.*

\*\*\*

*You can call it luck, or maybe even Divine guidance. You can call it anything you want but the day that Tim and I literally stumbled into the grand opening of the Science Center at Union Station, my life, and this book, stepped over the line from a collection of fairly vivid memories into a reborn reality!*

*I'd like to think that my visit there after so many decades happened because I was media savvy and heard all about it. That my keen sense of things that were going on around me had put me ahead of the information power curve. But any talk like that is rubbish. We just happened to be in the neighborhood, scouring the main lines just as we always did whenever I went home for a visit. For Tim and me, and sometimes my daughter Stacey when she can make it, going from one train-watching site to another is more than a hobby – it's an obsession!*

*Waiting for trains these days isn't a problem since Kansas City is arguably the second largest rail center in America. Those that rumble through are generally in a hurry just like everything else. For us, though, it's a time for father and son to chew the fat. Somehow, the problems that pop up living in today's cyber world sort of melt away as we peer down the tracks in the eastern Kansas countryside looking for the tell-tale sign of an approaching headlight. Once we get back into town it's only natural for us to pay our respects to the station. To me it's a trip to the* Taj Mahal.

*When I walked through the Union Station's front door and saw the magnificent finish work that so many people had taken on to complete with such devoted, caring attention, I knew that something spiritual had occurred here...I felt as if I were reborn.*

*What a wonderful achievement, I told Tim who stared at the 90-foot high ceilings as if he were looking at the ceiling of the* Sistine Chapel. *It was all there – the concourse, the big clock...the long spacious walkway that led to the track entrances below. Elegant...a monument to the strength and vitality of both Kansas City, Kansas and Missouri. Union Station belonged to everyone. That was a major pillar the founding fathers put into place when they set about to build it in 1910. It's still that way since its official opening in 1914.*

*Then I heard him...the raspy voice of the old man on the loudspeaker, whose Southern drawl echoed off the station's granite walls. The one who used to call the trains coming in and out of Union Station. Those times when Pops and I went inside to see* Mr. Dingworth *to buy our tickets to go to Omaha, Chicago – anywhere! The caller gave it all a sense of excitement and urgency as he announced the streamliners and their destinations.*

*"Attention...Rog Ahhhland...Train... Nummmber Threeee...the*
*Golllden...State...Li-mi-ted... deee-par-ting Track...Six...for*
*Lawwww-rence...*
*Toe...peee...ka - Hair...ring...done – Dall...harddd... -*
*Tu...come...care...eee -*
*El Passssoooo..."*

*He kept his cadence perfectly, slowly, deliberately and precisely, never missing a beat...never missing a destination until, finally...he got us all on time into* **Los Angeleeeezz....**

\*\*\*

*"Did you hear that?" I asked Tim who was absorbed by the station's splendor and trying as best as a 23-year-old could be to get more intimate with such a very special place.*

*"What Dad?"*

*"The voice...that man calling out the trains."*

*Tim looked me over. It was his classic stoic expression that instantly told me something was out of 'round with my comment.*

*"You didn't?"*

*"No."*

*"Oh," I said, coming to grips with the reality that it was all inside my head. That happened to me a lot every time I came home. The Spirit voices were hounding me again.*

*"There used to be a man who called out the trains. Nobody could understand everything real well, but it didn't matter. He was part of the excitement of going. It was him. I just heard him."*

*"You did? What did he sound like?"*

*"Well...he...." Then I stopped dead in my tracks.*

*"Hey, you know what? That's a good question. And you're right on. Maybe you oughta hear him for yourself."*

*A man on a mission, I scoured the concourse looking for someone who looked official. I spotted a young woman sporting a Robin's Egg blue suit coat with a nametag on the jacket. She was pointing to the ceiling and chatting with a couple of bystanders.*

*I tugged at Tim's arm and headed for her. He already figured what was coming. Just as he's always done when he saw me go into my lock-and-load mindset, he patiently took a backseat and more or less went along for the ride. He's a good son...and a lot more sensible than I sometimes give him credit for, but that's another story, altogether. Still, missions are missions...and this time I was on a real Lollapalooza!*

*"Hi," I said, smiling and pulling out a calling card that told her I was living in Singapore and working there as a public relations executive – a tactic that almost*

*always got peoples' attention and gave me the small window I needed to roll into my pitch.*

*"When I was a kid my father and I came here and there was this man who used to call the trains. I was wondering…do you think having something like that now would add to the ambience?"*

*The young woman thought over the suggestion, then smiled and nodded.*

*"Yes…it just might."*

*She looked around and spotted a man in his late thirties standing alone a few yards away.*

*"C'mon…."*

*When we approached, the man turned and smiled, and I sensed he had more than one thing on his mind. He was obviously caught up with seeing that the opening day went off without a hitch. The young lady introduced us. I was on the clock.*

*"What you could do," I said, "is call out the names of the trains at the exact times they arrived and departed. It would be more than background sound – it would be part of the station's factual history, and it would recreate the mood of the nation and Union Station when trains took us everywhere."*

*To me it all sounded perfectly sensible – no sweat, actually, in truth a basic no brainer. I studied his face hoping for some kind of understanding. What I saw was the same kind of practiced smile I had perfected over the years. I stepped closer trying to trigger all my skills to manipulate a better result.*

*"In fact, I used to be a color sports broadcaster for ESPN in Singapore…and I have the old editions of the* Official Railway Guide*…and I would be happy to look them up and put it all on a tape, or a CD," I said, trying to hide the desperation creeping into my voice. I thought about trying to offer an instant demonstration, but bit my lip when I saw the deadpan expression replace his deliberate smile.*

*"Well, that's certainly an interesting idea," he finally said. "We could think about that…. Yes, we could."*

*I was losing my grip.*

*"Of course…. It doesn't have to be me. After all, I realize I live in Singapore and I'm sure that somebody in town knows more than I do about such things…and they'd do it…free, just like I'm willing to do it."*

*I glanced at Tim and the girl, hoping to get an extra push along with my last salvo. The operative words: Free…no charge…zilch…on the house…a public service deal…get it?*

*"Thanks for that. We will certainly keep you and your idea in mind," the executive said, shuffling his feet, a sure sign that my audition was over. I gave him my calling card, shook his hand and he disappeared into the sea of humanity that was around us.*

*I glanced at Tim who quietly took it all in then nodded to the girl who shook my hand and scurried off in the other direction.*

*"He thinks you're nuts, Dad…" Tim said as we turned to go.*

*"He's not the only one."*

*We walked toward another part of the station in silence.*

*"But I still think it's a pretty good idea."*

*I skidded to a halt.*

*"You did? Really?"*

*For Tim, something that was "pretty good" really meant it was super. He wasn't much for using descriptive terms unless he was up to his behind in a college tennis match and things weren't going his way. Then he could be quite creative. More than once the chair umpire had expressed his "appreciation" at his choice of words.*

*"Yeah...it was...."*

*I studied his expression. He really meant it.*

*"Thanks for that."*

*He smiled and nodded. We turned and walked again, mulling over our thoughts. The "voice" was back. This time he was announcing the arrival of the Missouri River Eagle from: **Saint...Loooooois...** I laughed to myself. Whoever he was, he was damn good at his job and I hoped that one day I'd get the chance to tell him so myself. Then I laughed out loud. Who was I kidding? I'd have to settle for telling it to his great grandchildren. For me, time had stood still — but for the rest of the world it was business as usual.*

*Still, I wondered if they really knew what an important part he played in Kansas City, and the region's, colorful history...I know I do....*

# *Friends*

Whenever people don't see each other for a long time, there's always a little game that accompanies that first encounter. We each say to ourselves: "Boy, he's changed...he really looks old!" Then I convince myself that somehow the same thing hasn't happened to me. I don't look like that at all. Truth is...I do. Denial is a powerful force that psychologists tell us is necessary and useful because it protects us from even more painful fears. Yet as it does, at the same time it gnaws at our sense of reality. We start drinking our own bath water and convincing ourselves that it's really Champagne. Eventually, the inevitable happens: we all die from alkaline poisoning. We evolve into being our own disciples of creative fantasies and reality slips further and further into the background.

Each time I go to Kansas City one of the side effects is that reality comes back to me in bucketfuls. The faces that I have chiseled into my imagination that were once young and vibrant are now weathered and reveal the lines of strain that accompanied those hard times. Many are in their eighties now, but I swear there must be something in the water that keeps them so full of energy. During one of my trips my friend and associate, Dr. Robert Plancey, joined me. Old "Plance" is probably more nuts about trains than either Tim or me. All it takes is a phone call and somehow he finds a way to sneak away from his busy practice and hop on a plane in California to join us. The call to the rail frontiers in eastern Kansas is irresistible. Like us, he's become a Kansas City convert.

Once, after a day of heavy train watching, we went to a Serbian social and Dr. Plancey saw for himself about the resiliency of Midwestern folks. He shook his head in disbelief as he watched the piles of foods guaranteed to bring on strokes and heart attacks being dished out in force to the elderly who held up their plates, eager for more. The baked, ham, lamb, pork, greasy chicken and heavy potatoes – trimmings that were guaranteed to clog even the most well preserved and pampered arteries.

"It's gotta be in the genes," he finally concluded as he watched on in scientific wonderment at all the shenanigans. "That's it....It's the only answer. What they are eating violates every rule I know of in medicine to maintain health, especially in old age."

Obviously, somebody forgot to tell them. These hearty "grey panthers" are more preoccupied with buzzing around town, most of them still driving cars on their own. But even beyond this church group the imprint of longevity is evident elsewhere. Folks have discovered a great secret in the Midwest, and they probably don't even know it.

\*\*\*

*Friends in my age group haven't quite made it to the gerontology big leagues yet, but we're working on it. In fact, Kansas City is the only place I know of where I feel as if I'm young again. When there are three decades of living between you and the person you're looking at, it's not hard to get an attitude.*

*Truth is, I haven't seen the majority of those kids I wrote about for decades. Denny and I keep in close touch, though, much as I hate to admit it, thanks to new technology and the all-intrusive email. He lives in the East. He and his psychologist wife, Nell, have done something that few in his age group did during the back half of the century: They kept their marriage together, reared three kids, and as far as I know, they're still madly in love.*

*His sister Dee-Dee a.k.a.* screen star Dee Wallace, *also exchanges greetings with me from time to time via the Net, or mainly through her "forever optimist" mother, Maxine and second husband Jay. Aunti-Mac has a special talent: She's a* magnet. *The Spirits of Kansas City like to seek her out and then constantly buzz around her. Each time we meet, I feel the power of her energy and easily see them cuddled up and cozy under a quilt on the family couch right next to her, or at the foot of the old wooden post bed that once belonged to Gramps and Grams. They drive me nuts with all their antics, but it's all in fun. People who are lucky enough to sit a spell with Aunti-Mac better learn how to smile – a lot. Not a lot of time to spend on the pity pot.*

*Jay Heinemann, her devoted husband, is content to take the low road as he watches Aunti-Mac prattle over this and that. He deftly steps out of the Spirits' way along with putting in a fair bit of time trying to figure out how in the world he can convince her to give up her dream to win the* Reader's Digest Sweepstakes. *His mission is about as hopeful as somebody who spits into a prairie wind and thinks nothing's coming back. He tries, but he knows it'll never work – ever. It all has got something to do with her unshakable belief that anything's possible. So instead, all of us just bite our lips rather than offer advice we know will amount to nothing more than a distant echo along with a smile that hides her steely determination.*

*You see, when you are born a forever optimist, there's simply no alternative. Aunti-Mac doesn't know what it means to fail, at anything – and that goes for her sweepstakes dreams, which, if you were to ask her, is guaranteed to come in "any day now" on the mailman's delivery. She's so sure that it almost makes me want to pull out my wallet and get into the thick of it. So we all just leave her be…content to quietly thank her to ourselves for all the gifts that she has absolutely no idea she gave us for such a very long time.*

***

*Gramps and Grams Nichols are gone and I, for one, miss them very much. They were the descendents of an era that in the ensuing years were put to the test of change that is still evolving throughout America. Ironically, as it turned out, Gramps' heavy-handed views about race in America had an opposite effect on how his children and grandchildren eventually embraced the social changes that were on the horizon.*

*After graduating from the School of Journalism at Kansas University, Denny went on to become an ordained minister in the Methodist Church. His passion for helping others was more than mere words – he marched alongside Martin Luther King during the sixties and in a time that led to the awakening of America. He had seen first-hand, as many had, that something was wrong. He made his stand, and in the process helped to forever alter the American social fabric.*

*The twins went on to serve their country with pride and that later included Vietnam. Both died of cancer, a disease and timing that in later years hinted they had contracted it while flying helicopters in areas where* **Agent Orange** *was used. Still, they served with pride, and today their children carry their names into other parts of America.*

*Dee-Dee's contributions are, in fact, still very much a part of her life, and in some ways the most recent chapter of the Nichols-Bowers saga. Aside from continuing her successful career as a movie and TV star, she has redirected her creative energy to a new outlet: motivational speaking... yes... helping others recognize their potential and to build more fulfilling lives. The core of that burning desire, I suspect, came from her earlier experiences that no doubt included a deep sensitivity to help those who deserved better. In her own life she had come to understand how to cope with pain. Like her brother, she took those experiences and turned them into something positive, and the world is a happier place because of it.*

*And, of course there's the fountain of optimism, Aunti-Mac – whose reputation for her charitable nature – and along with husband Jay's quiet support, became the unofficial standard bearer of what care and concern for others was all about in Kansas City. For decades, her arms were perpetually extended to people of all races and creeds. She channeled that boundless energy into the formation of* **Cancer Action,** *a program that is still part of the community. Her graciousness and love for her community earns her accolades each time she visits the area – and these come not from just the officials sources, but from the common person hailing from all the ethnic groups. No honor could be higher.*

*No doubt there were thousands of families around the nation who made similar commitments. They challenged the strengths and weaknesses of America's values. They were the architects behind reshaping a nation's perception of itself in the decades that followed. But for my money, it would be a sure bet if you put it all on the doorstep of the Nichols family. In their own ways they saw America in a very different light – unlike many they could see far into its future, and they wanted to be part of it. Best of all they did it from where all good things emerge: They did it from the Heartland.*

***

*My childhood friend, Mikey, is out there, somewhere. His life was not an easy one in later years from what I learned, but he's always been a tough cookie. I would bet he survived even the hardest falls. He left Kansas City and settled in the West, maybe Las Vegas. But from that point it's all a blank sheet. I hope that somewhere along the way he hit the jackpot. He deserves a break.*

\*\*\*

*AJ got herself married and then had a ton of kids. She thought about going to work for an airline once, but then changed her mind, settling instead for a housewife's lifestyle with her salesman husband. Far as I know, she's hanging in just fine, and she's still very much a Kansan. She doesn't mind a little corn growing between her toes. I don't know what she's done lately with her whiz-kid Catholic teachings, but I'd bet it's still in her hip pocket... AJ can talk-the-talk, and when push comes to shove, she's got a compass in her head that points her to the nearest confessional booth whenever she thinks she needs it. I keep her close to me and I thank her for all that she did.*

\*\*\*

*The Fry boys grew up and eventually drifted away from their Lowell Avenue house. I often wonder how they all are doing and hope that whatever paths God laid out for them, it was full of joy and rewards. Maybe somebody who knows will tell them about this book, and when I go back again we can meet. That would be fun.*

\*\*\*

*And then there was Donald...big Don...the Washburn University graduate, and now a Chicago-based tax lawyer who made good and did us all proud. Years later I learned from one of our mutual best friends, Alex Supica, that Donald was probably too slow on the hard court to have amounted to much in his prime. You would have never convinced me. Besides, he kicked butt in too many other ways. He married a lady from Yugloslavia, had kids, kept his traditions close to his heart, and just rolled along, accumulating more successes than most, but also earning every one of them along the way. Donald Yovetich is a winner. He set the pace for all of us Serbs of the fifties whose parents worked so hard to put their offsprings into the world of higher education. He dove headfirst into the American Dream, and we followed, never looking back.*

# The New Immigrants

*T*he wedding was turning out to be everything everybody expected ... and
more....

"Look, see for yourself, Stevo. These are our young Serbs of today." Father
Alexander Bugarin said as he watched a small group standing together on the ground
floor of the St. George social hall. They were being led by a singer, himself a recent
immigrant from war-torn Kosovo. They were global travelers. People who had
bounced from one place to another in their own country, only to eventually find
their ways to Kansas City and the budding seeds of a new life.

For the first time ever, Kosovo really mattered to CNN. To many, it was really
a toss-up on who deserved to be there – the Christian Serbs or the Muslim offsprings
of a once powerful Turkish occupation that lasted for more than five centuries. Over
time, millions of Slavs had been converted into becoming soldiers of Allah during
the occupation of the Bosnia and Kosovo regions.

It was now evolving into a push-pull part of the world: pitting man's technology
to manage, and hopefully overwhelm well-entrenched cultural precedents, and a
people's mule-like stubbornness not to give an inch. It was also an old story being
played out once again in modern times – North and South Vietnam, Iraq and Kuwait,
Pakistan and India, Palestine and Israel, China and Taiwan, North and South Korea,
Northern versus Southern Ireland, East Timor and Indonesia, and now Kosovo and
the world.

As an American Serbian the actions pulled me at both ends like a piece of soft
taffy. I had been to Yugoslavia many times over the years and still had plenty of
family there. I spoke Serbian in our home so it didn't take much for me to integrate
into the society every time I visited. I also knew that I was an American, and so did
they. But there was a "relationship" and each time I came back I drew a tighter bead
on who I was and where it all began for me – and now for my children.

My cousin lives in Panchevo, a small town just outside Belgrade. Nobody
would have even bothered learning how to say the name except for the fact that it
was where one of the nation's most important refinery and chemical complexes was
located. Panchevo got whacked and I got worried.

This was the second major conflict that involved US forces and with me living
in Asia. Years earlier when America went to war in Kuwait, I fumbled through the
broadcasts offered by the BBC. Back then, Singapore's power elite had not yet accepted
the fact that CNN wouldn't undermine their orderly culture. Frankly, it was tough
finding out how the Americans were doing through the eyes and words of the Brits
and their BBC radio bulletins. Thankfully, Singapore's brain trust finally saw the

*light and the sporadic, hour-long CNN broadcasts of the past eventually blossomed into 24-hour coverage. It's been that way ever since.*

*With Kosovo, new technology became an unwitting ally that pushed me dangerously close to a reality that I wasn't sure I wanted to face so intimately. Only now, instead of television, it had everything to do with computer streaming and getting points of view from every direction.*

*I make no bones over my tenuous relationship with new technologies in general. In many ways they strangle us and create a homogenous look that pushes individuality to one side. It makes us slaves at mastering one process then having to learn another just to keep up. But in this case I have to admit I was grateful that it was here as I netted my way into* Radio Jugloslavia *and listened to the droning announcers talk about the NATO aggressors — the American war mongers (that's me), the imperialist invaders (me again) of a sovereign nation who every man, woman and child vowed to defend them to the death (my relatives).*

*It wasn't exactly the "Mother of all Battles" cry that Saddam had spun around the globe in his tirades. But as I listened to the never-ending demands for justice, I figured somebody had probably hired the same scriptwriter. I wondered, really, if they were talking about the same people I had visited so many times and whose warmth, graciousness and generosity overwhelmed anyone who was lucky enough to get in the way.*

*Then I remembered Pops' Sunday sermons and how he talked about this desolate land being the heart and soul of the Serbian people who fought and died there, and for centuries thereafter struggled to survive under unspeakable cruelties during the Turkish occupation; and where Serbian monasteries were built to preserve the faith, and still do. He did it all with power and persuasion, standing as he always did on the raised and carpeted floor in front of the altar. The* Holy Bible *tucked against his side and held firmly in place with his left hand, leaving his right free to draw sketches in the air as he spoke to his congregation. He was a Van-Gogh who didn't need a canvas, but the rendering was there anyway, crystal clear. His words conjured vivid impressions, colorful, vibrant, and full of energy. But good as he was, that wasn't the real story: he was getting help. And it was coming direct from the* Divine. *Just like the others who were mesmerized by his masterpiece of imagery and sound, I believed him. I believed it all.*

*** 

*The tamburitza group was playing on the small stage at the far end of the hall on the second floor. Singing in close harmony, the guests were enjoying the banquet hosted by the bride, groom and their families. Well-known and respected among American Serbs in the US, the Bajich Brothers represented a tradition of young Kansas City Serbs who took to the instruments and learned the songs of Yugoslavia's past, playing the music that inspired people to dance and sing into the early morning hours.*

*We talked and we ate and then somebody banged a steak knife on the side of their plate. Others joined in. The chatter got louder and more persistent until the groom finally stood and smiled. We stood, picking up our glasses in a toast. The plate banging was a cultural demand from the* narod *(people). We wanted reassurance that love was in the air on this…their wedding night. He obliged by giving his new bride a kiss as we applauded and drank.*

*Alexandra Campbell nee Crivakuca smiled and blushed just a little as all brides typically do. It was evident that she and her family were in their glory. Good friends had come to participate in her wedding to a young man – a hard working immigrant who was part of the most recent wave of Serbs from Yugloslavia. Through her selfless dedication she had worked as a social services volunteer to give a helping hand without fanfare. Now it was her turn to receive the recognition due her on their wedding day.*

*Tim and I had met her on one of my research trips for the book a year earlier. She offered us her home and over the next couple of weeks her sense of humor and warm, hearty laugh made us both happy that she had. Her near frenetic commitment to help the refugees adjust to their new environs was at times infectious. They had come to the region jobless, homeless, confused, and many were desperately homesick – displaced first by the bitter war fought in the Krajina region with Croatia, then later in Bosnia, and now the Kosovo debacle.*

*Communism, the economic system that had for decades supported their existences, had begun to unravel like a cheap Mexican rug throughout Europe. But in Yugoslavia, Slobodan Milosevic and his well-oiled pack of thugs, had managed to keep the old order in check. Like chameleons, they changed colors to adapt to the pressures for social and economic reform that were closing in on them. He cleverly attached himself to a simmering nationalism that he managed to heat up through his rhetoric, and in the end it led to pitting family members against one another over what Yugloslavia was all about, and where it should be heading.*

*His tactics in some ways reminded me of Joe McCarthy's antics in the fifties and his warnings to watch out for all those communists hidden in American closets. Lots of emotion, half-baked charges, media manipulation, but not a heck of a lot of facts. But people listened anyway, and many followed.*

*For Slobodan, Kosovo was the perfect bedrock on which to build a sturdy dictator's tower strung together by fear and repression – all in the name of nationalism. The province's continuing control by the Serbs became the focal point that rallied emotions and led to the death of thousands in a conflict that covered the nation's face over the next several years. It eventually ended there…in this lost land.*

*Those caught in the groundswell of the nationalism insanity were trying to survive in a country that could ill afford it. Entrapment was a reality for millions, but some were lucky. They were discovered by the* **Don Bosco Center,** *a relief organization that didn't bother to draw the line on what religion a person happened to be. They helped one and all. But in truth, it all got down to volunteers like Alexandra who took on the chores to help them settle in a new country where everything they saw and touched meant a lot of emotional renovation was required if they were going to make it.*

*As I watched her go about her tasks, I reflected on the fifties when a few kind souls also stood up and were ready to bring strangers into our homes and help them find new lives. George and Libby Zuzich, the Docman family, the Uzleac family, the Gerbas, the Supicas, the Vukas' and, of course, Pops and Mom, and many more – all of them had roots in Kansas City's past. Yet each felt a kinship with a people they had never met.*

*So here was Alexandra in the church hall, sitting next to the young man she had met in her volunteer work. Nenad, directly out of modern Yugoslavia, and now America. Like his predecessors, he came to the confluence of the Missouri and Kaw Rivers looking for a future. His dinner and the celebration were a milestone in his quest.*

###

*Now, with the dinner behind us and the festivities continuing in the church hall basement, I stood with Father Bugarin and watched this new generation of Serbs who no doubt had closeted their own images of this most recent war. There was no denying the fact that there was distance between us.*

*"What is it, father? What's missing here?" I finally said aloud, watching the small group as they locked arm-in-arm among themselves, oblivious to the rest of us. The American Serbs who once drove these kinds of festivities were now content to sit next to one another on folding metal chairs lined against the wall, watching from afar. The gap that separated them from the younger group wasn't totally due to their ages. It was also the presence of two very different cultures operating in the same space. Things had changed. The world had turned one too many times. The power of information and new ideas was spinning it even faster.*

*"They've taken our traditional music and turned it into something different," the priest concluded. "This is the new generation and they're making their own statements through their own kind of music."*

*Of course! It was so obvious that it blew right past me.*

*"Is that man playing the electric piano a Gypsy?" I asked as we continued watching this new wave creativity unfold.*

*"Da... He was hired along with the tamburitzas."*

*Indeed, therein was the part that had been troubling me. On one hand they were doing as Serbs always have done – sharing among themselves the beauty and spirit of their heritage through their songs. That part I related to and I felt a sense of comfort as the melodies tugged at my emotions. The songs were unfamiliar; yet again they were also compelling. I strained to pick up on the lyrics – of harmonies being supported by familiar sounding minor chords and being ably led by the male singer. It was a Serbian love song, but the rhythm and beat suggested a more cosmopolitan sound as if it could have could been sung, well, really anywhere, and by anybody. Part blues, part jazz, and part whole damn world. But still, there was something...very Serbian as well that kept it all together.*

*But then the melody suddenly turned upbeat and the small group formed into a tight circle and began to dance. It was a traditional kolo! The complicated steps belonged to music that emanated out of our deepest past, and yet here it was attached to a contemporary song. As I watched, I began to understand where my own* recollections really belonged.  Not here in the glaring reality of the present, and among these young people dancing to today's world beat.  That would never do. They were choreographing a different cultural message for the priest, the old timers along the wall, and yes, me too.  And in doing so they had successfully performed a case of stunningly effective musical surgery, these new Serbs.  They cut away precisely what they wanted out of their past and attached it to the here and now.  A surgical procedure that came right out of their souls.  And it was a young, one-man band Gypsy musician with long hair that was their musical surgeon leading them into this new zone of expression.  He was using his God-given talent along with a man-made electronic tool that used computer chips instead of treated wood and strings to usher us into this new reality.

I laughed at the irony of it.  Earlier, upstairs at the reception, I sat with a group of American Serbs at the long diner tables savoring the melodies and sounds coming out of the stringed tamburitzas that also told us about our past and honored the wedding couple on their day.  Now it was the Serbs of the old country here who were also united and also taking ownership of their identities.  Two Serbian cultures operating in parallel – two different peoples…really.  Both interpreting their centuries old traditions in very different ways…each taking from it whatever they needed to keep their identities in tact.

I wondered about my own past and what had happened to my family when that first wave of immigrants came to our shores after World War II.  I wondered and I watched.

***

Father Alexander Bugarin had a busy day in front of him.  First it was off to the hospital near his parish home in Kansas to visit a parishioner who had just returned from the Sun City retirement community in Arizona.

Inside the hospital room, Milan (Mike) Yaksic tried to connect to the little boy he remembered with the same name to the 6'2", 210-pound middle-aged man who stood before him now.  Mike had been admitted to the hospital over concerns that his heart had become infected with a virus that was putting a strain on his 78-year-old body.  He had opted to return to Kansas City from his retirement home in Arizona to attend to his advancing medical problems.  His sisters, Mary and Dorothy, were still living in the area.  Staying close to his remaining family was a priority now….

As he spoke about the years Pops served the Serbian community, I felt the same energy swirling around him when I was a kid, and when he came around the church.  Mike is a fiesty personality, passionate about his views, maybe even at times downright ornery, but always willing to put himself up for scrutiny to anyone who had a mind to bump up next to him.  His recollections about those years, and Pops, were still vivid.

"Your dad was a very intelligent man," he said in a high-pitched voice that cracked from his advanced years, but still had an edge to it.  "He had a lot of guts, I'll give him that."

The way he said it told me the two probably had more than their fair share of run-ins – but despite that, he saw Pops as a man not to be taken lightly.  I glanced at *the priest whose surprised expression told me he knew we were entering into uncharted waters of Kansas City's often-raucous history.*

*"I remember once when one of our Serbian boys who worked as a cop got himself into serious trouble with the Police Chief. We were all worried. We were pretty sure he was going to get fired," he said. "Your dad was on his way out of Kansas City as our priest, but he went down to see the Chief, anyway. He told him he was leaving town, but before he did, he wanted to talk to him about what happened. He used all of his markers to help him out. He asked the Chief to give him another chance – as a personal favor. He did."*

*Mike Yaksic's temper was well known, but he certainly wasn't alone when it came to making loud noises. In those robust years the majority of the Serbs were bona-fide West Bottoms or Kansas City, Missouri, cardholders that had since moved into other neighborhoods and were generally living better lives. But the propensity to fire up over issues was something that came with the turf, and it's evident among the old timers, even today. They do speak their minds.*

*His clarity of events of those first original American Serbs who settled in the Bottoms – coupled with what I had earlier learned about the first wave of immigrants who came to Kansas City in the early fifties, reinforced what I had been suspecting for a long time, and what Father and I also discussed concerning the group that was here today. There were indeed undeniable parallels in their collective experiences and attitudes. Yet there were also glaring differences. And that was where the seeds of conflict grew that eventually led to my father leaving the church, essentially forever.*

*One constant both groups shared who arrived in the back half of the century was that many were damaged goods, emotionally speaking. They were victims to events no American Serb in modern times had ever experienced first hand in their own land.*

*Interestingly, what also linked these groups was the same communist ideology and economic system that had been initially imposed on the society in 1945. But the results of the exposure and its impact on them over subsequent generations engendered very different attitudes and behaviors.*

*Among the fifties immigrants, it was their passion for defending the monarchy and their church that was centermost in their thinking; that in turn carried over into their perceptions of what needed to be preserved in their new homeland at all costs. Many saw themselves as Freedom Fighters against communism and defenders of the Mother Church.*

*They brought with them perceptions and beliefs that were unshakable and linked to the horrors of a lost land that represented the very dirt they had given their all to preserve. Many had been officers in the King's free Yugoslav Army, and who were eventually outnumbered, humiliated and routed by the combined forces of Hitler's armies, Tito's communist Partisans, and the civil war with the Croatian Ustashi. Underlying their futile attempts to preserve the old order, the church was as it always has been among the Serbs – the singular institutional linking pin holding the pieces of a centuries old tradition firmly in place. It was all they had.*

*To these men and women who had given up so much, only to end up as emotionally shell-shocked wanderers throughout Europe after the war, the impact was no doubt devastating.  Those that came to Kansas City brought along these memories, and with it passionate, if not at times totally irrational views of their church, and what it should be.  In truth, they were defending – and then attempting to re-create and impose the very culture and lifestyles that had been systematically eradicated in their homeland.  As such, their interpretation of the church, its teachings, and in fact their Divine right to comment on the very Cannon Laws of the institution itself, eventually led to conflict of a very different kind.  And Pops was right there in the middle trying to somehow find a way to negotiate the changes that were already underway, but even by then difficult to manage.*

*Yet that was only half the paradigm.  There were other factors that set people into opposition with one another, and this had more to do with separating reality from fantasy.  It began with a basic premise:*

**Where people come together whose cultural values seem to be similar, yet in truth they are vastly different, and where the collective will of these men and women are determined to impose themselves, one over the other, then one can assume that the prospects for peaceful co-existence are in jeopardy.**

*Pops understood the anxieties that accompanied those fifties immigrants into the community.  He also knew the Kansas City Serbs. He arrived at a time when ninety-nine percent of the American Serbians he was told to lead had never even been to Yugoslavia. His job was to re-construct an image of home, – the stari krai…and that's just what he did with his words, the music, and St. George giving him Divine back-up.*

*They were first generation Serbs, the children of those turn-of-the-century arrivals.  They had created a Pollyanna perception of the "old country." With each song, each story passed on by their parents, each lesson learned in Serbian school, the mountains of Yugoslavia became higher, the grass greener, and the sky more azure.  It was to me as I recall it, a Serbian version of Shangri-La, punctuated by the bigger-than-life Serbian heroes that we were all taught to revere as if they were standing next to Abraham Lincoln.*

*No doubt we had crossed the line. We were left alone for fifty years to nurture our own perceptions about Serbianism until the arrival of those first DPs. When that happened life changed for everybody. We were put on an irreversible path leading to culture clash.  They challenged us about how we had always done things – what Serbian tradition was really all about, and who our heroes really were supposed to be, and why – nothing was sacrosanct.  Emotions ruled and enemies were made that lasted a lifetime.  It was not a pretty time, but it was our time, nonetheless.  And it was to last well into the next decade, a phenomenon that eventually led to a schism in the Orthodox Church in America.*

*The reality is that all ethnic groups share similar perceptions about what and who they are: the Irish with their emerald green isles and stories of Leprechauns; the Greeks with their Gods and Goddesses mythology; even the traditionally reserved English with their Robin Hood and King Arthur folklore.*

*But I suspect ours pushes it the edge of the envelope.  We stand at the pulpit as Pops did and tell of ourselves, readily mixing the myths and realities of our traditions with our religious beliefs, all in one serving. We talk of the brave souls who died defending Serbian causes, and Christianity, over the centuries. We cherish our historical mosaic: Our church, our heroes, and our Serbian-Slav heritage. This is the triad that binds our ironclad system of beliefs. These cannot be broken, at any price. It's so deeply entrenched in our Serbian psyche that it can lead to the adoption of incredibly powerful acts of social defiance – actions that can, and do, fly in the face of reasonable thinking.*

*Ask the politicians in Washington who scratched their heads in bewilderment when they discovered how an affable nation – a society that seemed to have a penchant for producing good basketball players – would intentionally follow a dictator they openly despised rather than abiding by the rule of law and avoid the massive aerial ordnance that was dumped over Kosovo, then throughout the country, and ultimately in their nation's capital. Where people were willing to endure hardships and major lifestyle adjustments – casually pointing out that all the "racket" going on outside was interfering with their sleep. The racket, by the way, was Belgrade's buildings being pulverized, along with a Chinese Embassy, and a host of chemical plants and a refinery around the fringe of the city.*

*It was our heroes and the stories of our past that were in part responsible for these incredibly blasé attitudes that seemed to pervade throughout the general population. No matter what happened, there were some things that were non-negotiable. Beliefs, really, that you never, ever give up. You hold your mud…. Kosovo is one of them. And because of a dictator who intimately knew the depths of those beliefs and commitments (another priest's son, incidentally), he played a political poker game in Yugloslavia from a deck of cards that everybody knew was loaded. Some asked how that could have happened? The answer is simple: It's the only game in town.*

***

*(Editor Post Script: On October 5, 2000, the world watched as thousands of Serbs gathered in Belgrade. Collectively, they sent a defiant message: <u>Gotovo</u>…they finally had enough of more than a decade of struggles. Slobo, the Pariah, was summarily ousted and in the celebrations that followed, millions cheered them on. Whether, or how long, this newfound freedom will be preserved is still an open book. The forces opposed to it are resistant and cunning in what they can do. Slobo is still in town. We are all watching, waiting…and wondering.)*

***

*"Is this the place?" I asked Father Bugarin, as I looked up at the four-story brick apartment building that had seen better days.*

*"Da…up there," he said pointing to the higher floors. "I think he's on three. I've only been inside once or twice – we shall see."*

*As we walked toward the cement steps leading into the building, I saw several knots of kids just hanging out – Hispanics mostly, but also a sprinkling of African Americans. My years of training as a police officer heightened my awareness that we were entering a zone that could spell trouble, but when they spotted Father's cleric uniform, they quickly lost interest.*

*I shifted my focus when we entered the front door and entered the building's main hallway. The echoing sounds inside the old building told me it was an active tenement life that probably could have existed in fifty of America's larger cities. The heavy, dank odor of mildewed carpets and dirty wallpapers blended with spicy foods that suggested far-away places. I followed the priest as he climbed the creaking wooden stairs, passing still more teenagers and old men along the way.*

*"Evo," he said, looking at the tarnished and partly bent apartment number plate on the door and comparing it to the piece of paper he held in his hand. He glanced at me and smiled as he knocked on the door. His short stature in some ways reminded me of Pops. When he smiled I sensed that despite the fact he was serious-natured and intellectually drawn, there was also a little boy lurking inside that couldn't wait to get out.*

***

*Milan Bauk's rapid-fire responses were pithy, probably nothing more than a nervous reaction of someone who was uncomfortable speaking his mind so openly in front of a stranger. Perhaps it had something to do with years of conditioning in the old country. In his former village of Kaldrma near the town of Donji Lapac in Lika, he was continually reminding himself that if he didn't watch out, communist informants might overhear him and file a report. It could mean more headaches than he and his wife, Sladjana, had already. Even though he now sat in the comfort of his living room in the heart of America, I sensed he felt the shadows of the past were still lurking somewhere in the darker corners of their drab and sparsely appointed apartment.*

*Milan is a working man, unashamed to wipe the sweat off his brow in his quest to put food on the table for his wife and two children. Since his arrival to the region two years earlier, he managed to find work in a car wash.*

*To others, the simple job is anything but a statement of unqualified success, but to Milan Bauk it was a declaration – a watershed achievement that meant he had finally found his way to the front door of economic salvation. The car wash job, in fact, signaled the end of years of fruitless search for employment in his own country. His is a story of the modern Serb immigrant who in many ways mirrored those who came into the region a hundred years earlier, and during Pops' time following the war. But now here it was again on the threshold of a new century.*

*Each day he stood along the car wash running track and wiped down the shiny new Fords, Chevies, BMW's and Cadillacs. Milan worked extra hard to make sure the dollars the customers spent were a worthwhile investment. He happily took his place in the great machine of Capitalism. Previously a farmer and laborer on the railroad, now he turned that same willingness to using his hands to build his new life. He knew there was something more waiting for him than the countless promises the communist leaders put at his feet in the past, yet rarely delivered. Those turn-of-*

the-century Serb settlers who slaughtered cattle in the West Bottoms packinghouses would have certainly understood where all that drive came from. Escape and economic freedom are powerful stimulants. Milan is one of them.

Now, as he sat in his living room and his wife quietly tended to her customary role offering wine to us, he looked back at his life and what had evolved up to now. Like many of the newcomers, Kansas City offered him much, but if the truth be known, Serbs are a lot like pigeons – once they fly out of the coop there's an instinctive desire to fly back. Father Bugarin's visit was in a way an effort to keep that compulsion in check.

"There was a priest who lived near our village, and I guess the officials more or less just put up with him," he said. "Every once in a while somebody would want to baptize their newborn babies. They would invite him over to their houses because going to the church would tell everybody what they were doing."

As he spoke I watched his wife quietly move around the fringes of the discussion, studying her husband's expression and, I assume, recollecting in her own way what she'd seen. She grew up in the town of Drvar, in Bosnia, a community that for whatever reason was considered to be a communist stronghold. Among these citizens, the idea of Christianity, church and religion had undergone a particularly severe assault. It left its mark on the lifestyles of an entire generation.

"What they would do is bring the priest inside their homes and then into a back room. Then they'd turned up the house radio so loud that it would drown out his voice as he chanted the prayers and baptized the baby. The neighbors couldn't hear," he explained.

Bauk's eventual arrival into Kansas City was a part of a thirty-family contingent. But unlike the staunch Serbs and self-declared patriots who came in the fifties, these were a looser confederation composed of a cross-section of ethnic groups – Serbs, Croats, Gypsies, and even Muslims. Many were involved in mixed marriages, an after effect of the socialist teachings of the times. When it came to the church, their attitudes were much different from their predecessors. Many were essentially indifferent. Others, however, were receptive and saw their faith as an anchor in surviving in a new land.

Lika is a part of the Krajina and it perhaps came as no surprise that Milan began his nomadic life in search for work among a population who he saw as his own kind. When war broke out between the Croatians and Serbs, he and his family were expelled. Virtually all of the Serbs who lived in this enclave were surrounded by Croatians. They naturally sought sanctuary, traveling south into Serbia proper.

"We were forced off our land by the Croatians," he explained. "We were Serbs and all we wanted was a chance to work – maybe to farm as we had always done."

He soon discovered that what they were embarking on was nothing more than the life of a drifter family. Wherever they went in their own country they were met with suspicion, resistance, and sometimes even outright rejection. There were no jobs to be had in Yugoslavia, and no time, really, to entertain helping Serbs who came from such a remote part of the country. They were as Americans might call them nothing more than country bumpkins who were part of the hinterland of a country that already had too many problems to deal with in its core population.

"We were unwelcome in our own country," he said, "so we moved on, hoping that somewhere we could finally find a place to start again."

The search eventually led many of them to Kosovo where they, like the others, moved into an occupied a region of Yugoslavia, a land that that was also under a growing dispute. Once again their stay was short-lived.

Bauk studied his wineglass carefully as he chose words. Then he looked at us. There was a curious mix of pain and anger in his expression.

"This problem that now goes on in Kosovo, the killing...everything today...this all began because of Tito..." he declared.

"What do you mean?" I asked.

"It was Tito and the communists that invited them back (from Albania) after World War II — the communists believed that all of Yugoslavia's people who once were there were welcome to return in this new society. He opened the doors...and now this is what it led to."

His simple assessment was shockingly to the point and frankly unlike the myriad of explanations and debates that were flying around the world on TV, the Net – the droning "NATO Aggressor" propaganda stories that were being pumped out of Belgrade's government station; or the counter charges by NATO forces and America's media factory working overtime to defend (maybe occasionally even trying to understand) its actions.

The intellectuals and opinion leaders ripped and tore at the historical fabric of the Kosovo region and the Serbs in general, offering flimsy anecdotes, along with their haughty, whiz kid analyses. Only a few weeks before Mr. Clinton had resorted to using a map to show everybody where the hell Kosovo was. The information scramble was on.

I remember decades earlier when JFK told us all about Vietnam and the headaches there. He got all my attention. At the time, I was stationed in Goldsboro, North Carolina, in the Air Force. He used a map, too. But now, as I watched Mr. Clinton, I wondered why his PR team hadn't taken full advantage of technology to put his story forward – doing a high-tech, multimedia demonstration that drove home his concerns and explained his actions. I guess he thought he could get the job done by just relying on his words. Clinton was really good with words, especially his ability to split hairs on what they meant. I learned a lot there. Now he would enlighten us all again, right from the Oval Office – a place in the White House we had all come to appreciate more than we needed to in recent months. Kosovo would be handled. He was where he wanted to be, holding his pointer in his hand...ready to go.

As I watched and listened to Clinton point to the Balkans and mispronounce Kosovo, a haunting worry crept in. Mr. President was in a sales mode and building up a head of political steam. If unchecked, it could put us on a war footing in a cause that frankly few Americans really knew that much about. Kosovo was, in fact, a cultural war that was erupting into a civil conflict. Ugly, hell yes.... Complicated...? you bet...but once you peeled the onion, it got down to that.

There was work to be done. Americans go to war only when the heroes and villains are clearly defined, and fully in view. I think that's because we've been *steeped in sports. We're conditioned to categorize results in being either winners or losers...We argue about it on* Imus in the Morning...*the never-ending war games of the sports world. Heroes and villains...it's an American passion. That's what makes them turn up the volume. That was Iraq.*

*But Kosovo wasn't like that. There were...complications. For one thing it wasn't that easy finding a Kosovo expert as the on-air stumblings from all the networks confirmed in boring redundancy. Only the open arguments among current and former military leaders began to show there were genuine flaws in the strategy. President Clinton did what he always did – he covered his keester with a high altitude, almost outer space bombing directive. Nobody dies...nobody gets shot down.... The kill rate on the cardboard tank effigies was impressive. The phony roads made of plywood and leading to nowhere were pummeled. Sometimes, though, they hit moving trains with civilians on them. That was news.*

*Kosovo was starting to smell like a military cesspool. Politicians dusted off their old, "I oppose Vietnam" speeches and used stickers to paste in the new name: Kosovo. Everybody got out their world gazettes one more time to take a closer look.*

*But the Serbs knew, and that meant both sides of the Atlantic. The idea of being the heavy in a global "sports" game made them uncomfortable. Hell, it made me uncomfortable and I was living in Singapore! When Kosovo got ugly we all noticed it...even out there – in the cheap seats of the world stadium. With a little help from media it eventually become a centerpiece for a battle of wills involving nations and a military machine, all being played out on a Balkan social fault zone that owed its genesis to centuries of historical cultural brick smashing, with no change in sight as we entered the threshold of a New Millennium.*

*Yet here, now, in this spartan apartment listening to this ordinary working man – someone who had nothing at stake in the big picture, yet everything to lose as a result of it, Milan Bauk had managed to hone a razor-sharp conclusion to what had inspired a war that was showing no signs of letting up. This wasn't an essay presented by Harvard intellectuals; or analyses developed by State Department Ivy League hot shots. It was Milan Bauk sitting in his simple chair and cooling his jets after a hard day's work putting elbow grease on a Cadillac hood. He simply had his antenna up. He knew what it was like to live under a system that had engineered an entire country into an economic flat spin. The problem was that Milan didn't have a parachute, and he knew it.*

*People like Milan Bauk spend a lot of their time trying to figure out how to avoid putting ten pounds of crap in a five pound bag, mostly thanks to the stupidity of others. They see the world a lot clearer than we do because it's really a matter of bottom-line survival. They get...well, ring-wise...at figuring out where their priorities really belong. They focus most of their energy looking around for ways to survive, all the while doing their damnedest to sidestep whatever obstacle is in the way. Milan Bauk could cut the lanes and juke with the best of them. Not only that, he did it with a wife and two kids hanging on his shoulders. He may have been born in Yugoslavia, but as far I'm concerned his moves were primetime All-American.*

\*\*\*

*"What you heard is something that many people in the old country now believe, but they rarely speak about it," Father said, as we rode together down* Independence Avenue *toward the* City Viaduct *to the Kansas side. To them, the idea of permitting thousands of Albanians to move into the same place where it had taken decades to get them out were the seeds that eventually led to the conflict that we erupted today.*

*"These are uncomplicated people," Father Bugarin explained. "Most only have fourth to eighth grade education. But I would say they are generally decent and honest. They are not all that religious, though. Remember, many generations have been brought up under the rule of communism. They simply lost their ways. My job is to help them back to Christ and our Mother Church."*

*I first detected that same determination in him when we met a year or so earlier. The son of a priest who came from central Yugoslavia, he followed his father's footsteps, taking up the cloth and a conviction to duty that would have earned High-Fives from Mother Teresa. Being that I was a priest's son and from the same parish that he was only now coming to fully unravel, we quickly became friends and, I assume, formed a bond of trust built along an understanding that only priests' sons can rightfully appreciate. It was, as I later discovered, to be a process that would benefit us both.*

*For me, his succinct, direct beliefs about Orthodoxy, his fervent commitment to traditions that reflected the Serbian culture, and his obligation to remind each of us that we must do our share to preserve our heritage – these were all thoughts and obligations that I had long ago put on the back burner in my life*

*To him, the life I had experienced as a world traveler, the varied cultures I had studied and had been challenged to understand and embrace, and in particular my own definition of what an American Serb is in comparison to those who came from the old country – these were issues he was also trying to understand more completely. The challenge as I saw it was for him to somehow temper his cultural biases on Serbianism from his homeland, as they may not be totally in synch when viewed in the American perspective. It's a difficult tightrope to walk.*

*These points of debate often led to brisk exchanges between us but we soon discovered something my cultural research was confirming more clearly with each visit to the region: both of us were Serbs to the core – **but at the same time our own national cultures defined what, and how, that was to be perceived and individually demonstrated. Occasionally, that put us on opposite ends of the spectrum.***

*As a priest who came to America eleven years earlier in response to a need for clergy to fill the depleting ranks in the Orthodox Churches throughout North America and Canada, Father Bugarin had paid his dues. Those early years had taken their toll on the young man. Lonely and out of touch with all that gave him cultural balance and comfort, he only had his faith to keep him on track as he tried to cope with what, and where, he really belonged in this new land. To that end, those early experiences were no doubt useful now as he met the latest wave of immigrants who had come out of the war torn regions of the Krajina, Bosnia and now Kosovo.*

*Yet even now as we rode together, I sensed that Yugoslavia and where it is today was far from Father Bugarin's most pressing agenda. His energy and focus had more to do with re-inculcating an entire generation into the Mother Church. In re-establishing the patterns of regular church going, of ensuring that children – the lifeblood of the church, were baptized, of upholding Serbian traditions and passing them on to a new generation; and finally, of making the church a pillar of life in everyone's thinking. That was – and continues to be, a full-time job. His marriage to the American-born, Gordana, and their task of rearing their two children has since gone far to ease the pain of those earlier years. He has made his way.*

*The young priest was recruited by the retiring **Milan Bajich**, the priest who replaced Pops in 1956 when he left Kansas City. Father Bugarin came to St. George's to teach the scriptures and re-inject youthful energy into his calling. But he had a big pair of shoes to fill. Father Bajich came to Kansas City when the white-hot tempers and cultural clashes were still very much a part of the church scene in the early fifties and in the decade that followed. But he was not without his own capabilities. What Kansas City needed was a priest whose firm hand was unshakable, and whose mission was to lead his flock out of ignorance and into baseline enlightenment about what it was to be Serbian, and of the Orthodox faith. He made no apologies about his tasks and his direct approach and getting the job done. Those that resisted soon discovered that he was a man of conviction and considerable inner resolve. He reared a family of eight, moved out of the inadequately small parish house I grew up in and into another larger home across the street, then set about tending to his clerical duties with military-like punctuality. No doubt over the years his approach generated a few grumblers, but Milan Bajich proved himself more than capable at managing the affairs of a Serbian colony that had a reputation of being headstrong, if not at times down-right contentious.*

*He also had another gift that came direct from God: a booming baritone voice that sounded so much like Pops', when he led the Divine Liturgy you'd have thought it was my father who was inside instead of him. In the priorities that invariably accompany Serbian life, a good singing voice and the ability to play a stringed instrument were prized talents. Like Pops, Father Bajich was as comfortable leading a choir in concerts throughout the US as he was offering communion during Lent. When his four sons later picked up the tamburitzas and earned a widespread reputation among the Serbs that they were a cut above most, for him the circle of tradition had been closed. Of course, the point here is that the boys were, in fact, all-American Serbs who also took the best out of their cultural heritage and made it work. I guess you could argue the same could be said for any ethnic group and its preservation of cultural traditions. Fair enough.... But since this is my Epilogue, I'll exercise my right in taking a little editorial license to do some home-court bragging for ours. Serbs can walk the walk....*

***

*My father left Kansas City a broken man. He initially went to Bisbee, Arizona, to take a parish there, but the hounds of conflict continued to pursue him, even to this remote mining town near the US-Mexico border. Eventually we ended up in Los*

*Angeles in a simple apartment not much different from the Bauk's. We had our backs against the wall. Only our inner will to survive and my mother's tower of strength prevented us from falling even further. I knew how it felt to cry yourself to sleep, desperately wanting to return to the only home I had ever known. But it wasn't to be, until now, decades later.*

*In the years that followed, Pops dabbled with his clergy profession, working primarily as an Assistant Priest at the* St. Stevan's Cathedral *in Alhambra, California. A man whose charisma always swirled around him, over the years Pops was offered churches throughout California, but he never accepted, nor did he fully recover from the troubled times that led to his leaving Kansas City. Instead, he created a life with my mother that increasingly made him a recluse, and over time separated him from the opportunity to celebrate the Liturgy that had once been so much a part of his life.*

*For many years I held a deep resentment about his decision not to re-engage his calling as a cleric, and I had told him so. He had the gift, and in later years whenever I spotted a student or an athlete who had something special, the same irritation would overwhelm me. We are, it seems to me, only the custodians of whatever God chooses to give us inside. Some have more than others. In that light we are all obliged to develop whatever these gifts are to their fullest.*

*Pops' decision not to use his talents was troublesome in other ways. His isolation led to advanced stages of alcohol abuse. And it put added pressure on Mom who was a lioness when it came to her duties. But despite all this she remained devoted to Pops until she died suddenly of a brain hemorrhage in 1973.*

*The event proved to be perhaps his most painful episode in a string of trying events. As a priest I think he believed he had a special relationship with the* Divine. *I suspect he thought God had played him out. He thought that no matter what, he would go first and allow Mom to live out the rest of her life in relative peace. But that wasn't to be. Her passing drove him even deeper into isolation and into his addiction. He died two years later in Pasadena, California, while having himself a boilermaker in a bar. Not long after that the bar went out of business. It was replaced by a glass shop owned no less than by a Greek Orthodox businessman. Their specialty? Making stained glass windows for churches. It's hard to keep a good man down....*

*Today, both of my parents lay side-by-side in the Serbian cemetery next to* St. Sava's Church *in East Los Angeles. I'm sure that if anybody happened to be in the neighborhood they'd love to see you. Pops and Mom always enjoyed the company of their Serbian brothers and sisters. And everybody knew that Pops loved a good time.*

*The truth was that Pops probably shouldn't have been a priest at all. He always wanted to be a lawyer and was well on his way until a world depression forced him to change his mind. He was a man who I can honestly say was an enigma in how he embraced life with such complete courage at times, while at others grappled with a fragile ego and sometimes distorted self-perception. He could be a total stranger to those who were closest to him; at other times we could see right through him. We could feel the beat of his heart.*

But in his prime no one could argue that he didn't embrace life with gusto. At times his passion to savor all of life's beauties took him beyond the grounds of reasonableness and clashed with his expected role in the community. Just like all of us, he made his fair share of mistakes. He was, as we all are…only human.

On the other hand, he had an inner strength that could allow him to gently close the eyes a final time of his best friend, Pete Stepanovich; or explain to a confused and devastated family why their little child had been taken from them so early, and tragically; or writing plays in Serbian for others to enjoy and perform; or leading a choir to use their collective voices to reach for the very gates of Heaven. He could do all of these things, and he did them well. He could do it because aside from his human frailties, there was a touch of the Divine in Pops. Everyone who came into contact with him felt it. I love my father, and I miss him. I'm sure that if he were here with us today he would touch us all again with his vitality. He was a good man.

To my knowledge, Pops and Mom returned to Kansas City only once in the ensuing years. It was at the tail end of a trip to visit me in North Carolina. Father Bajich in his customary, decent and honorable way, accorded Pops all the dignity deserving of a man and his wife who had given so much to this little church. I would have loved to hear them celebrating the Divine Liturgy together with their booming voices echoing throughout the Bethany Street neighborhood. Kind of like double-headed steam engines thundering out of town, hell bent for leather.

As for me it's taken a while to sort things out about those years and a multitude of emotional readjustments I made along the way. I went through my own turbulent times, and part of that included rejecting my heritage, only to discover that in the end, and aside from our loved ones, it's really all we have.

I recall once sitting in the living room of my friend, Alex Supica, a relative of Pete Stepanovich, a man who today in many ways reminds me of him. We talked about the years that had passed and the very different paths life had taken us – he, pretty much staying close to his Kansas City roots and eventually marrying a gentle soul, Jan, an educator, and someone who willingly converted into Orthodoxy. As a result, adopting the customs of a people that were not hers through birthright, but was taken in all the same. Today her place in the Serbian community is assured – she's affectionately known among her friends as "Yaya…."

In recent years other converts have bolstered the church congregation, and if you were to ask Father Bugarin, they're doing quite a fair bit to show others the way. It's a phenomenon that I suspect emerges from a society that finds itself increasingly looking for ways to put form and substance in the place of generalities and hype that bombard us from every corner of our lives. For some, the appeal of Orthodoxy and all that it embraces in the Serbian tradition is the perfect solution and I, for one, want to thank them for that. Their commitments remind me that whereas they had to search out a new direction through trial and error, it's already been given to me by Providence.

\*\*\*

*"Yes Alex, I've done many things in my life, you're probably right about that. And, I suppose looking at all of that from the outside in, it could be something different, and maybe even exciting," I said. "I've been an educator and worked for six CEOs of global corporations; I've been an ESPN color broadcaster and I was a reporter, and a magazine writer. I've seen much of the world and know a little about how to read its pulse. But the truth is, if I had to do it all over again, I would have gladly traded places with you. Right here...in this lovely home...on your quiet street, and in this neighborhood...and among the Serbian people that have been with you for a lifetime."*

*Alex shook his head and laughed, convinced that I'd finally gone completely mad. Yet in truth I couldn't have said it any clearer, or meant it any more deeply. As a result of events that were completely out of my control, my current life angled into a different tributary that in forty-five years taught me more than I probably needed to know, some of which I would just as soon forget. But in the process, I also experienced the joys of getting a decent education, which in turn set the stage for interpreting the world in my own way. These streams of experiences took me into the slums of Los Angeles, and into the rice paddys of Vietnam. It taught me how to work and hold my own with minds that were more supple than mine – of dealing on equal ground with the captains of industry, of meeting Presidents, Senators and Congressmen; and the celebrities of the silver screen and famous athletes from around the world. Then back into the heart of Asia again where my only son was properly reared thanks to the help of a beautiful Eurasian woman whose quiet ways brought me peace and, yes, the emotional equilibrium that had eluded me for such a long time. And the pride of my only daughter who chose to follow her school teacher father's footsteps. No joy is greater than seeing the values we teach our young to pursue their own dreams in any way they choose. Or a son who proudly stood to take a commission in the army and wear his country's uniform.*

*When I think about all of these events and all of my childhood friends, I imagine myself seated inside a speeding train heading for all points west. Outside, and just beyond the rails, I see the meandering Kaw River. Sometimes it flows next to me, but then it drifts away, out of sight, only to reappear again when we glide into a long, sweeping curve.*

*It's been that way in my life. I've meandered to many places just like that old river. It began in my Kansas City home, then I drifted far, far away. Now I'm back. The Kaw is there to quietly greet me. It comes to my side – a life-long friend that never really left.*

*So if you'll excuse me, there's something I need to do now. I have an appointment to keep with the Spirits of Kansas City, Kansas. They've asked to see me, again. There's something they're dying to tell me...and I really do need to listen. Maybe it's another railroad story that's buried in the past. Maybe it's about someone I haven't thought about for a very long time. No matter. All my life I've been a sucker for a good story, and now I think I finally know the reason why....*

*They tell us about ourselves....*

*The End*

# Acknowledgments

*My deepest appreciation to the following individuals who graciously gave their time searching their attic trunks, scouring through old church documents, offering interviews, and encouraging me to complete this work.*

Maxine Heinemann-Bowers
Retired
Kansas City, Missouri

Dennis Bowers Ph.D.
Minister, Methodist Church
Philadelphia, Pennsylvania

Reverend Alexandre Bugarin
St. George Serbian Orthodox
Parish Priest,
Kansas City, Kansas

Ann Dodig-Chandler
Retired
Kansas City, Kansas

Kannan Chandran
Editor
Republic of Singapore

Susan Conway
Hospital Administrator
Hesperia, California

Jay Heinemann
Retired
Kansas City, Missouri

Vasa Mihailovich Ph.D.
Professor Emeritus, University of
North Carolina
Chapel Hill, North Carolina

John Monchil
Retired
Kansas City, Kansas

Tom Hogan Ph.D.
Professor
Sydney, Australia

Joey Gerba
Retired
Kansas City, Kansas

Margaret Huebner
Human Resources Executive
Los Angeles, California

Carl Lande Ph.D.
Professor, Political Science
University of Kansas

Linda Leong
Proof Reader
Republic of Singapore

Miodrag Milakov
Cousin & Engineer
Panchevo, Yugoslavia

Jeanie D'Conceicao Milakov
Human Resources Director
Republic of Singapore

Stacey Anne Milakov
Elementary School Teacher and
Loving Daughter
Brea, California

Tim Milakov
Officer Candidate
US Army

Robert Plancey MD
Physician
Monrovia, California

Milka Plecas
Retired
Kansas City, Missouri

Verica Milakov-Rankovic
Cousin, Journalist and Mom
Beograd, Milakov

Research Staff
Strawberry Hill Museum
Kansas City, Kansas

Research Staff
University of Kansas Photo Archives

Research Staff Attendants
Wyandotte County Historical Society

Georgia Slaughter
Librarian, Kansas Room
Kansas City Kansas Public Library
Kansas City, Kansas

Danica' Dodig-Solich
Housewife and Mother of Five
Outstanding Sons
Colorado Springs, Colorado

Helen Gerba-Stonestreet
Retired
Kansas City, Kansas

Alex Supica
Executive, Social Security
Department
Kansas City, Kansas

Joe Vaughan
Editor
Prairie Village, Kansas

Dorothy Vukas
Retired
Kansas City, Kansas

Milan Yaksic
Deceased
Kansas City, Kansas

Milo Yelesiyevich
Author, Publisher
New York, New York

Sam Zuzich
Retired Trucking Executive
Kansas City, Missouri

# Bibliography

## Books

Ball, Don. *America's Railroads,* New York, Norton & Company, 1980

Colias, Joe G. *The Missouri Pacific Lines,* Crestwood, Missouri, MM Books, 1993

Dorin, Patrick C. *Everywhere West The Burlington Route,* Seattle, Washington, Superior Publishing Company, 1976

Luse, William R. *Railroad Town,* Fort Scott, Kansas, Sekan Printing, Inc. , 1988

McCall, John B. and Schultz III, Frank A. *Katy Southwest,* Dallas, Texas, Kachina Press, 1985

Spivak, Jeffrey. *Union Station – Kansas City,* Kansas City, Missouri, Walsworth Publishing Co., Inc. 1999

Taylor, Loren L. et al, A *Short Ethnic History of Wyandotte County,* Kansas City, Kansas Ethnic Council, 1992

The First Catholic Slavic Ladies Association, Anniversary, *Slovak-American Cook Book,* Chicago, Illinois, Tylka Brothers Press Inc., 23rd Edition, 1952

Siebenthaler, O., & Taylor, Warren T. *Aftermath – A pictorial record,* Kansas City, Missouri, S&W Publications, 1951)

## Periodicals, Brochures, Government Reports, Internet, Operating Books, Ethnic Reports, Annual Reports and Religious Materials

Mathewes-Green, Frederica, *12 Things I Wish Had Known,* Ben Lomand, California, Concilliar Press, (date unknown)

Kansas City, Kansas Chamber of Commerce, *The Part That Doesn't Show,* 1951

Magnuson, Carl R. *The Keepers, — a ten-month humanities project to investigate the perpetuation or loss of cultural traditions in the Serbian, Slovenia and Croatian ethnic communities of Kansas City,* Kaw Valley Arts & Humanities, 1990

Matejic, Mateja, Ph.D. *Orthodoxy: Courage to be different,* Monroe, Michigan, Ex-Cel Printing, 1994

Missouri – Kansas-Texas Railroad. *Rules and Instructions of the Transportation Department,* Parsons, Kansas, October, 1943

Schriver, Errett P. Representative, 2nd District. *The Kansas-Missouri Flood of 1951 – Ninth Intermediate Report of the Committee on Expenditures in the Executive Departments,* Washington, US Government Printing Office, 1951,

The Serbian Cathedral. *Mystery of the Touch #7*, New York, Obid Press, 1956

St. George Church. *Divine Liturgy Handbook*, date unknown

St. George Church. *Srpski Glasnik*, Kansas City, Kansas, 1999, Year 5, Issue 18 - Year 3, Issue 9

St. George Church. *75th Anniversary Book*, Kansas City, Kansas, 1981

St. George Church. *90th Anniversary Book*, Kansas City, Kansas, 1996

St. George Church. *A Time Line of Church History*, Mount Hermon, California, Counciliar Press, (Year unknown)

St. George Church. *What on Earth is the Orthodox Church?* Ben Lomand, California, Counciliar Press, 1994

St. Lazarus, "Ravanica" Orthodox Cathedral. *How Old is the Orthodox Church?* Detroit, Michigan, 1997

Union Pacific Railroad. *System Timetable No.3*, Omaha, Nebraska, 1980

United States Justice Department, FBI Internet Home Page. *Conspiracy to Deliver a Federal Prisoner*, Washington DC, 1999

Hudson-Essex-Terraplane Historical Society. *Internet Home Page*, Watertown, Ct, 1999


## Historical Articles

Belt, Mike. *Flood of '93*, Kansas City Kansas, 1993

Burnes, Brian. *Kansas City's Big Floods*, Kansas City Star, July 7, 1997

Dysart, Patty. *Armourdale Came Out Better in Flood of 1993*, Kansas City, Kansan, Aug. 12, 1993

Spivak, Jeffrey. *Science City Designers Dffer a Peek*, The Kansas City Star, Sept. 24, 1997

Steifer, Georgie. *People of the Kaw Valley Before the Flood*, letter, 1951

Unknown. *Havoc Mounts in Kansas*, The Kansas City Star, 1951

Unknown. *Flood Briefs (map)*, Kansas City Star, 1951

Unknown. *River Crests (high water statistics summary)*, Unnamed multiple newspaper sources, Year Unknown

Unknown. *Check Fire Loss*, Kansas City Times, July 17, 1951

Unknown. *When Firemen Thought The Oil Fire Was Under Control Yesterday, (photo and deep caption)*, Kansas City Times, July 17, 1951

Unknown. *Oil Still Burns*, Kansas City Star, July 17, 1951

Unknown. *Oil Fire Is Still Burning*, Kansas City Times, July 18, 1951

Unknown. *Disaster As The Kaw Spreads*, Kansas City Star, July 13, 1951

Unknown. *Kaw Rolls Into Argentine*, Kansas City Times, July 13, 1951

Unknown. *Raging Kaw Into Armourdale*, Kansas City Star, July 13, 1951

Unknown. *As Homes Come Down Over Strawberry Hill*, Kansas City Kansan, June 9, 1957

Unknown. *Final Run Near For Interurban*, Kansas City Star, 1961

Unknown. *Changes in the Weather*, Kansas City Star, 1997

Wire Service Report. *Serbs May Let Montenengro Leave Yugoslavia*, American Srbobran, Nov. 10, 1999